Digital Humanities and Buddhism

# Introductions to Digital Humanities – Religion

Edited by
Claire Clivaz, Charles M. Ess, Gregory Price Grieve, Kristian Petersen, Sally Promey

## Volume 1

# Digital Humanities and Buddhism

An Introduction

Edited by
Daniel Veidlinger

DE GRUYTER

ISBN 978-3-11-051836-8
e-ISBN (PDF) 978-3-11-051908-2
e-ISBN (EPUB) 978-3-11-051839-9

**Library of Congress Control Number: 2019933231**

**Bibliografic information published by the Deutsche Nationalbibliothek**
The Deutsche Nationalbibliothek lists this publication in the Deutsche Nationalbibliografie; detailed bibliografic data are available on the Internet at http://dnb.dnb.de.


Cover image: Social network visualization. With friendly permission of Martin Grandjean.
Printing and binding: CPI books GmbH, Leck

www.degruyter.com

# Table of Contents


Daniel Veidlinger
**Introduction — 1**

Ilona Budapesti
**Past, Present, and Future of Digital Buddhology — 25**

Part One: **Theoretical and Methodological Issues**

Daniel Veidlinger
**Computational Linguistics and the Buddhist Corpus — 43**

Gregory Price Grieve
**An Ethnographic Method for the Digital Humanistic Study of Buddhism — 59**

Part Two: **Digital Conservation, Presentation and Archiving**

Kuo-Ming Tang and Shu-Kai Hsieh
**Ontologizing Buddhist Digital Archives: Two Case Studies — 77**

Paul G. Hackett
**Digital Encoding, Preservation, Translation, and Research for Tibetan Buddhist Texts — 91**

Miroj Shakya
**The Digital Sanskrit Buddhist Canon Project: Problems and Possibilities — 111**

David Wharton
**Digital Libraries of Lao and Northern Thai Manuscripts — 127**

A. Charles Muller
**The Digital Dictionary of Buddhism and CJKV-English Dictionary: A Brief History — 143**

## Part Three: **Digital Analysis of Buddhist Documents**

Christopher Jensen
**Mapping Religious Practice in the *Eminent Monks:* Theoretical and Methodological Reflections — 159**

Christopher Handy
**A Context-Free Method for the Computational Analysis of Buddhist Texts — 183**

James B. Apple
**Digital Filiation Studies: Phylogenetic Analysis in the Study of Tibetan Buddhist Canonical Texts — 209**

**Appendix: Selected Digital Humanities Resources — 227**

**Index — 231**

Daniel Veidlinger

# Introduction

The Digital Humanities are a new way of approaching traditional Humanities disciplines using the analytic and display powers of computers and digital networks to gain novel and in many cases deeper insights into questions at the center of Humanities research. Some view Digital Humanities as a way to assist more traditional research projects, perhaps using more heavily data-driven methodologies, but others hail it as an entirely disruptive enterprise that seeks to fundamentally alter the way the Humanities are done (Gold 2012, x). While the tools may be different, the traditional focus on language, texts, art, culture and ideas remains the same. There is no one definition of what Digital Humanities are and no one methodology that all Digital Humanities scholars use, but what they all have in common is a willingness to implement the latest technological developments to assist in the archiving, analysis and dissemination of the subjects in which they are interested, and to supplement the critical and speculative perspectives associated with the Humanities with a more empirical and data-driven approach.[1] However one defines it, there is no doubt that, as Eileen Gardiner and Ronald Musto announce in their primer for the Digital Humanities, "The array of platforms, applications, techniques and tools, all developed under the rubric of 'digital,' have been dramatically changing the way that humanists work, how they do research, gather information, organize, analyze and interpret it, and disseminate findings" (Gardiner and Musto 2015, 3).

Just as the idea of the "Humanities" spans a vast and contested field, so there are many valences of the term "Digital." At root, digital information is information that has been encoded and reduced into a binary series of ones and zeros that represent the original data and can be displayed once again through appropriate decoding. Because Digital Media reduce all text, images and sounds to numerical codes, they can consequently be described in mathematical terms,

1 Geoffrey Rockwell at the University of Alberta has brought together a number of scholars and asked them to define Digital Humanities. Their varied responses include such definitions as "Anything a Humanities scholar does that is mediated digitally, especially when such mediation opens discussion beyond a small circle of academic specialists", "The process of modeling, inserting raw information available through books, journals and other resources into a database and visualizing it to the user", "The digital humanities is whatever we make it to be" and "A delimiting hiatus (an anagram of 'digital humanities')." For the full list see http://www.artsrn.ualberta.ca/taporwiki/index.php/How_do_you_define_Humanities_Computing_/_Digital_Humanities%3F

https://doi.org/10.1515/9783110519082-001

manipulated algorithmically, and subjected to an almost infinite variety of computational procedures, many of which are described in lucid terms in the excellent introductory text edited by Constance, Lane and Siemens (2017). Computers armed with digital information don't just make representations of the world as literary or artistic works do, but rather they supplement this with the ability to manipulate these representations and model new possibilities (Smith 1995, 460). These models, operating within the heuristic sphere of the Humanities, take "imperfectly articulated knowledge" (McCarty 2005, 194) and help us to cultivate better comprehension of the subject through further computational operations upon the model.

The various features of the digital open up vast new vistas for analysis, manipulation and transformation of the information so encoded. For example, whereas it is quite difficult to alter a photographic negative on film using hand-retouching or chemical agents, a digital image can be altered programmatically by changing the binary code that represents the image (Manovich 2001, 10). Amongst the ones and zeros that encode and describe the image, there may be a series 001100 that represents the color green, and this can be changed to blue by simply replacing this with the code for that color, say 000011. An item that is digitally encoded resists decay over time (as long as technologies exist to decode it) and maintains a high degree of fidelity during the copying process, features which make digital media ideal for the preservation and dissemination of information. Whereas an audio recording on magnetic tape loses some quality and fidelity each time it is played and even more so each time it is copied, a digital MP3 music file, for example, can be played or copied over and over without suffering any loss of quality, and each copy stands as a perfect replica of the original, sounding exactly the same. Likewise, a manuscript can be damaged or smudged with each reading and the leaves, paper, bark or other material can rot over time. A photograph of the manuscript on film may help this situation somewhat, but it can also bleed color over time, curl and get otherwise damaged. However, a digital image of the manuscript remains the same forever (again, as long as technology remains to decode it). Of course, as Johanna Drucker, director of UCLA's Digital Humanities program reminds us, "The benefits of being able to encode information, knowledge, artifacts, and other materials in digital format is always in tension with the liabilities—the loss of information from an analogue object, or, in the case of a born-digital artifact, its fragility to migration and upgrade" (Drucker et al 2014, 9).

Another key feature of Digital Media that bears mentioning is that they enable random access to data just like human memory does. This is quite different from older forms of electric communication, such as cassette tapes or films, which have to be played through in a linear manner in order to find the information for which one is searching. Digital Media also can be connected into complex networks of exchange that communicate with each other through binary code and open up unprecedented opportunities for collaborative research. This networking feature allows digital archives, for example, to store an enormous amount of material that has been centralized from locations all over the world, obviating the need to travel to these archives in order to do research using their collections. Digital technologies are distinct for being highly scalable, meaning that they can be expanded relatively easily to perform larger and larger quantities of work as necessary, and for being modular, meaning that they can be separated as discrete units and combined in different ways in order to be customized for different tasks. All of these features of digital technologies will be covered in the various chapters of this volume, and their application specifically to Buddhist studies will be addressed.

There has been a fair degree of debate about the usefulness, desirability and effectiveness of the Digital Humanities, and there are differing views on this from different sectors. Some Digital Humanities techniques that at first seemed promising have perhaps led to poor or inadequate results, but open-minded inquiry and continual iterations may well serve to improve those areas in the future.[2] This is a field that, while not as new as some might think,[3] can nevertheless be said to be in its infancy, if only in terms of the untapped potential that it has, and with thoughtful development of the various methods associated with this field, it is likely that ever greater contributions will be made.

It may very well be that digital and computational approaches will eventually become so integrated into the Humanities that the idea of the Digital Humanities as a separate discipline or mode of inquiry will coalesce into the Humanities more generally, and the techniques that now come under that rubric will be just another set of tools for Humanists to use (Gardiner and Musto 2015, 2). To some extent, we are all Digital Humanists now, and the identification of a scholar or project as associated with the Digital Humanities may really be

---

2 Tom Scheinfeldt has discussed some of the successes and failures of Digital Humanities to pose and answer consequential questions. He suggests that it may be that, like other new technologies, it may take some time before their full use becomes apparent, and the theoretical issues salient to these specific methods may also make themselves clearer with the passage of time (2012).

3 The first project that is generally associated with the Digital Humanities, or Humanities computing as it was first called, was headed by Jesuit scholar Roberto Busa who built the *Index Thomisticus* starting in 1949. This is a massive concordance of the works of Christian theologian Thomas Aquinas that enlisted IBM and its computers to assist in lemmatization of the words being indexed as well as search and retrieval of information for the project from the massive body of material produced by this medieval scholar.

one of degree rather than kind. How many of those who rail against the Digital Humanities insist on using a card catalogue instead of web-based digital library catalogues? The electronic catalog is really just one kind of Digital Humanities tool that reflects many of the key elements of Digital Humanities: it is easily accessible from any location with an Internet connection, it uses computerized search to unearth data in seconds rather than a lengthy and laborious manual examination of text, and it includes a copious amount of metadata, that is, data about the data that allows for easier sorting. It also, incidentally, requires an enormous amount of human-performed work to be done in order to enter the data in the initial phase, which has also been typical of Digital Humanities projects. In fact, one of the reasons that Digital Humanities is gaining such traction now is that so much has already been digitized that we can often skip these labor-intensive initial phases and go right into analysis of the digitally available material. As Matthew Jockers points out, "Though not 'everything' has been digitized, we have reached a tipping point, an event horizon where enough text and literature have been encoded to both allow and, indeed, force us to ask an entirely new set of questions about literature and the literary record" (Jockers 2013, 4).

There are some very fundamental epistemological questions that lurk in the background of discussions about the analytic side of Digital Humanities that ought to be laid bare. A human reader can never read or digest all the information about any topic, and there is consequently always far more data available than can be used in any one study done by a person. In general, Humanities scholars are not able to look at more than just a small amount of what they consider representative documents to provide evidence for their claims and they must hope that these are able to stand in some meaningful way for the rest of the subject under study. Over time, this bottleneck has become such an intrinsic feature of the scholarly landscape that somehow we forget that ideally we would like to look at more documents in order to avoid building vast intellectual edifices based on what amounts to anecdotal evidence. The problem with anecdotal evidence is that it can be cherry-picked from a sea of information to prove or support a variety of different points.

For example, in writing a book about Buddhism, the author of *What the Buddha Taught* had necessarily, in a 150 page book, to take a small selection of texts and ideas from the corpus of over 15,000 pages that constitutes the full Pāli canon or *Tipiṭaka* which the book is intended to represent. Ideally, this is done through a careful selection of representative examples of the text, but there is invariably a large amount of personal bias that goes into such a selection. Within such a large corpus, other passages and ideas could have been selected that would provide a very different view about what the Buddha taught. In fact, many scholars have argued just that – that this book and others of its ilk have privileged one group of themes from one kind of text within the vast Buddhist corpus at the expense of other kinds.[4] Namely, they have highlighted the texts that focus on meditation, self-transformation and philosophical speculation at the expense of the more devotional, magical, and apotropaic texts that can also be found therein. Is there a way to settle this argument, and demonstrate what the Buddha really did teach? Speaking from a purely textual standpoint, perhaps if one could account for *all* the occurrences of *all* the words or phrases in the entire corpus, and manipulate them using a topic modeling algorithm or some similar unsupervised data mining algorithm, one could get to a statistically informed idea of what the text is about, devoid of human bias.

Likewise, it has for a long time now been understood that just focusing on major historical factors like great men, kings and battles provides a skewed understanding of history; extending one's domain of knowledge far beyond these subjects is necessary to get a better picture of what transpired in the past. But how far must one extend? How many personal records or household quotidian activities must be studied to get a sense of how people were living in those times? In theory, studying a certain representative sample should give one a good sense of the state of the whole population,[5] but the 2016 surprise election of Donald Trump in the USA has shown just how wrong even conclusions based on expertly sampled data can actually be. Ideally, one would want to eschew sampling and learn about every person or entity in the population under study. This has of course been impossible in the past, but the dream of analyzing each individual entity under study at a low cost is becoming possible with the aid of digital technologies. In the past, interviews with a few people had to stand in for the opinions of everyone else in their category, but now with social

---

4 David McMahan in his masterful study of modernism and Buddhism states "Elements of Buddhism that many now consider central to the tradition – meditation, internal experience, individual authority – are so constructed because of the gravitational pull of modernity. Modernity has attracted particular elements from the vast corpus of the tradition and not only made them central – leaving out others that have actually been more typical of Buddhist experience throughout history – but also reconstituted them in terms of modern discourses" (2008, 44). A large amount, if not a majority of contemporary Buddhist scholars seem to agree with this presentation. Jeff Wilson claims that "Written while he was staying at the Sorbonne after eight years' residence in the West, *What the Buddha Taught* reveals Rahula to be most interested in presenting Buddhism as a rational, humanistic religion that uncannily fits with modern times. He therefore cherry-picks from the Buddhist tradition elements that best demonstrate this ideal." (2014, 26).

5 For a concise introduction to selecting sample sizes, see https://www.itl.nist.gov/div898/handbook/ppc/section3/ppc333.htm [Accessed September 27, 2018]

media such as Facebook, Twitter, Snapchat and the like, we can actually begin to get a sense of what each individual in a group under study thinks about a given issue. Until now, we have had to represent our object through synecdoche, but

> in the digital realm the nature and truth claims of this representation are undergoing radical shifts. Because of vast new quantities of source material, search accessibility and aggregation and analysis tools, our representations are becoming more extensive and more accurate, offering us what might be a closer approximation to at least the complete historical, literary or visual record (Gardiner and Musto 2015, 19).

Rather than relying on whatever books happen to be in the local library or otherwise available, digital techniques allow us to operate on much larger scales than ever before. Google Books (https://books.google.com/), or the Hathitrust (https://www.hathitrust.org/) provide instant access to millions of documents that can be searched for relevant passages while sitting at one's own computer. This greatly reduces the chance that we might miss some document that could change our whole understanding of an issue, and brings us that much closer to the ideal of full access to an entire corpus. Surely if interpreting some literary movement based upon fifty books is good, then examining its expressions in ten thousand books is better and greatly reduces the incidence of sampling bias as well. There are many different techniques that can be used to analyze entire corpora and gain insight into statistical features of the language therein (Kytö and Lüdeling 2009). As Matthew Jockers writes,

> Instead of conducting controlled experiments on samples and then extrapolating from the specific to the general or from the close to the distant, these massive data sets are allowing for investigations at a scale that reaches or approaches a point of being comprehensive. The once inaccessible 'population' has become accessible and is fast replacing the random and representative sample. In literary studies, we have the equivalent of this big data in the form of big libraries... Science has welcomed big data and scaled its methods accordingly. With a huge amount of digital-textual data, we must do the same (2013, 7).

While digital techniques might offer a solution to the sampling problem, in cases where the texts are not just located and accessed digitally, but also processed algorithmically rather than read by a person, a difficult semiotic problem arises. Stanley Fish has argued that large scale statistical analysis of texts is a purely formal exercise that does not really tell us anything about their "meaning," inasmuch as meaning is not a fixed entity lying in wait within the text but rather emerges through engagement with the reader (1980, 70–73). If there is no conscious being who becomes aware, through the normal reading process anticipated by the author of the book, of whatever patterns the computer is finding, then how can the computer's findings really mean anything about the work? Are such studies not just spinning circular arguments that reference nothing beyond themselves? Fish is suspicious of the scientific claims made by such studies, and of their seeming elimination of the human from the reading process. These critiques should be seriously considered, and as humanists, we must do our best to relate statistically derived data to the human experience as much as is possible. The marriage of all the techniques at our disposal in contemporary times is a work in progress.

## Buddhism and Digital Humanities

As this volume is dedicated to Buddhism and the Digital Humanities, it behooves us to examine not only various definitions of the Digital Humanities, but also of Buddhism. Scholars recently have come to speak of *Buddhisms* in the plural, rather than Buddhism, because the forms of this religion differ so much from one another that it may be challenging to think of them as the "same" religion. Helen Tworkov, an editor with the Buddhist publication *Tricycle Magazine*, puts it very well when she observes:

> There is no one way to be a Buddhist. Like other world religions, Buddhism has proved capable of providing something for everyone. The many sects that now exist ... reflect the compelling and flexible dimensions inherent in any body of ideas that has been tested by time and has crossed continents (Tworkov 1991, 4).

Buddhism is usually divided into two main schools: Theravāda and Mahāyāna. The Theravāda school claims to reflect the earliest teachings of the historical Buddha, and its canonical texts are preserved in an Indic language related to Sanskrit called Pāli, which is similar to the language that the Buddha would have spoken. These texts highlight a number of ideas as the key teachings of the Buddha, and these have been endorsed by the tradition as containing the core doctrines of Buddhism. An early expression of the Four Noble Truths can be found in the *Dhammacakkappavattana Sutta* which is said to be the first sermon of the Buddha shortly after he became enlightened. Here, he says that all things are characterized by *dukkha*, or "suffering." This suffering is closely connected to the state of flux where whatever comes into being will eventually cease to be, whether it is a person, a mountain, an idea, or even a god. This entails the denial of any permanent, eternal substrate that forms the core of the human being, such as a Soul, and endorses instead the idea that we are constituted by five separate and ever-changing aggregate parts that include the physical body, sensations, perceptions, mental formations and consciousness. The Second Noble Truth explains that desire is what leads to suffering. Since all things are impermanent, including the objects of our desire and the human being itself, we can never permanently come to have the things we want, leading to the unsatisfactory state of *dukkha*. The Third Noble Truth states that by ceasing our desires, we can stop suffering and escape from the eternal cycle of *saṃsāra*. *Saṃsāra* denotes a cycle of rebirth that is governed by the law of karma which holds that all morally charged actions have a related effect: good deeds will lead to good results in this life or in a future life, and bad deeds will lead to bad results. As long as one has karma, one will be reborn, but when desire is completely overcome, the force that binds karma to oneself is destroyed and one is reborn no more. The Fourth Noble Truth outlines an eightfold path to achieve this blissful, desire-free state, known as Nirvana, that includes disciplined living, moral behavior, and meditation.

Mahāyāna Buddhism arose in the first few centuries of the Common Era with a focus on the idea of the Bodhisattva who, out of great compassion, vows to help all beings achieve Nirvana, rather than striving to reach the ultimate state for his or her own benefit. Because the Bodhisattva was viewed as being able to transfer good karma to the devotee, Mahāyāna Buddhism also became more devotional in tone than Theravāda, although devotion has also been a feature of Theravāda in practice from the earliest times as well. Philosophical schools of Mahāyāna often focus on the idea that all things lack any unchanging, self-existent substrate but rather are characterized by emptiness. Some took that to mean that nothingness is the fundamental ontological reality and that the world of our senses is a kind of illusion, without substantial reality. The notion of two truths was developed to account for the apparent opposition between the conditional reality of the world as we perceive it, replete with real substances that are different from each other, and the ultimate reality of undifferentiated emptiness. Other Mahāyāna schools such as Yogācāra focused more on the role of the mind in the creation of the world of experience and has been taken to be a form of idealism by some philosophers.

The Buddhist teachings were originally memorized and transmitted orally and were only laid out in writing for the first time in the first century BCE, according to traditional chronicles such as the *Mahāvaṃsa*. Both written manuscripts and oral traditions were brought to Central, East and Southeast Asia over the centuries, where they were often translated into the local languages.[6] The Digital Humanities scholar who is interested in Buddhism is thus blessed

6 For a good overview of the history of Buddhist texts, see Mizuno (1982).

with an abundance of material,[7] and in fact the unusually large size of the Buddhist canonical works and the wide distribution of its many artifacts led scholars to develop an interest in using computer storage and retrieval systems from early on in the computer age. As displayed by the broad range of chapters in this volume, there are many avenues that one can go down and many insights to be pursued. In terms of texts, the Buddhist canon as preserved in China is perhaps the largest collection of religious works in the world, containing over 3000 titles, some translated into Chinese from Indic originals and others written originally in Chinese.[8] The Theravādin canon in the language of Pāli is the only complete surviving canon from the pre-Mahāyāna mainstream sects and it consists of over 180 volumes. There are also thousands of works in a variety of other languages, such as Tibetan, Mongolian, Uighur, Sogdian, Thai, Burmese, Sinhalese, Cambodian and of course Sanskrit that are either translations of Buddhist canonical texts, or other works associated in some way with Buddhism. A great deal of this material has already been digitized, some of it in machine readable formats, and some of it as static images, as noted by the contributors to this volume. There are also enormous stores of Buddhist art, artifacts and archeological reports covering its 2500 year history in Asia, where many countries had in the past or still continue to have large Buddhist populations and governments interested in promoting the religion. This vast amount of material, then, makes Buddhism a rich subject for Digital Humanities, as many digital techniques are optimal for storing, curating and examining extremely large quantities of data.

The history of digitization of Buddhist texts begins in 1988, when, in honor of the Buddhist *Vesak* holiday, the entire Theravāda *Tipiṭaka* canon in Pāli was published on a disc drive as well as CD-ROM. This project was directed by Professor Supachai Tangwongsan of Mahidol University in Thailand and was based on a Siamese edition of the text. It also included a program called BUDSIR (Buddhist Scriptures Information Retrieval) that was designed to facilitate reading and searching the text. In 1994, additional texts including the traditional commentaries known as *Aṭṭhakathā* were released, leading in a stroke to a system that now could easily replace travel to the few libraries in the world that housed this complete set of Pāli texts. Soon, Thai, Burmese and other Southeast Asian

7 The best place to start investigating the wealth of digital Buddhist materials is in the series of encyclopedia articles written by Lewis Lancaster (2010), himself a pioneer in the field.

8 Aming Tu (2016) discusses the process of digitization of the Chinese Buddhist texts, the various stages that the project went though over the last twenty years, and the standardization efforts that have been going on to facilitate more academic exchange and research. The online canon comprises more than 150 million Chinese characters encoded in the XML language according to TEI standards.

script versions became available alongside the Roman one, and some versions were even equipped with a built-in Pāli dictionary. This effort was followed by a similar project to digitize the canon headed by the Vipassanā Research Institute in India that allowed for sophisticated search and retrieval functions in a variety of Asian scripts. This project was based on a slightly different edition of the canon that was redacted in 1956 in Burma as part of the Sixth Buddhist Council (by Burmese reckoning) known as the *Chaṭṭha Sangāyana*. Another project based in Sri Lanka at the Sri Vajiragnana Dharmayatanaya monastic training center also digitized a version of the canon that was published in the island in the 1960s. Since the late 1990s, all of these editions have been available on the Internet in addition to CD-ROM.[9] The Pāli Text Society, in turn, has also released a CD-ROM version of its Roman edition of the Pāli canon known as EPaliText. Despite a great deal of interest, a digital version of the complete English translations published by the Pāli Text Society has not yet been produced, and in fact no complete English versions of the Pāli Canon are yet available online. However, a number of individual texts and *suttas* can be found in various forms on the Internet, in particular at https://www.accesstoinsight.org/. Access to Insight started in 1993, when John Bullitt set up a dialup computer bulletin board service in his home with the support of the Barre Center for Buddhist Studies in Massachusetts. Later that year it joined with DharmaNet, another Internet-based bulletin board service based in California and initiated the Dharma Book Transcription Project, which digitized and distributed over a hundred books on Buddhism using the transcription efforts of a team of volunteers from around the world. In 1995 the overworked bulletin board service was moved to a website and since then AccessToInsight.org has grown into a well-organized library of over a thousand *suttas* and several hundred articles and books.

Besides these machine-readable text versions of the Pāli canon, there are a number of projects that are currently publishing digital images of Pāli manuscripts found in monastic libraries and other repositories all over Southeast Asia, in particular the Digital Library of Lao Manuscripts (http://laomanuscripts.net) and the Digital Library of Northern Thai Manuscripts (http://lannamanuscripts.net). The Fragile Palm Leaves Project (http://fpl.tusita.org/) maintains a database of thousands of Palm Leaf Manuscripts from Southeast Asia in their collection, and digitization efforts have begun with the help of the Buddhist Digital Resource Center (http://www.tbrc.org).

9 The Thai edition can be found online at https://www.mahidol.ac.th/budsir/budsir-main.html, the Sri Lankan edition at https://what-buddha-said.net/library/Pali/SLTP.htm, and the Burmese edition at https://www.tipitaka.org/.

A major early project to digitize the Tibetan Canon was initiated by Geshe Michael Roach who helped to found the Asian Classics Input Project (ACIP) (http://www.asianclassics.org/). Also in 1988, the ACIP began hiring Tibetan refugees in India to input Tibetan Buddhist texts into computer systems. Large catalogues of Tibetan woodblock prints have also been compiled, based largely on the collection of the Russian Academy of Sciences Institute of Oriental Studies, covering well over 50,000 titles, dwarfing similar catalogues available in print and emphasizing thereby the power of digital information storage to transform the way scholars do their work and research. Work is also being done on Mongolian and other collections housing hundreds of thousands of texts.

The Drukpa Kagyu Heritage Project which has now merged with the Padma Karpo Translation Committee (https://www.pktc.org) was another early project to use computerized methods in order to collect, preserve, archive, and publish Tibetan Buddhist texts. Tsoknyi Rinpoche III of the Drukpa Kagyu lineage saw the power of computers to preserve the Tibetan heritage and was able to enlist Lama Tony Duff, who already had experience programming Tibetan word-processing software and fonts, to manage a project to digitize Tibetan texts. The project got underway in Nepal in 1993 and by 2000 had transcribed and digitally edited approximately 2,500 titles. The software that was developed specifically for Tibetan texts, including dictionaries, grammars and word processing has been distributed to many monasteries and text preservation projects around the world and much of it is available at https://www.pktc.org.

Another important player in the early days of digitization of Buddhist texts was the International Research Institute for Zen Buddhism that published not just digitally entered Buddhist texts, but also material about the digitization process itself. Their journal *The Electronic Bodhidharma*, (http://iriz.hanazono.ac.jp/frame/book_f0.en.html) that began publication in 1991 dealt with such things as the challenges faced by those wishing to use non-Roman characters or diacritical marks, the problems caused by computer memory limitations, the various features of different kinds of computer operating systems, how to use markup languages, and other issues that helped to train and inform many scholars even beyond Buddhist studies about the art and science of bringing the Humanities into the digital realm. All of the digitization projects related to Buddhism faced particular challenges because fonts for Asian languages or transliteration and diacritics were often not standardized and different systems were not compatible with each other. A wrong choice of coding or platform could lead to great amounts of lost work and time.

In the early 1990s, the digitization of the Chinese canon faced some of the problems mentioned above because many of the characters used in the classical language of the Buddhist texts were not available in any commonly used fonts for modern Chinese. Therefore, entirely new fonts had to be developed prior to any attempts to digitize the content. Professors Lewis Lancaster, Urs App, Christian Wittern and Sungtaek Cho began a project to digitize the oldest complete set of wooden printing blocks for the Chinese canon from the Song period, which is actually held not in China but in Korea at the Jogye Order's Haein Monastery, where its 83,000 blocks from the 13th century have survived the ravages of war and climate until today. Eventually the Samsung Corporation agreed to help sponsor the project, and the works were released on CD- Rom in 1996, known as the *Tripitaka Koreana* (http://kb.sutra.re.kr/ritk_eng/index.do).

The most commonly used digital version of the Chinese canon is that of the Chinese Buddhist Electronic Text Association (CBETA), led initially by Ven. Hui Min and Aming Tu (http://www.cbeta.org/). It is based on the standard scholarly canonical resource, the Taisho Shinshu Daizōkyō (which was itself based largely on the Tripitaka Koreana). The print publisher of the classic volumes, Daizo Shuppansha Inc had initially wished to sell CD versions of the digitized text as a commercial undertaking, but they proved to be so expensive that a market was not apparent for the discs. Through an innovative agreement that pioneered some features of later intellectual property arrangements for information on the Internet in general, the CBETA acquired permission to distribute the texts online while Daizo Inc retained the copyrights. A project in Japan known as Saṃgaṇikīkṛtaṃ Taisho Tripiṭaka (SAT) housed at the University of Tokyo (http://21dzk.l.u-tokyo.ac.jp/SAT/index_en.html) has also published a digital version of the Daizōkyō online and has put a lot of work into ancillary tools for dealing with variant readings, translation and other issues.

Interestingly, the digitization of Sanskrit Buddhist texts has lagged behind that of Chinese, Pāli and Tibetan works because there is not an active community of Buddhists that still use them. Here we see one feature of contemporary religious life that bears some similarity to the way things have been done for centuries: the patron's interests largely dictate what religious artifacts get made. However, in the early 2000s a project got started that has made a great deal of headway at the University of the West in Los Angeles. Professor Lewis Lancaster from UC Berkeley in collaboration with Professor Min Bahadur Shakya of the Nagarjuna Institute of Exact Methods in Kathmandu began to digitize and publish online Mahāyāna Buddhist texts in Sanskrit, and that project has developed into the Digital Sanskrit Buddhist Canon that is described in detail in this volume in the chapter by Shakya.

Many of the Buddhist manuscripts, inscriptions and other fragments that have been unearthed in the Pakistani and Afghan regions that were known as Gandhāra in the classical world and were major centers of Buddhist learning are archived online at https://gandhari.org/. Here, one can find catalogues and Roman transliterations of a large amount of material from this important region, as well as several helpful reference resources.

A number of digital reference resources exist that can be used in conjunction with the digitized canons. One of the earliest major reference works to be digitized was the multi-volume *Fo Guang Buddhist Dictionary* (Hsing Yun 1988–99) that was made available on CD-ROM in the 1990s. Other projects were started to make dictionaries available for use directly online. Some of the largest such dictionaries are the Digital Dictionary of Buddhism (http://www.buddhism-dict.net/ddb/ ) and the Chinese, Japanese, Korean, Vietnamese – English Dictionary (http://www.buddhism-dict.net/dealt/ ) that first came online in 1995 with about 3000 terms and have now grown to over 100,000. These were developed by Charles Muller while at Toyo Gakuen University who writes a chapter about them herein. The University of Chicago hosts a Digital South Asia Library that includes a digitized version of the standard Pāli Text Society Pāli – English dictionary (http://dsal.uchicago.edu/dictionaries/pali/). The University of Cologne, under their Cologne Digital Sanskrit Lexicon project (http://www.sanskrit-lexicon.uni-koeln.de/), has digitized a number of Sanskrit dictionaries, including the Sanskrit – English dictionary by Monier Williams and the Buddhist Hybrid Sanskrit Dictionary by Edgerton. A Gāndhārī-English Dictionary produced by Stephan Baums and Andrew Glass is available at Gandhari.org, along with Monier Williams' Sanskrit Dictionary, Edgerton's Buddhist Hybrid Sanskrit, the Pāli Text Society's Dictionary and other materials (https://gandhari.org/n_dictionary.php). A searchable PDF of a scholarly Tibetan-Sanskrit-English dictionary edited by Jeffrey Hopkins is available for download at http://uma-tibet.org/pdf/greatbooks/UMA_Dictionary_May2016.pdf. Lama Tony Duff has also produced a digital Tibetan-English dictionary known as *The Illuminator* whose entries are organized by semantic fields and parts of speech, providing a great deal of context and lexical data for each entry (http://www.pktc.org/dictionary/).

The Digital Pāli Reader (https://pali.sirimangalo.org/) is an open source tool that provides an easy-to-use interface as an add-on to the Firefox Internet Browser with basic keyword search, navigation, bookmarking and automatic dictionary look-up as well as conjugation and declension look-up tools. It allows for instant lookup of words, simply by clicking on a word in the passage being read.

Digital photographs have also been made of thousands of manuscripts, many of which pertain to Buddhist subjects, drawn from archeological findings along the Silk Road. This project has been carried out under the auspices of the International Dunhuang Project (IDP.bl.uk) headed by Dr. Susan Whitfield and this has given scholars the ability to access scanned documents that were previously available only to those who travelled to the libraries such as the British Library where these items were housed. Digital maps have also been prepared that allow scholars to learn more about the provenance of many of these manuscripts, and related artifacts have also been digitally photographed.

An important and wide-ranging resource to mention is Buddha Net (http://www.buddhanet.net/), which was founded in 1992 in Sydney, Australia by Ven. Pannyavaro. It views itself as a cyber-sangha that provides a shared space housing thousands of text, visual and audio documents about all forms of Buddhism so that "an ancient tradition and the information superhighway will come together to create an electronic meeting place of shared concern and interests" (http://www.buddhanet.net/about_bn.htm). Here, one can find a Buddhist e-library with hundreds of machine readable books in a variety of Western and Asian languages, links to brick and mortar Buddhist resources around the world, guides for Buddhist studies, images of important Buddhist monuments, videos of Buddhist rituals, audio files of chanting and much more.

A number of tools are being developed to aid in the computational analysis of many of the online digital collections of texts. Two that will be mentioned here are TACL and READ. TACL is a free software tool developed by Michael Radich and Jamie Norrish (https://github.com/ajenhl/tacl/). The tool is intended to help discover such things as the sources of a given text, the impact of this text through citations, stylistic features distinctive to a given author or text and other inquiries along these lines. The tool uses the CBETA Chinese Canon and analyzes the texts into "n-grams", which are strings of characters whose length is determined by the user. The tool compares the texts in question and looks for all the strings of characters that are shared exactly by the texts, or all of the strings that are unique to each text. These results can then be sorted and analyzed in various ways and summary statistics can be generated that can show various ways in which these texts are related.

The Research Environment for Ancient Documents (READ) is a system currently being developed by a team lead by Mark Allon at the University of Sydney and Ian McCrabb at the Prakaś Foundation (http://sydney.edu.au/arts/research/read/). It is a comprehensive multiuser philological toolset for the transcription, translation and analysis of ancient Sanskrit and Prakrit manuscripts, inscriptions, coins and other documents. It also serves as a publishing platform and facilitates detailed annotation and tagging of textual corpora. In addition, it can link images, glossaries, bibliographies, catalogs, and dictionaries in a well-designed visual editor that also allows for flexible metadata, search and Text Encoding Initiative (TEI) support, amongst other features. READ incorporates a paradigm shift in data structure from strings of marked-up text to a semantically-linked network of objects and aggregates some of the latest developments in digital philological tools.

Various techniques can extract information from digitized corpora and display it in ways that allow one to derive new insights from the data. For example, Marcus Bingenheimer, Jen-Jou Hung and Simon Wiles (2011) have used computerized network analysis to visualize social network data derived from a TEI-encoded corpus of texts. Using a PREFUSE toolkit (http://www.prefuse.org), they derived a dataset of nexus-points from the markup information in the digitized *Biographies of Eminent Monks* that represents the social network implied in this text. Each 'nexus-point' is based on the data found in the encoding of the *Biographies* that had been previously made for other purposes, and represents a specific place and time at which some monks had some sort of interaction. This then provides information about 'who knew whom' in a certain period of Chinese Buddhism, and can greatly improve our understanding of the Buddhist society of the time.

Other work being done by Bingenheimer with his colleagues Jen-Jou Hung and Jieli Kwok includes stylometric analysis of Chinese Buddhist texts in order to ascertain an estimated time frame during which they were produced, along with the possible translators involved in the project. This is important in order to begin to establish the provenance of the scores of anonymous texts in the Chinese Buddhist canon. Stylometry applies statistical methods and artificial intelligence algorithms to the analysis of text and seeks to discover word-usage patterns that are not evident to the human reader but mark the "style" of the author. Stylometry can be used to attribute an anonymous text to a certain author by comparing it with a corpus of texts by possible authors and then identifying the authors with whose texts it shares the most features (Bingenheimer, Hung and Kwok 2012).

Since this volume will focus specifically on Buddhism and the Digital Humanities, it is important to note Buddhism's own contribution to the development of digital technologies. The translation of information into a series of ones and zeros that is the hallmark of the digital is only possible due to the invention of the very idea of zero by Indian mathematicians in the middle of the first millennium who were inspired by the Buddhist idea of emptiness. The very word *zero* derives from the Sanskrit Buddhist term *śūnya*, meaning "nothing."

Interestingly, throughout its long history Buddhism itself has also developed techniques with features that resonate with some of the more modern digital technologies. For example, the complex system of oral transmission that was – and to some extent still is – the main way that Buddhist texts were transmitted,[10] allows a human being to mimic the search capabilities of a computer. With a written text, one must spend long hours poring over the work in order to find relevant passages that shed light on whatever question it is that one is interested in. However, in the case of a memorized text, the person retains in memory the complete text and can mentally search for the relevant passages in an instant.[11] In contemporary times, the computer becomes an extension of human memory, and actually brings us back, not forward, to the way texts used to be engaged, as the computer can instantaneously bring up a passage that is relevant to whatever issue one is concerned with, just as the wise men of yore could quote relevant textual passages as needed, seemingly out of thin air.

Another analogue with digital frameworks can be found in the copious use of lists and matrices, called *mātrikās* in Pāli, that give structure to the Pāli canon. In this case, we find that these lists are linked together in much the same way as the tables of a relational database. The lists emerged by necessity in the oral world of early Buddhism as mnemonic devices to facilitate the memorization of key features of the Buddha's teaching. But in Buddhism, they achieved a state of sophistication and interrelationship that is unparalleled in the world's literature, with some lists being subsumed by others, and other lists expanding upon the data in yet others. For example the Four Noble Truths are often listed in the simple form "The Noble Truth of Suffering, The Noble Truth of the Origin of Suffering, The Noble Truth of the Cessation of Suffering and the Noble Truth of the Eightfold Path." Each of these elements, however, links to another list that expands on the phrase in question. So we find a list of features of suffering: "birth, aging, illness, dying, sorrow, grief, pain,..., in short the five aggregates of grasping are suffering." One can then, of course, turn to a list that includes details about these five aggregates, "Form, feeling, perception, mental formations and consciousness." As in a relational database, each of these lists is maintained separately in the memory, but they can be joined by way of the elements that they share in common. "The lists essentially are not just lists to be listed one after another, but fit together to form a pattern. Thus to learn and know the lists is to learn and know how they fit together, how they interconnect to form the structure and pattern of the Dhamma" (Gethin, 1992, 155). These interrelated lists can be seen as a pre-modern instantiation using human memory instead of computer chips of what we would now call a relational database.

10 For a discussion of oral techniques in premodern times, see Veidlinger (2006) and for contemporary times, see Klein (1994).

11 For a detailed study of the ways pre-modern people retained texts in their minds, see Carruthers (1990).

We might also point out that *maṇḍalas* attempt to encapsulate and encode a large amount of information into a much smaller field, as these colorful diagrams house a shockingly complex welter of ideas, cosmological principles, mythological tropes, salvific technologies and esoteric knowledge, a microcosm just waiting to be unpacked by those with the correct hermeneutical key (Brauen 1997). The impetus is remarkably similar to the obsession amongst many computer scientists with compressing data into more compact formats, the most well-known one being the zip file. The question of how to house as much information as possible in as small a space as possible is one which evidently interested the pre-modern Buddhists as much as it does contemporary signal processing researchers. *Maṇḍalas* also, of course, transform a large amount of knowledge into a series of concentric circles and other geometric shapes, as such essentially displaying their information in what could be considered a precursor to the creative data display programs that are often used by Digital Humanists, such as pie charts, network node-link spheres or the weather pattern chart shown in Figure 1.

I would like further to dwell upon the ubiquitous digital practice of tagging for a moment. Tagging grew out of the related markup process that records "information formally distinct from the character sequence of the digital transcription of a text, which serves to identify logical or physical features or to control later processing" (Renear 2004, 219). Markup developed out of traditional publishing practices where an editor might mark <heading> or <italics> next to a block of text to indicate that this text will be set in these ways in the final print version. Markup has blossomed into sophisticated tagging schemes using languages such as XML (eXtensible Markup Language) that allow one to define features of a document that one wishes to highlight using tagging elements. This is an incredibly powerful tool for textual scholars who now have the ability to add information about a text right into the document as metadata that is readable by both humans and machines, in ways analogous but functionally far superior to the interlinear commentaries that can be found in classical Chinese texts, for example (Gardner 1998). There is virtually no limit to the information that can be encoded in this way into a file. One can encode with XML the name of the <author> of a text, the <year> it was written, its <provenance>, its main themes, its main characters, and whatever else the scholar wishes to highlight. The Text Encoding Initiative (http://www.tei-c.org) has developed a scheme of scholarly standards to use when encoding a text in XML, and it is very helpful in setting up and laying out these texts, as well as allowing for easy collaboration and utilization by different scholars.

What is remarkable is that the process of tagging – of simply recording some details about an item – is also a key feature of the core Buddhist practice of

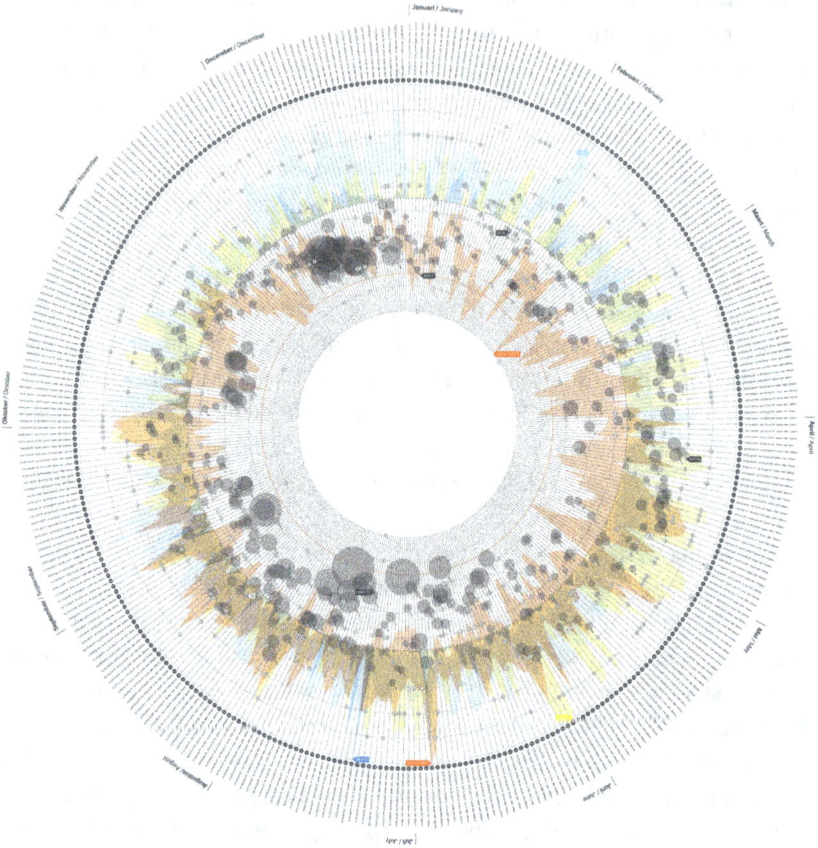


**Fig. 1:** Weather Chart courtesy of CLEVER°FRANKE

mindfulness. Mindfulness, also known as *sati* or *vipassanā*, asks us to analyze each breath as it goes in and out, marking short breaths in our mind as <short breath> and long breaths as <long breath>. We are then invited to expand this process to other aspects of our body, our thoughts and our feelings. We make a mental note of what they are, note some of their features such as <pleasant> or <painful> and move on to experience the next one (Hart 1987, 67–74). It is asserted that the simple act of tagging these experiences brings us to a deeper state of awareness and thereby closer to the bliss of Nirvana. There is little doubt that tagging a text can bring us closer to an ideal state as well, although dare we say that in this case, it is an ideal state of scholarly knowledge?

**Fig. 2:** Kalachakra Mandala https://en.wikipedia.org/wiki/Mandala#/media/File:Kalacha kraSera.jpg

## Outline of the Volume

This volume brings together scholars of Digital Humanities and Buddhism from around the world for the first time to address key issues in the field, disseminate the results of their research, and suggest ways forward. As a supplement to this Introduction, Ilona Budapesti presents a brief survey of the past, present and future of digital Buddhology. She identifies three stages in the development of this field, the first of which she calls the 'conservation/preservation' era, characterized by the labor-intensive work of taking high quality images of Buddhist manuscripts or typing Buddhist texts manually into a computer. This set the stage for the present state of digital Buddhology, the 'database' era. Current efforts in creating digital databases, semantic webs, optical character recognition, parsing, tagging, statistical methods in natural language processing and computational linguistics represent very courageous attempts at automating some of the drudgery of textual scholarship and extracting meaningful connections unseen (or even invisible) before. She then examines some possible future issues, challenges and opportunities such as the importance of standardization of data which can lead to reduced costs in development, sharing and reuse of resources, and finally, the potential benefits of vertical integration amongst web, database, and machine learning applications.

The next section of the book focuses on the theoretical and methodological issues associated with Digital Buddhology, with chapters that discuss various methods that can be deployed for analyzing text computationally, as well as ethnographic methods that can be used for examining expressions of Buddhism in Virtual Worlds. Daniel Veidlinger focuses on some of the more popular computational language processing techniques and explains how they can be used to further our understanding of Buddhist texts and reveal new perspectives on their meaning. Computers are able to digest enormous amounts of text – millions and millions of words that would take many lifetimes for a human to read – and apply various algorithms to the text in order to find relationships between the words, the ways they are used, as well as various hidden patterns and stylistic features that are not immediately evident to a human reader. The systems that he examines are Term Frequency-Inverse Document Frequency (TF-IDF), Collocation Analysis and Vector Space Semantic Mapping. Focusing on the practice of Buddhism in Second Life, Gregory Grieve in his chapter outlines an ethnographic method based on the field of virtual worlds, illustrating the salient issues with a case study of Buddhist objects, places, avatars, groups, and events as they are encountered in the Virtual World of Second Life.

The second section of this volume deals with digital conservation, preservation and archiving. A key archival problem in the Digital Humanities generally is how to relate and cross-reference texts that are in different languages. In Buddhist studies this problem is particularly acute because of the extraordinarily wide variety of languages in which the texts are written, including Sanskrit, Chinese, Thai, Sinhalese, Tibetan, Uighur and many others from entirely different language families. In their chapter, Kuo Ming Tang and Shu-Kai Hsieh introduce an *OntoLex* (Ontology-Lexicon) approach for the integration of cross-language Buddhist Scriptures that is informed by traditional Buddhist taxonomic knowledge structures. The approach originated from the Semantic Web community and uses ontologies, which are structured frameworks that record semantic information connected to a lexicon, in order to relate words across languages through a deeper understanding of their meaning in concert with a scholarly standard semantic network known as WordNet.

Paul Hackett discusses the variety of projects to encode, preserve and translate Tibetan Buddhist texts. His chapter begins with an introduction and overview of the needs of the community that regularly engages with Tibetan Buddhist literature including practitioners, translators, and scholars. It then surveys the various text initiatives and digitization projects and their scope, as well as the tools being developed to manipulate and analyze those resources in order to provide multiple points of access to that data, from syntactic parsing and semantic analysis to machine (assisted) translation. In addition to tools for direct text manipulation, secondary lexical and related resources such as digital dictionaries, multimedia archives, and basic computer resources (fonts, input methods, etc.) are also discussed.

Miroj Shakya contributes a chapter on the Digital Sanskrit Buddhist Canon Project at University of the West in Los Angeles and the Nagarjuna Institute in Nepal that is preparing a Sanskrit Canon for the modern world. While there is no unified collection or catalogue of Buddhist texts in Sanskrit, the source material of DSBC comprises printed editions of Sanskrit Buddhist texts published from the end of the nineteenth century onwards. This chapter discusses the development of the DSBC Project and examines the challenges that the project has been facing related to the digitization and preservation of Buddhist Sanskrit Texts.

David Wharton presents an account of a groundbreaking project that will likely change the face of Southeast Asian scholarship by making a large number of primary sources for the study of Lao and Lan Na culture freely accessible for study online. Since 2007, the National Library of Laos has collaborated with the University of Passau and with the Universities of Pennsylvania and Chiang Mai to produce the Digital Library of Lao Manuscripts and the Digital Library of Northern Thai Manuscripts, which together contain images of over 18,000 manuscripts, many of which deal with Buddhism. These collections, which went online in 2009 and 2016 respectively, rely heavily upon previous manuscript survey and preservation projects, and the majority of the images are digitized from microfilms produced by Harald Hundius, Chiang Mai University and the National Library of Laos in the 1970s, 1980s and 1990s, together with more recent images of directly digitized manuscripts.

With so many Buddhist texts available online, as outlined in the preceding chapters, the section ends with a study of an important tool to assist in reading this material. Over thirty years have now passed since the beginning of the pair of lexicographical compilations that are the Digital Dictionary of Buddhism [DDB] and the Chinese-Japanese-Korean-Vietnamese/English Dictionary [CJKV-

E], and over twenty years have passed since their installation on the Web. Charles Muller explores this pair of compilations that now contain together more than 110,000 entries, based on the contributions of more than 300 dedicated individuals who worked without major funding in one of the first examples of scholarly crowdsourcing in any field. This chapter will be particularly helpful for those wishing to establish other collaborative projects as it identifies successful strategies that might be further developed and applied elsewhere.

The third section of this volume focuses on what we can do with the data once it has been digitized. We must remember that the digitization of resources is only the first step in the scholarly endeavor, and it is hoped that further analysis will be performed on this material once it has been reliably converted to a digital format that can be manipulated algorithmically. In his chapter, Chris Jensen charts out the geographical biases of the *Gaoseng Zhuan* (*Biographies of Eminent Monks*) by plotting density maps of all locations named therein. In doing so, he situates this problem within the broader theoretical landscape of Historical GIS (Geographic Information System) scholarship. A geographic information system is designed to capture, store, manipulate, and communicate spatial or geographic data with the aim of helping thereby to recognize patterns that may shed light on the phenomena under study. Jensen proposes a statistical test that would allow researchers to more confidently base geographical conclusions upon these Chinese sources, and finally offers a case study of the utility of this test, using it to explore the geographical extent of a specific set of practices (namely, those related to visionary dreaming) in comparison with these texts' overall spatial distributions.

Recent advances in computing have enabled researchers to digitize large amounts of Buddhist texts in various languages, but analysis of these texts is still mainly limited to traditional methods that do not take advantage of the unique capabilities of the computer. A major problem with closing this gap involves the automation of word boundary selection for the purpose of constructing text concordances. Chris Handy presents a novel and scalable method for constructing such concordances without requiring user input, by searching for repeating character strings. He demonstrates how to apply this technique to sample texts in Sanskrit, Pāli, Tibetan and Chinese, and explains how the data gained from the concordance generation can provide seed material for more complex pattern analysis.

James Apple's chapter discusses the results of applying phylogenetic analysis, a computer-based method derived from principles of evolutionary biology supported by philological study, to select examples of Mahāyāna Buddhist scriptures found in Tibetan canonical collections (Tib. bka'-'gyur). The chapter initially outlines the methodology for utilizing computer-assisted cladistic techniques in investigating the genealogy of textual witnesses found in literary texts. Evolutionary biology and textual criticism have in common the principle that species or texts share derived characters in their evolutionary history that indicate relationships between ancestors and descendants. The chapter then provides an overview of the results of philological and phylogenetic analysis of select Tibetan versions of Mahāyāna scriptures. Based on these results, the chapter considers the costs and benefits of utilizing phylogenetics for the study of Tibetan texts.

We hope that this initial foray into Buddhism and Digital Humanities will be a useful introduction for those wishing to get involved in this field and look forward to the new insights that will arise in the coming years using these tools.

## References


Bingenheimer, Marcus, Jieli Kwok and Jen-Jou Hung. 2012. "A Computer-Based Approach for Predicting the Translation Time Period of Early Chinese Buddhism Translation." In *Digital Humanities 2012 Conference Abstracts*, edited by Jan C. Meister, 230–231. Hamburg: Publishing House of the Hamburg State and University Library.

Bingenheimer, Marcus, Jen-Jou Hung and Simon Wiles. 2011. "Social Network Visualization from TEI Data." *Literary and Linguistic Computing* 26(3): 271–278.

Brauen, Martin. 1997. *Mandala.* Boston: Shambala Publications.

Carruthers, Mary. 1990. *The Book of Memory.* Cambridge: Cambridge University Press.

Crompton, Constance, Richard Lane and Ray Siemens (eds.). 2017. *Doing Digital Humanities: Practice, Training, Research.* New York: Routledge.

Drucker, Johanna, David Kim, Iman Salehian and Anthony Bushong. 2014. *Introduction to Digital Humanities Course Book.* http://dh101.humanities.ucla.edu/wp-content/uploads/2014/09/IntroductionToDigitalHumanities_Textbook.pdf

Fish, Stanley. 1980. *Is There a Text in this* Class? Cambridge, MA: Harvard University Press.

Gardiner, Eileen and Ronald Musto. 2015. *The Digital Humanities: A Primer for Students and Scholars.* Cambridge: Cambridge University Press.

Gardner, Daniel. 1998. "Confucian Commentary and Chinese Intellectual History." *Journal of Asian Studies* 57(2): 397–422.

Gethin, Rupert. 1992. "The *Mātikās:* Memorization, Mindfulness and the List." In *In the Mirror of Memory*, edited by Janet Gyatso, 149–172. Albany: SUNY Press.

Gold, Matthew (ed.). 2012. *Debates in the Digital Humanities.* Minneapolis: University of Minnesota Press.

Hart, William. 1987. *The Art of Living: Vipassana Meditation as Taught by S.N. Goenka.* New York: Harper & Row.

Jockers, Matthew. 2013. *Macroanalysis: Digital Methods and Literary History.* Champaign, IL: University of Illinois Press.

Klein, Anne. 1994. *Path to the Middle: Oral Mādhyamika Philosophy in Tibet.* Albany: SUNY Press.

Kytö, Merja and Anke Lüdeling (eds.). 2009. *Corpus Linguistics: An International Handbook.* Berlin: De Gruyter.

Lancaster, Lewis. 2010a. "Computers and the Buddhist Cultural Heritage." In *The Encyclopedia of Buddhism,* edited by Damien Keown and Charles Prebish, 241–244. New York: Routledge.

Lancaster, Lewis. 2010b. "Cyber Buddhism." In *The Encyclopedia of Buddhism,* edited by Damien Keown and Charles Prebish, 254–258. New York: Routledge.

Lancaster, Lewis. 2010c. "Digital Input of Buddhist Texts." In *The Encyclopedia of Buddhism,* edited by Damien Keown and Charles Prebish, 288–296. New York: Routledge.

Lancaster, Lewis. 2010d. "Digital Research Resources." In *The Encyclopedia of Buddhism,* edited by Damien Keown and Charles Prebish, 296–299. New York: Routledge.

Lancaster, Lewis. 2010e. "Electronic Publications." In *The Encyclopedia of Buddhism,* edited by Damien Keown and Charles Prebish, 307–310. New York: Routledge.

Lancaster, Lewis. 2010f. "Technology and Buddhism." In *The Encyclopedia of Buddhism,* edited by Damien Keown and Charles Prebish, 726–733. New York: Routledge.

Liu, Alan. 2011. "The state of the digital humanities: A report and a critique." *Arts and Humanities in Higher Education* 11(1) :8–41

Manovich, Lev. 2001. *The Language of New Media.* Cambridge, MA: MIT Press.

McCarty, Willard. 2005. *Humanities Computing.* London: Palgrave MacMillan.

McMahan, David. 2008. *Buddhist Modernism.* New York: Oxford University Press.

Mizuno, Kogen. 1982. *Buddhist Sutras: Origin, Development, Transmission.* Tokyo: Kosei Publications.

Renear, Allen H. 2004. "Text Encoding." In *A Companion to Digital Humanities,* edited by Susan Schreibman, Ray Siemens and John Unsworth, 218–239. Malden, MA: Blackwell Publishing.

Scheinfeldt, Tom. 2012. "Where's the Beef? Does Digital Humanities Have to Answer Questions?" In *Debates in the Digital Humanities*, edited by Matthew Gold, 56–58. Minneapolis: University of Minnesota Press.

Schreibman, Susan, Ray Siemens and John Unsworth (eds.). 2004. *A Companion to Digital Humanities.* Malden, MA: Blackwell Publishing.

Smith, Brian C. 1995. "Limits of Correctness in Computers" In, *Computers, Ethics and Social Values*, edited by Deborah Johnson and Helen Nissenbaum 456–469. Engelwood Cliffs, NJ: Prentice Hall.

Snow, Charles P. 1964. *The Two Cultures and A Second Look.* Cambridge: Cambridge University Press.

Tu, Aming. 2016. "The Creation of the CBETA." In *Spreading the Buddha's Word in East Asia,* edited by Jiang Wu and Lucille Chia, 321–336. New York: Columbia University Press.

Tworkov, Helen. 1991. "Many is More." *Tricycle Magazine* 1(2): 4.

Veidlinger, Daniel. 2006. *Spreading the Dhamma: Writing, Orality and Textual Transmission in Buddhist Northern Thailand.* Honolulu: University of Hawaii Press.

Wilson, Jeff. 2014. *Mindful America.* New York: Oxford University Press.

Ilona Budapesti

# Past, Present, and Future of Digital Buddhology

*"Die Eule der Minerva beginnt erst mit der einbrechenden Dämmerung ihren Flug."*
Hegel, Preface to the *Philosophy of Right*

## Introduction

The goal of this chapter is to endow the digitally curious Buddhist textual scholar with the benefit of hindsight based on projects already underway that focus on the Pāli, Chinese and Tibetan Buddhist Canons. It should also be of benefit to the funding bodies, libraries, technologists, graduate and undergraduate students, the faith community, and the general public who wish to engage with Buddhism through the aid of digital devices and applications.

One of the thorniest issues that confront those thinking of a new Digital Humanities (DH) project is *what the research question should be.* It is often easiest to start with the *supply side* and establish what technologies we have in order to decide what the next step in digitization should be. For example, we might have manuscripts and wish to produce high quality photographs, or we might wish to go from photographs to a transcribed and machine-readable e-text, or from an e-text to a tagged corpus or from a corpus to a database, or we might wish to apply a specific statistical method or machine learning algorithm. The IDP,[1] TBRC,[2] THLIB,[3] CBETA,[4] SAT,[5] and the CST[6] are all, at the time of this writing, such supply side projects, laying down the data, infrastructure, and application layers first, with the aspiration that others will be able to benefit from these efforts. Starting from a specific question in mind about the text, or

1 International Dunhuang Project. (1994). Retrieved from http://idp.bl.uk/

2 Tibetan Buddhist Resource Center. (2009). *eTexts*. Retrieved from TBRC website http://tbrc.org/#!etexts

3 The Tibetan & Himalayan Library. (2010). *Tibetan Literary Encyclopedia Overview.* Retrieved from THLIB website http://www.thlib.org/encyclopedias/literary/

4 Chinese Buddhist Electronic Text Association. (1998). http://tripitaka.cbeta.org/

5 University of Tokyo Digital Database of the Taisho Canon (1998). http://21dzk.l.u-tokyo.ac.jp/SAT/index_en.html.

6 *Chaṭṭha Saṅgāyana Tipiṭaka* edition of the Pāḷi Canon. (1954). Retrieved from Vipassana Research Institute website http://tipitaka.org/chattha

https://doi.org/10.1515/9783110519082-002

being a *demand side* project is much rarer, examples[7] being *TACL*[8] for Chinese Buddhism by Michael Radich, and Śāstravid,[9] "a web-based electronic research tool for the study of Indian philosophy" connecting Sanskrit and Tibetan primary sources by Jan Westerhoff.

This chapter provides a survey of *textual* projects in the Digital Humanities in Pāli, Chinese and Tibetan. It pinpoints the major tension between technology and funding lifecycles and provides a set of recommendations for those who are currently involved with or wish to embark on a digital Buddhology project, for the sustainability and preservation of the knowledge created, and the ease of reuse for future research. It closes with some possible future trends that we can see across the board in terms of technological advancements.

## Distinguishing Humanistic Computing and Digital Humanities

Being a relatively new term, the definition of Digital Humanities is still in flux but can be broadly stated as "the intersection of humanities and computing" (see Figure 1). I will call this the *wide definition of Digital Humanities.* On one hand this includes applying humanistic approaches to the study of computing and looking at such things as the question of representation and the epistemology of computing through the lens of media studies, game studies, cultural analytics and other newly emerging fields; on the other hand it means "employing technology in the pursuit of humanities research."[10] Let us call the prior one *Humanistic Computing*, and restrict our interest to the latter, which we can call the *narrow definition of Digital Humanities.* We define it as the study of traditional

7 The Oxford Corpus for Old Japanese. (2016). A good example of a demand driven digital project initiated by linguistics research on Japanese verbal syntax such as bigrade transitivity. Although not Buddhist in focus, it is a prime example of textual analysis in an East Asian classical language. Retrieved from http://vsarpj.orinst.ox.ac.uk/corpus/publications.html

8 Textual Analysis for Corpus Linguistics. (2015). Retrieved from TACL git repository https://github.com/ajenhl/tacl/

9 Śāstravid. (2014). *Indian Philosophy Research System.* Retrieved from Śāstravid website http://sastravid.theology.ox.ac.uk/ . This database contains both high quality data that has been manually proofed by expert editors and connection between translations and commentaries allows one to see connection between texts effortlessly. A semantic organization of philosophical concepts also allows one to move the level of analysis to a higher level of abstraction not possible before. Users can view multiple languages, tag passages, create and share notes.

10 Source: https://en.wikipedia.org/wiki/Digital_humanities [Retrieved January 8, 2017]

humanities disciplines such as history, philosophy, linguistics, literature, art, archaeology, music, cultural and area studies (including Buddhism), with tools provided by computing such as Hypertext, Hypermedia, data visualization, information retrieval, data mining, statistics, text mining, corpus linguistics, digital mapping, natural language processing, machine learning, artificial intelligence, and digital publishing.

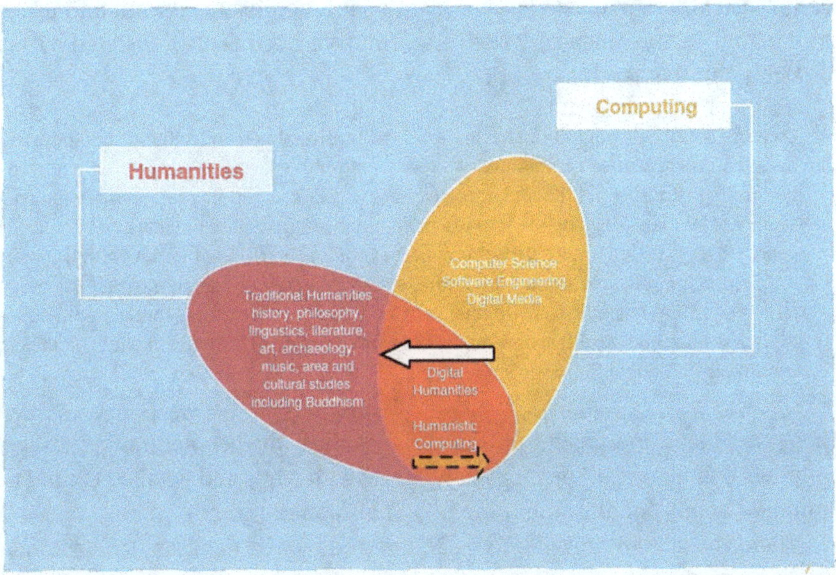


**Fig. 1**

This chapter, then, will focus on digital output or digital technology, defined as an activity that involves the creation, gathering, collecting and/or processing of digital information from a specific domain of humanity.[11] In short, we will narrow our definition of Digital Humanities to the *use* of computing technologies for traditional humanities; I am thus excluding "humanistic computing."

The textual Digital Buddhology scholar will discover that besides manuscripts, other media are now being investigated with previously unimaginable technologies. Multi-spectral images of non-textual artifacts and material culture

11 Technical Plan, Research Funding Guide, AHRC http://www.ahrc.ac.uk/funding/research/researchfundingguide/attachments/technicalplan/ [Retrieved January 8, 2017]

such as architecture,[12] sculptures, paintings, musical instruments, costumes and garments, ritual implements, altars and *maṇḍala*s are being produced. Auditory and visual media including recordings of current practices, recitations, melodies, music, and ritual dancing are just beginning to be investigated digitally as well. Some very exciting examples of non-textual Digital Buddhology are the virtual Thai and Tibetan monastery projects that are available online. These sites provide photographs, maps, videos and interactive media that allow the user to virtually "visit" these monasteries and learn about their history, layout and usage. On the Thai Digital Monastery site (http://tdm.sas.upenn.edu/), directed by Justin McDaniel, the developers write:

> Creating a monastic digital library for Thailand involves interconnecting technology, field data, and a supportive community of experts and enthusiasts. We strongly adhere to the notion that exposing hidden and scattered data to a large multi-lingual international community of learners can generate new research initiatives, juxtapose previously disconnected concepts and discourses, and inspire new students in the fields of anthropology, history, art, linguistics, religious studies, literature, etc. The knowledge community that is generated out of virtual interactive environments can question stereotypes, reconfigure old epistemic structures, and postulate new notions of what it means to be both a modern global citizen and a traditional monastic student.

There are videos and images on the site that cover the people, murals, *stūpas*, buildings and images at the monastery, along with maps and detailed textual information about Buddhism and life at a Thai monastery.

There is a similar project (Figure 2), directed by Jose Cabezon, to construct a virtual representation of the Sera monastery of the Gelukpa order in Tibet (http://www.thlib.org/places/monasteries/sera/ ). The project directors tell us that

> The Sera Project is a research and pedagogical initiative employing state-of-the-art digital technology in the service of creating the most comprehensive, interactive, multimedia database of a Tibetan Buddhist monastery ever attempted. The various nooks and crannies of this website allow you to explore the different facets of Sera, one of Tibet's most important monasteries. You will find sections on its physical layout, history, material culture, educational system, and ritual life – in short, all of the various aspects that together constitute the richness and complexity of Tibetan monastic life. (http://www.thlib.org/places/monasteries/sera/about/wiki/sera%20monastery%20project%20overview.html#ixzz4X1ZWZzU7)

12 How LIDAR Scans Reveal Angkor's Hidden City, Smithsonian Channel, https://www.youtube.com/watch?v=o6Kq4XF1zKU

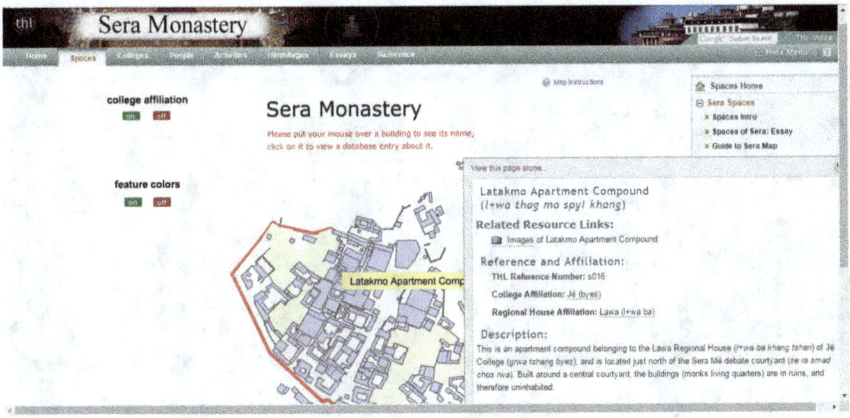


**Fig. 2:** The Sera Project (http://www.thlib.org/places/monasteries/sera/)

Two new emerging technologies which should also be mentioned are 3D imaging of sculptures[13] (Figure 3) and laser assisted drone-based mapping of archeological sites. These can both help to preserve important information about Buddhist artifacts and their find sites, as well as help us to see elements that might not be discoverable with the naked eye. Here we have technology assisting us to gain a deeper understanding of Buddhist history and material culture that can open a new era of knowledge production that could only have been dreamt of prior to the development of these technologies.

## Conservation Era, Database Era, Statistical Era

Textual digital projects can be broken down into three main eras. The past 'conservation' era consists of taking high quality images of Buddhist manuscripts and then creating transcripts of their content. I call the present the 'database' era because most projects with access to a machine readable e-text then took the next step to either create a tagged corpus or to put their text into some form of database for specific search and retrieval purposes. The future is likely to be the 'statistical' era, which includes both classic statistics such as corpus linguistics and more advanced forms using artificial intelligence or machine

13 Body of Devotion: The Cosmic Buddha in 3D January 30–December 2016 Arthur M. Sackler Gallery in Washington D.C. https://www.freersackler.si.edu/press-release/the-cosmic-buddha-in-3d-exhibition-to-open-jan-30/ For a 3D visualization see https://www.youtube.com/watch?v=pl2oAfaSlPg

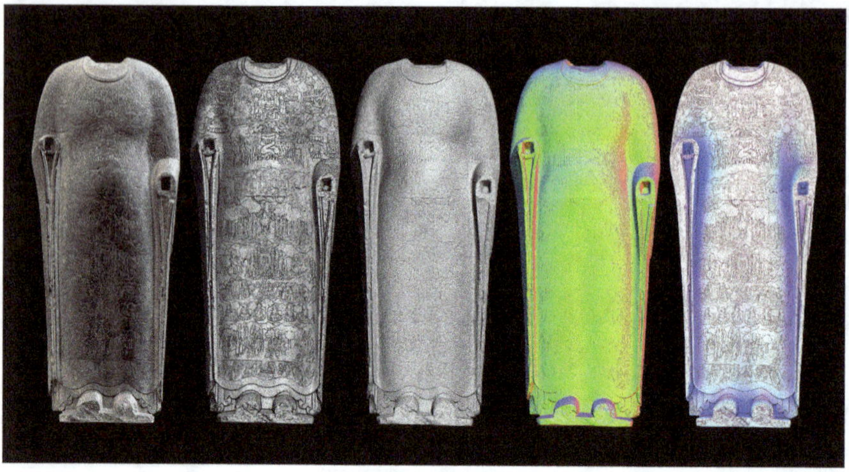

**Fig. 3:** The Cosmic Buddha 3D Scanning (Used by permission of the Freer Gallery, Washington, D.C.)

learning and most recently deep learning for natural language processing. Let us now survey projects in each language separately, after which we will draw up common themes, pitfalls as well as lessons learned.

## Pāli

Pāli has a very mature e-text: the whole Pāli Canon is available in high quality, machine-readable format, boasting text that has been proofread and accurately reflects the content of the manuscripts upon which it is based. The largest 'past' or 'conservation' project is the *Chaṭṭha Saṅgāyana Tipiṭaka* (CST) CD and website published by the *Vipassana Research Institute,* which has made the whole Pāli canon available in Roman and several other scripts in a digital format and is both highly proofed and comprehensive. The *Digital Pāli Reader* (DPR) is an open source tool[14] that provides an easy-to-use interface with basic keyword search, navigation, bookmarking and automatic dictionary look-up as well as conjugation and declension look-up tools. Although this e-text lacks a comprehensive database, nevertheless the quality and quantity of the data make it a prime candidate for statistical and algorithmic treatment of the text which may allow us to study morphology, authorship styles, chronology, poetics and

14 Digital Pali Reader. (2012). Retrieved from Sirimangalo website http://pali.sirimangalo.org/

other features in new ways that were not possible previously. At present there are several other projects involving Pāli texts such as the Thai and Lao manuscript preservation projects[15] as well as Canonical editions published by Mahidol University in Thailand[16] and the Sri Vajiragnana Dharmayatanaya Bhikkhu Training Center in Sri Lanka,[17] although none of these have attained the popularity of the CST.

A brief mention of Buddhist Hybrid Sanskrit is in order here. Computational work has begun on Classical Sanskrit[18] and we also see digital attribution studies in Indian philosophy,[19] as well as the Sanskrit Manuscripts project at Cambridge[20] and the Search and Retreival of Indic Texts (SARIT)[21] project, but the resources for Buddhist Hybrid Sanskrit (BHS) are limited. Franklin Edgerton's classic dictionary is available as searchable PDF, as well as a dictionary file[22] from Cologne Digital Sanskrit Dictionaries,[23] and a version is also available at Gandhari.org.[24] Edgerton's grammar and reader are available as scanned PDFs, however no further resources for BHS are currently available online. Thinking ahead, a reader similar to the DPR would be a good next step linking Edgerton's dictionary to machine readable e-text. Ideally a dictionary with both the Pāli, BHS and Sanskrit dictionaries combined would be the next supply side project to enable the adoption of BHS.

## Chinese

A good example of conservation efforts is the *International Dunhuang Project* (IDP), an international collaboration to "make information and images of manuscripts freely available on the internet for research and educational purposes." According to Susan Whitfield, Director of the IDP at the British Library, however, there is not enough funding in place to turn the high quality images into text. This unfortunately greatly limits the possible uses and the audience of the

15 http://lannamanuscripts.net and http://laomanuscripts.net. These are both described herein in the chapter by David Wharton.
16 https://www.mahidol.ac.th/budsir/budsir-main.html
17 https://what-buddha-said.net/library/Pali/SLTP.htm
18 Sanskrit Computational Linguistics Symposia. (2007, 2008, 2009).
19 Helleswig, Oliver. Indology mailing list. (Nov 5, 2015). http://listinfo.indology.info/
20 http://sanskrit.lib.cam.ac.uk/
21 Search and Retrieval of Indic Texts. http://www.tei-c.org/Activities/Projects/sa02.xml
22 http://www.sanskrit-lexicon.uni-koeln.de/scans/BHSScan/2014/web/index.php
23 http://www.sanskrit-lexicon.uni-koeln.de/
24 https://gandhari.org/n_dictionary.php

data, so it is to be hoped that this situation will change as Digital Humanities gains popularity (and funding) in order to make the texts available in machine readable format in the near future. The use of Intelligent Optical Character Recognition (iOCR) combined with crowd-sourcing should be able to turn the data into machine readable format, which could greatly reduce the cost compared to manual entry and proofreading.

A large body of Chinese primary texts is available in the *Thesaurus Linguae Sericae* (TLS)[25] and Buddhist texts in CBETA. For the latter the goal was to digitize the whole Taishō Tripitaka, which they did, with high accuracy, and the quantity and quality of the text increases each year as more texts are keyed in and proofed. Several manuscripts are included with their differences noted. The project made it possible for the current generation of Buddhologists and the general public to run basic searches in the Chinese sources. One of the advantages is that the data is available in XML, however, the complicated UI[26] has a somewhat long learning curve. For example, sometimes conducting a search requires various steps and some workarounds on the organization of the underlying texts, which are organized by Taishō volumes, and further broken down by so called 卷 (Chinese: juǎn) or scrolls. Working with the CBETA online can sometimes be a manual and time-consuming endeavor if one wishes to perform analyses from a historical or a philosophical perspective. However, their downloadable CBReader allows for a far easier and more productive search process. In both systems, one is able to locate the matches of a single search term, or use "&" (means AND), "|" (means OR), "-" (means NOT) to perform a search on more than one search term. There is also a useful function called near ("~"), which can search the document where terms A and B appear within a certain distance from a number of Chinese characters. After the user has specified *what* they want to search in this manner, they can then specify *where* they want to search by specifying the search range. For example, they can search in the entire CBETA corpus, only in the current text or they can set a custom search range by text collection, book volume or in the online version, by author or time period.[27] There are also a number of useful ancillary tools such as a term usage statistics chart and connections to the Buddhist Studies Authority Database and the Digital Library and Museum of Buddhist Studies. Finally, it should be mentioned that the code underlying the tool is not open-source and thus it is not possible for those with programming skills to contribute improvements to

25 Thesaurus Linguae Sericae 漢學文典. An Historical and Comparative Encyclopaedia of Chinese Conceptual Schemes. http://tls.uni-hd.de/home_en.lasso

26 User Interface

27 Thank you to Dr. Jen Jou Hung for clarification on these search capabilities.

the project. From a purely scholarly standpoint it might be beneficial to develop an easy-to-use, open-source user interface.

Another example of databases is the Digital Dictionary of Buddhism[28] (DDB) by A. Charles Muller. It is notable for two excellent aspects, first that contributions from users are encouraged and the living database is updated monthly, and second that the DDB thought to make progress on the integration problem by becoming interoperable[29] with the online SAT Taishō Text Database[30] thereby greatly increasing its utility. Words found in the SAT texts can thus be easily looked up in the DDB in a seamless manner during the reading process.

The *Chinese Buddhist Canonical Attribution Database* (CBC@)[31] is another database initiative that possesses excellent potential for bringing together philologists, philosophers and historians by allowing user-contributed attributions, including multiple hypotheses alongside each other for comparison.

## Tibetan

A Tibetan conservation effort that has made progress in turning manuscripts into editable, electronic text or *e-text* is the *Tibetan and Himalayan Library (THLIB)*, which includes a manually keyed in *Derge Kangyur* and some associated reference works. The drawbacks of this resource for computational analysis are that the data is behind a proprietary interface making it costly and complicated to get to the data source for corpus-level machine processing. The THLIB data has also not been subjected to as rigorous a proofreading regimen as the Pali and Chinese databases and has also introduced some romanization errors. The digital textual scholar should thus be aware that the content of the THLIB files may be somewhat less faithful to the content of the manuscripts they intended to digitize than might be desired in an ideal situation.

The e-texts of the *Tibetan Buddhist Resource Center (TBRC)*, which has recently changed its name to the *Buddhist Digital Resource Center*, constitute a deep catalog of available Tibetan texts. Over 995,000 pages had been scanned

---

**28** Digital Dictionary of Buddhism. (1995). Retrieved from DDB website http://buddhism-dict.net/ddb/. DDB is "a compilation of Chinese ideograph-based terms, texts, temple, schools, persons, etc. found in Buddhist canonical sources"

**29** Through the help of the *International Institute of Digital Humanities*.

**30** SAT Daizōkyō Text Database. (2008). *Saṃgaṇikīkṛtaṃ Taiśotripiṭakaṃ*. Retrieved from University of Tokyo website http://21dzk.l.u-tokyo.ac.jp/SAT/ddb-bdk-sat2.php

**31** Chinese Buddhist Canonical Attributions database. (2015). Retrieved from CBC@ website https://dazangthings.nz/cbc/

by 2015 and some 600,000 pages are in queue, consisting not only of canonical and commentarial texts, but also of historiographical, philosophical, literary, legal and other genres. Of course, with such a massive amount of material being digitized mostly through OCR,[32] there are transcription inaccuracies of which the scholar should be aware. In future, it is a desideratum for this and other massive text projects to have a mechanism in place for proofing and correcting the data, using expert crowd sourcing when appropriate as well.

Although the TBRC e-texts are proprietary, there is currently a freely available Tibetan corpus in the ACIP[33] data set. It is raw text-only,[34] available for download and consequently requires programming skill to use it such as ability to tag,[35] parse, or build custom searches. However, the texts are readily readable by both humans and machines in this form and can thus be efficiently used for a variety of traditional and digital purposes. A culture of Tibetan texts has arisen over the years from small projects, various monasteries, and "gray-market" e-texts from Chinese publication houses, but unfortunately none of those are systematic or could be taken as a coherent corpus.

## Cross-linguistic Comparison

As we saw above, the three canonical languages of Pāli, Chinese and Tibetan share this pattern of undergoing first a *preservation* era (past), are now roughly all undergoing a *database* building era (present) including building semantic webs,[36] and a few recent and upcoming publications are attempting *statistical* methods.

Some unique challenges arise with regards to each primary language. Pāli is ready for statistical and machine learning because of the available high quality e-text but we are discovering new/unknown primary texts for which more pres-

32 Optical character recognition is the process of scanning images into a computer and letting software convert the image file into a text file.

33 Asian Classics Input Project. (1988). Retrieved from ACIP website http://www.asianclassics.org/

34 The Buddhist Canons Research Database. (2013). Retrieved from AIBS website http://www.aibs.columbia.edu/databases/New/?sub=about

35 Dr. Paul Hackett at Columbia has tagged the text which provides the underlying data on his website. http://www.columbia.edu/~ph2046/RnD/Hackett/

36 A framework to extend the Web (Internet) through standards so that data can be shared and reused across applications.

ervation work will need to be done in order to bring them into the universe of digital processing.

Both in Pāli and Sanskrit we need to lemmatize, that is, disambiguate word boundaries and find core lexical elements that surface in different morphological forms before semantic analysis can be fruitful. In Chinese, specifically the case of the CBETA we need separation of the application layer from the data layer. Finally, in Tibetan the quality of e-texts needs to be raised.

## Technology versus Funding Lifecycle

The technology lifecycle if simplified could be divided into planning, development and maintenance phases. The problem, however, is that funding bodies do not like to fund existing projects or maintenance phases, the preference being to fund "new" research. It is not possible to use research grants to endow projects in perpetuity either, as all funds must be spent. This basic misalignment of funding versus technology lifecycle is one of the major causes of failure for digital projects.

A case in point is Śāstravid mentioned earlier. The search tools were built with proprietary software making it costly and difficult to maintain, update and sustain development. Once funding ran out, this project faced the same problem that many digital database efforts faced, which is that their data was entangled with the technology and could neither be built upon nor reused for further work.

Most academics and funders do not understand the capital required for software development: a grant of $50,000 is considered large when in reality building and providing quality content for a *CMS (Content Management System)* can cost in the millions. Maintaining software can run in the hundreds of thousands of dollars a year to keep up-to-date including both technology costs and the employment of skilled human resources. Funders thus put a death sentence on any project they fund if there is no continuity plan that would endow the project in perpetuity, which however is disallowed by funding guidelines: usually only costs can be covered not endowments.

## Sustainability versus Data Preservation

If we follow the simplified software development lifecycle of "plan, develop, maintain" we will see that academics are caught in a conundrum, namely that there is no explicit funding available for the "maintain" part yet they are asked to submit sustainability plans with their grant applications. In reality the academic technical project lifecycle looks more like "plan, apply, fund, develop, publish, die." Sometimes death happens before publication.

When funding runs out most project owners try to reach out to libraries and ask their IT departments to take over their data. On speaking with Dr. Christine McCarthy Madsen, Head of Digital Resources at the Bodleian Library I found out that more than 30 digital projects were looking for an owner/maintainer to take over just this last year. There is no funding available for that, however, nor is there skilled IT personnel to do so at libraries. Even at the Bodleian, technician jobs remain unfulfilled for years because software engineers with sufficient technical knowledge are employed in industry at 3x-10x more than what a library can offer. In short, once funding runs out, many projects die.

A useful – and vital – distinction that is made in the UK's Arts and Humanities Research Council technical guidelines separates project sustainability from data preservation. Sustainability is how long the project's website and front-end will be available to users, whether there will be continued editing permitted after the end of the funding process or whether it will be frozen with editing suspended. Preservation is what will happen to the data at the end of the project, for example if it is parked in a low-cost, well-established data store it could theoretically last for many decades or even centuries. Preservation is easier than sustainability and should be performed regularly throughout the lifetime of the project. Whether there is a migration plan to park the completed dataset and findings of analysis in a destination is what I define as an *exit strategy*. A good example is the relatively new Oxford Research Archive (ORA),[37] which aims to provide the same function that libraries have provided for books historically by being a repository for digital assets. To further improve the usability and utility of the ORA I propose a) publication of *explicit standards* that each media type has to be stored in – e. g. text, image, audio, video, b) an *automated validation tool* from the side of the ORA that researchers can keep running their data against before and during their development, to validate and correct their data structures while the development phase is still underway and c) *storage cost calculators* to help with grant applications. This would allow researchers to build clear and precise exit strategies even before starting development, instead of becoming an afterthought in which one tries to find a data storage solution after publication has already been undertaken.

A set of minimum positive recommendations for maximizing the reusability of projects follows. As a corollary these recommendations will lower total cost of

---

**37** https://ora.ox.ac.uk/

ownership and maintenance, the key to overcoming the death trap set up by the systemic problem of funding misalignment.

1) decide on demand vs. supply side project
2) have a clear exit strategy
3) clear separation of concerns: data should be separate from the database layer, which should be separate from the application layer
4) maximize in-house technical skills and documentation
5) standardize and simplify

In short, the digital project lifecycle would have these suggested phases "Plan, Apply, Fund, Develop Iteratively, Backup Incrementally, Migrate Regularly, Archive/Preserve/Deposit, Publish, Close." Agile[38] style continual publishing is also suggested, if possible.

For simplicity, a good example is the Cuneiform Digital Library Initiative[39] where researchers opted for ASCII only character encoding. Even UTF-8 caused unnecessary computational load. The advantages of simple data structure were long-term accessibility and lower (negligible) cost of maintenance, which directly translated into sustainability as well as preservation.

## Future

First and foremost, more standardization of data in the preservation/conservation area would be invaluable. An extensible but well-defined XML standard is needed similar to what the hospitality, flight, travel, supply chain, and virtually all commercial industries have created. Text Encoding Initiative (TEI) standards have been developed for Western manuscripts and happily many of the elements defined in the manuscript description module can also be used to describe Buddhist texts.[40] There is now a TEI Special Interest Group (SIG) that is dedicated to developing encoding solutions to challenges facing scholars dealing with East Asian materials. The SIG hopes to create guidelines for encoding Japanese, Chinese, Korean, Taiwanese and Vietnamese texts that are TEI P5 compliant in order to establish shared standards that can be used by communities

38 Collier, Ken W. (2011). *Agile Analytics: A Value-Driven Approach to Business Intelligence and Data Warehousing.* Pearson Education.

39 http://cdli.ucla.edu

40 The TEI manuscript description module can be found at http://www.tei-c.org/release/doc/tei-p5-doc/en/html/MS.html

interested in texts from the region, including Buddhist texts.[41] An impressive amount of work has also been done on text encoding for Buddhist studies by the TBRC, which is now rebranding itself as the Buddhist Digital Resource Center (BDRC) as its efforts continue to branch out of Tibetan texts into those in all Buddhist languages. The BDRC has a legacy text encoding schema for its archival files and has supplemented this with a very extensive Buddhist ontology in the Web Ontology Language (OWL) that is aimed at capturing as many features of the Buddhist cultural heritage as possible.[42] For example, the OWL ontology that they have built includes ways to identify the monastic lineage of a Buddhist author, along with who his parents were, where he was born, and many other such details that can be shared across websites that adhere to this same OWL schema, and can also be used for performing deep searches on their material. The BDRC also aims to connect multiple resources in Buddhist studies leveraging linked data through their Buddhist Universal Digital Archive (BUDA) that aims to collect and connect all available digital Buddhist Resources. BUDA will offer a suite of research tools with access to multiple repositories of Buddhist texts and artifacts and will boast deep and dynamic search capabilities including multi-language queries. Once it is complete, it will no doubt represent a great leap forward for Digital Buddhist studies.

BUDA will also use the International Image Interoperability Framework (IIIF) standards that allow image level metadata to be shared across the Internet and for annotations to be made and stored with the data. In fact, IIIF will likely be used by many digital Buddhist projects in the future, as it serves:

> 1)To give scholars an unprecedented level of uniform and rich access to image-based resources hosted around the world. 2) To define a set of common application programming interfaces that support interoperability between image repositories. 3) To develop, cultivate and document shared technologies, such as image servers and web clients, that provide a world-class user experience in viewing, comparing, manipulating and annotating images.[43]

As such, the IIIF offers a standardized method of describing and delivering images over the Internet, and it even allows for structured metadata that explains how the images should be sequenced, which would allow a manuscript whose different pages are held, for example, in different repositories, to be displayed on the screen in the proper, seamless sequence if one is using IIIF compliant viewing software. This kind of capability will greatly enhance the viewing expe-

41 http://www.tei-c.org/Activities/SIG/EastAsian/
42 https://github.com/BuddhistDigitalResourceCenter/owl-schema
43 http://iiif.io/about/

rience and usability of Buddhist artifacts, manuscripts, and other cultural materials that are spread across the world in separate digital silos.

Another future trend will, of course, be increased use of mobile technologies. BDRC has again paved the way by releasing a mobile app *BDRC Lib*, providing a new way to interact with the library. The app, available on the App Store and Google Play, allows users to search BDRC's library offline and then share and download texts when connected to the Internet. BDRC also offers an API that can allow for detailed computerized searches through their catalogue.

In the future there may be more adoption of semi-automated (and eventually with the use of AI, fully automated) classification and meta-data tagging. We will likely also start to see more corpus linguistics and statistical methods where computers take a set of inputs and employ various algorithms to supply answers to questions about word usage patterns, author attribution problems and many other subjects that cannot be answered using only human readers. Some linguistic examples are the *ARTFL (American Research on the Treasury of the French Language)* Project which has used *Philologic,*[44] their main software, for term-frequency and usage-over-time analysis on the *TFL (Treasury of the French Language)* and the Oxford Corpus for Old Japanese.

We will most likely see wide adoption of crowd-sourcing systems such as Amazon's Mechanical Turk.[45] It has been shown that large quantities of non-expert judgments can perform as well as, or even outperform, expert-judgments, which means we can achieve the same quality of data at a fraction of the cost.[46] The cost implications[47] are huge, as well as time implications. This does not mean that expert readers will not be needed, but that they can focus on developing research questions and working on analysis, rather than doing low-level, repetitive tasks for long periods of time. The ideal world of DH is

44 PhiloLogic4. (2014). *The ARTFL Project.* Retrieved from ARTFL website https://artfl-project.uchicago.edu/

45 Amazon's platform for on-demand scalable workforce. An example of using the Mechanical Turk would be this: users are shown an image of a word, and are presented with a few possibilities. They have to choose which word the image actually is showing. Each user is paid a tenth of a penny per image or less making it very cheap to employ large numbers of readers. By combining the answers of hundreds of relatively low skill users, we can get as good a result as with expert readers because the task of seeing an *image* and reading a word from it is very easy for humans, but very difficult for computers (at the moment).

46 Studies have compared MTurk workers to offline workers doing similar tasks and have found that the highly rated workers perform about as well as the offline workers. See https://featuredcontent.psychonomic.org/high-quality-mturk-data/.

47 Potentially thousand-fold cheaper or more.

where computers can do what they do well and humans can focus on building knowledge.

Open source software and open source mentality for collaborative, decentralized development will likely gain more and more momentum. As we see Google open sourcing their machine intelligence suite TensorFlow[48] we will also see in academia that researchers will be able to gain better data and better tools more cheaply if they rely on the crowd.

Open source also would imply doing away with "waterfall"[49] development in favor of "agile"[50] style development; in Digital Humanities today resources are being wasted because sometimes a 2–3 year long planning phase precedes development. In three years' time a well defined list of requirements is created and then the project starts. However, by the time the software is created it is already several years out of date. We should learn from software companies and use best practices where development is done in small increments and user feedback is immediately looped back into the work.

After the exploration of static statistical methods, machine learning could be brought in to the picture once machine-readable high-quality data is available. We should thus make use of the freely available, off-the-shelf, cutting-edge algorithms for natural language processing. Combine this with crowd-sourcing, so that even non-professionals can contribute and we have thousands, perhaps millions of devoted people from faith communities around the world who can help solve the problem of digitizing millions of lines of manuscript images.

In short, having these three elements combined: standardization, open sourcing and crowd-trained machine learning is the optimal path for the future of Digital Buddhology.

48 https://www.tensorflow.org/

49 Every feature is carefully scoped in advance with full specifications being written before development starts. Then project schedules are drawn up that look similar to a 'waterfall' with each stage completed before proceeding to the following stage.

50 A working hypothesis of the user's behavior and needs is made and development is started immediately then small but complete features are released approximately every two weeks incrementally. Then user behavior is observed and adjustments are made to keep up with current trends and needs.

# Part One: **Theoretical and Methodological Issues**

Daniel Veidlinger

# Computational Linguistics and the Buddhist Corpus

The process of reading and interpreting religious texts has been going on for millennia, and in fact many of the hermeneutical techniques that scholars throughout the humanities use today were developed over the centuries in attempts to get at the meaning – hidden, metaphorical or otherwise – of various religious texts. Many of the greatest advances in communication technology have also taken place in the effort to preserve and transmit religious texts, from the astonishingly accurate oral transmission of the Hindu Vedas to the legends of Egyptian deities depicted in hieroglyphs, and on through the block printing of the Buddhist sutras and later the movable type of Gutenberg's Bible. Many people's first encounter with the radio was through hearing a preacher's voice emanating from the speaker, and in contemporary times over a quarter of Americans regularly use the Internet to find information about religion (Pew Foundation 2001). It is now possible to use computers and other related digital technologies to help in the hermeneutical enterprise. This chapter will focus on some of the more popular computational language processing and text mining techniques and explain how they can be used to further our understanding of Buddhist texts and reveal new perspectives on their meaning.

A human scholar might read all of the words in a passage and examine their individual meaning, then consider the context in which the words occur, what is known about the author, the historical circumstances surrounding the creation of the text, and perform many other intellectual maneuvers in order to understand the passage. On the other hand, a computer at the current stage of development is not able to understand the piece in the same way. However, computers are able to digest enormous amounts of text – millions and millions of words that would take many lifetimes for a human to read – and apply various algorithms to the text in order to find relationships between the words and hidden patterns and stylistic features that are not immediately evident to a human reader. As John Burrows, an important pioneer of this kind of analysis, states,

> Statistical analysis is necessary for the management of words that occur too frequently to be studied one by one... they constitute the underlying fabric of a text, a barely visible web that gives shape to whatever is being said... An appropriate analogy, perhaps, is with the contrast between handwoven rugs where the russet tones predominate and those where they give way to the greens and blues. The principal point of interest is neither a single

https://doi.org/10.1515/9783110519082-003

stitch, a single thread, nor even a single color, but the overall effect (Burrows 2004, 323–324).

The digital techniques are not intended to replace human readers, but rather are best used in tandem with the insights gained by close human reading, for invariably the human scholar is forced to draw conclusions about a corpus based on only a sampling of the texts within it. Ultimately, of course, all literary analysis depends upon massive processing of data and detecting of trends. However, the traditional way relies upon years of research that lies collected in the human critic's head who over time achieves the ability to reliably detect meaningful patterns, whereas a computer does it explicitly and in an instant. A human critic, in other words, is never just reading one document in isolation, but is processing that document through a neural net constructed in her own brain from previous readings of hundreds or thousands of documents that have left a latent impression. As Burrows puts it,

> literary analysis often rests upon seemingly intuitive insights and discriminations, processes that may seem remote from the gathering and combining and classifying on which [digital humanities] have concentrated and in which computational stylistics is usually engaged. But those insights and discriminations are not ultimately intuitive because they draw, albeit covertly, upon data gathered in a lifetime's reading, stored away in a subconscious memory bank, and put to use, as Samuel Johnson reminds us, through processes of comparison and classification, whether tacit or overt (Burrows 2004, 344).

Digital techniques can help scholars expand the data that they are able to examine using the insights gained from the initial close reading. They can be confirmed or contradicted by the statistical analysis of the entire corpus, and then new insights gained from the mechanical reading process can be cycled back and used to check the texts through a close reading. Ideally, therefore, the two techniques should be used to complement each other. In this chapter, I will examine a few of the more popular statistically based methods and provide some examples of how these techniques can be used to discover new insights about Buddhist texts.

The techniques that will be examined in this chapter have been used for some time already in the fields of Digital Humanities, Machine Learning and Natural Language Processing and there are several publically available systems that can be used to deploy them. These techniques are Term Frequency-Inverse Document Frequency (TF-IDF), Collocation Analysis and Vector Space Semantic Mapping.[1] Each of these techniques is able to process very large amounts of text and look for relations between the words that can tell us many things about the overall topic of the text, and different ways words are used within it.

Of course, for any of these techniques to work, the text that one wishes to examine must be machine readable and properly formatted. The first task, then, is to identify a good machine readable text that one wishes to analyze. Ideally, the text should be in a raw text form, such as a file ending with .txt. There are then various transformations that must be effected on the text during the preprocessing phase, including sentence boundary detection, punctuation cleansing, stemming and normalization of spelling. The punctuation marks can cause a lot of confusion for the algorithms and skew the results significantly if they are not dealt with properly. For example, in the sentence "The Buddha taught the Dharma, and the Dharma lives on today in many forms" we would want the computer to recognize that "Dharma," (note the comma) and "Dharma" are the same term. Although this might seem straightforward, a number of complicated issues arise that must be resolved, because sometimes the punctuation may carry important semantic meaning, such as in a hyphenated word, so that removing it will lead the computer down the wrong path. However, one of the benefits of working with an extremely large corpus of material is that these issues should hopefully resolve themselves in many cases, as the number of correct hits far outweighs the number of improperly parsed terms. Stemming involves associating the different forms of a word with the same stem or lemma, which, again, can greatly skew the results if not done correctly. Should plural and singular forms of the same noun be associated with each other, for example, so that three occurrences of the word "ox" and two of "oxen" would count as five occurrences of the lemma "ox"? What about different tenses of the same verb? It is also important to associate various contractions with the correct longform term, for example *isn't* and *is not*. These are all questions that need to be resolved, although the answer may be different depending on the nature of the text one is dealing with and the kinds of questions one wishes to ask.[2]

Associated with these issues is the question of determining the size of the entities that one wants to examine in the analysis. One may wish to process each word separately, or one may wish to process 2, 3, 4 or more words together in order to retain the meaning of phrases, as Chris Handy discusses in his chap-

**1** Source code for TF-IDF in Python is available at https://code.google.com/archive/p/tfidf/. Code in R for Vector Space mapping is available at (http://bookworm.benschmidt.org/posts/2015-10-25-Word-Embeddings.html#fn14) .

**2** Miner, Elder and Fast provide a good summary of the various issues involved in preprocessing of text (2012, 46–50).

ter herein. For example, the phrase "the four noble truths" would obviously be processed very differently by an algorithm that allows for 4-gram phrases than by one that just looks at each word individually. There is no single "correct" way to process texts, and the determination of the amount of words to be examined as a unit should be up to the researcher, with trial and error often being the best or even only way of knowing which one works better. A lot depends on exactly what the purpose of the analysis in question is. For some lines of research, a uni-gram parse might be best, and for others, a multi-gram parse might fare better. The results, as any responsible Digital Humanities scholar will admit, always have to be judged and tweaked based upon the learned opinion of the researcher. There will almost always be results in any language processing or data mining project that do not seem to make any sense and can be discarded. However, it is important at least to try to understand why the system would have provided the problematic output, because perhaps therein might lie some of the most useful insights due to the fact that they go against what was previously held to be the case.

For Buddhist studies, there are many sources of digitized texts that can be used for machine assisted language processing, and many of these are discussed in other chapters in this volume. Some of the existing locations where the interested scholar can find a great deal of Buddhist texts in a variety of languages, including English translations are:

http://www.sacred-texts.org; http://www.Tipitaka.org; http://www.cbeta.org; http://www.tbrc.org; http://www.dsbcproject.org; http://www.buddhanet.net http://www.accesstoinsight.org; http://www.asianclassics.org/; and http://gretil.sub.uni-goettingen.de/#RLBuddh. Some of these sources contain texts that are formatted to be mined and analyzed effectively by computer algorithms or accessed easily in machine readable form, and others will need more intensive pre-processing by the researchers. For the examples that will be discussed in this chapter, I will be using English translations from Pali as found at www.sacred-texts.org or at www.accesstoinsight.org, in order for the examples to be useful to all readers of this volume. Of course, one must be very careful when making determinations about what the original texts say based on a translation, as the translation itself might be of poor quality or might not adequately represent the contents of the text. However, for the current demonstration purposes it should suffice.

## TF-IDF

Statistical analysis of word frequency such as TF-IDF (Term Frequency-Inverse Document Frequency) is a form of corpus analysis (Froehlich 2015) that expresses how important a word is to a document without the need for complex machine learning algorithms. In TF-IDF, a word or term is always compared against the overall corpus, so that its relevance to a particular document is highlighted against its presence in all the documents in the corpus. For this kind of scoring, the raw frequency value increases along with the frequency of the word in the document being examined at the moment (the "term frequency"), but this frequency score must be offset by the overall frequency of the word in the corpus (the "inverse document frequency"), which gives rare words more value, and decreases the value of common ones. For example, in a particular text, one might find the word "meditate" x amount of times and the word "speak" 2x times. However, since "meditate" is a much rarer word in general, occurring in far fewer documents than "speak," it would still score higher than "speak" even though it occurred less often in the particular text under examination. TF-IDF can produce a rich comparative map of the various themes within different bodies of religious texts. These models can serve to highlight how different traditions emphasize different features of the texts that a computer might not recognize as central, and vice-versa, how a computer might recognize certain themes as central that a human would not.

Formally, there are two parts to TF-IDF. The first calculates the number of times a word appears in a document, divided by the total number of words in that document to give the term frequency (TF). The second part is the inverse document frequency (IDF), which is usually calculated as the logarithm of the number of documents in the corpus divided by the number of documents where the term one is interested in appears (Miner, Elder and Fast 2012, 50 – 51). As mentioned already, this formula has the benefit of lessening the weight of common terms and heightening the weight of rare ones, giving a good sense of which terms are most relevant to a document. There are various different ways of achieving roughly similar results, with different ones being appropriate in different contexts.

I will go through an example of TF-IDF as applied to Buddhist texts in order to demonstrate its usefulness to humanities scholars. For this example, I have used the English translations of some well-known Pali Suttas from the *Dīgha Nikāya* that can be found at the AccessToInsight.org website, the *Āṭānāṭiya Sutta* and the *Mahāsatipaṭṭhāna Sutta*. Using a publicly available website that provides a word frequency analysis of a webpage or block of text (http://

www.online-utility.org/text/analyzer.jsp), I performed a word frequency analysis on the texts. The list of individual words and their raw frequencies in each *sutta* was then input as a table called *occurrences* into a relational database built in MS-Access (that comes with most versions of Microsoft Office). The percentage score was then calculated using the frequency score as a percentage of the total number of words in each *sutta*, and this table was called *Individual Sutta*. I had previously built a table in this database called *General Corpus* with all the words and the amount of *suttas* they occur in within the texts of the *Dīgha Nikāya* collection available on AccessToInsight.org. This was used to calculate the number of texts (or documents) within which each word occurs, as required for calculation of the inverse document frequency. I then created an "inner join" between the words from each *sutta* and the words as they appeared in the larger list of words and their global occurrence rates in all the documents of the *Dīgha* corpus. An inner join is a database term that refers to a connection between entries in one table and the identical entry in another table. It allows those tables to be joined so as to use information in both tables in a seamless way in reference to the same entry. It is important to keep in mind that there are slightly different approaches that one can take to producing TF-IDF results, with slightly different results and scores, and there is no right or wrong method within the accepted group of methods. It is always a good idea to look over results of this nature to ensure that they look basically correct, and that no major errors or inappropriate methods were employed. Having said this, I will show my results and hopefully the reader will agree that they do seem reasonable given the topic. Note that these results only include words that occur at least twice in the *suttas* in question, in order to weed out errors and noise. First I will present two word lists ranked in order of their TF-IDF score from the *Āṭānāṭiya Sutta* and the *Mahāsatipaṭṭhāna Sutta*. I ask the reader to guess which *sutta* each list comes from before I reveal it. The *Āṭānāṭiya Sutta* is a popular *paritta* text that is used to protect the reciter from bad occurrences and malevolent forces. The *Mahāsatipaṭṭhāna Sutta* constitutes one of the most important sets of meditation instructions in the Pali canon:

**Tab. 1**

Sutta One

| Keyword | Occurrences | Percentage | Docs | TFIDF |
|---|---|---|---|---|
| yakkhas | 26 | 1.0129 | 3 | 0.014041776 |
| reverence | 12 | 0.4675 | 2 | 0.008376476 |
| homage | 14 | 0.5454 | 4 | 0.005991831 |
| quarter | 8 | 0.3116 | 2 | 0.005583123 |
| conqueror | 9 | 0.3506 | 3 | 0.004860348 |
| gotama | 14 | 0.5454 | 5 | 0.004774806 |
| mighty | 13 | 0.5064 | 5 | 0.004433374 |
| protection | 7 | 0.2727 | 3 | 0.003780425 |
| men | 8 | 0.3116 | 4 | 0.003423276 |
| male | 8 | 0.3116 | 4 | 0.003423276 |
| pay | 8 | 0.3116 | 4 | 0.003423276 |
| laywoman | 8 | 0.3116 | 4 | 0.003423276 |
| mount | 6 | 0.2337 | 3 | 0.00323977 |
| attendants | 7 | 0.2727 | 4 | 0.002995916 |
| salute | 4 | 0.1558 | 2 | 0.002791561 |
| ocean | 4 | 0.1558 | 2 | 0.002791561 |
| attended | 4 | 0.1558 | 2 | 0.002791561 |
| nuns | 4 | 0.1558 | 2 | 0.002791561 |
| looked | 4 | 0.1558 | 2 | 0.002791561 |
| harming | 4 | 0.1558 | 2 | 0.002791561 |
| attendant | 4 | 0.1558 | 2 | 0.002791561 |
| birds | 5 | 0.1948 | 3 | 0.002700501 |
| retinue | 5 | 0.1948 | 3 | 0.002700501 |
| direction | 6 | 0.2337 | 4 | 0.002567457 |
| named | 7 | 0.2727 | 5 | 0.002387403 |
| called | 8 | 0.3116 | 6 | 0.002159847 |
| sons | 4 | 0.1558 | 3 | 0.002159847 |
| sovereign | 4 | 0.1558 | 3 | 0.002159847 |
| sun | 8 | 0.3116 | 6 | 0.002159847 |
| glory | 4 | 0.1558 | 3 | 0.002159847 |
| eminent | 3 | 0.1169 | 2 | 0.002094567 |
| kuvera | 3 | 0.1169 | 2 | 0.002094567 |
| names | 3 | 0.1169 | 2 | 0.002094567 |
| fierce | 3 | 0.1169 | 2 | 0.002094567 |
| gandhabba | 3 | 0.1169 | 2 | 0.002094567 |
| king | 13 | 0.5064 | 8 | 0.002053275 |
| happy | 7 | 0.2727 | 6 | 0.001890212 |
| blessed | 26 | 1.0129 | 10 | 0.001846735 |
| afar | 4 | 0.1558 | 4 | 0.001711638 |
| enjoys | 4 | 0.1558 | 4 | 0.001711638 |
| live | 5 | 0.1948 | 5 | 0.001705413 |
| magadha | 3 | 0.1169 | 3 | 0.001620578 |
| against | 3 | 0.1169 | 3 | 0.001620578 |
| nagas | 3 | 0.1169 | 3 | 0.001620578 |
| chief | 3 | 0.1169 | 3 | 0.001620578 |
| silence | 3 | 0.1169 | 3 | 0.001620578 |
| placed | 3 | 0.1169 | 3 | 0.001620578 |
| lies | 3 | 0.1169 | 3 | 0.001620578 |
| kings | 7 | 0.2727 | 7 | 0.001469843 |

Sutta Two

| Keyword | Occurrences | Percentage | Docs | TFIDF |
|---|---|---|---|---|
| focused | 54 | 1.6698 | 2 | 0.0299188 |
| discerns | 58 | 1.7934 | 6 | 0.012430902 |
| externally | 19 | 0.5875 | 2 | 0.010526587 |
| internally | 19 | 0.5875 | 2 | 0.010526587 |
| reference | 23 | 0.7112 | 3 | 0.009859325 |
| unsustained | 13 | 0.402 | 2 | 0.007202873 |
| breathing | 12 | 0.3711 | 2 | 0.006649219 |
| flesh | 15 | 0.4638 | 3 | 0.006429633 |
| bone | 11 | 0.3401 | 2 | 0.006093774 |
| remains | 45 | 1.3915 | 8 | 0.005642047 |
| feeling | 37 | 1.1441 | 8 | 0.004638926 |
| clinging | 10 | 0.3092 | 3 | 0.004286422 |
| qualities | 34 | 1.0513 | 8 | 0.004262655 |
| trains | 6 | 0.1855 | 2 | 0.003323714 |
| factor | 6 | 0.1855 | 2 | 0.003323714 |
| origination | 15 | 0.4638 | 6 | 0.003214817 |
| mental | 35 | 1.0823 | 9 | 0.003113583 |
| remain | 9 | 0.2783 | 4 | 0.003057438 |
| monk | 33 | 1.0204 | 9 | 0.002935508 |
| tendons | 5 | 0.1546 | 2 | 0.00277006 |
| feelings | 10 | 0.3092 | 5 | 0.002706949 |
| awakening | 10 | 0.3092 | 5 | 0.002706949 |
| pleasant | 12 | 0.3711 | 6 | 0.002572269 |
| passing | 12 | 0.3711 | 6 | 0.002572269 |
| furthermore | 9 | 0.2783 | 5 | 0.002436429 |
| sensual | 7 | 0.2165 | 4 | 0.002378496 |
| bodily | 4 | 0.1237 | 2 | 0.002216406 |
| factors | 4 | 0.1237 | 2 | 0.002216406 |
| media | 4 | 0.1237 | 3 | 0.001714846 |
| blood | 4 | 0.1237 | 3 | 0.001714846 |
| short | 5 | 0.1546 | 4 | 0.001698455 |
| repeated | 3 | 0.0928 | 2 | 0.001662753 |
| months | 3 | 0.0928 | 2 | 0.001662753 |
| skin | 3 | 0.0928 | 2 | 0.001662753 |
| gnosis | 3 | 0.0928 | 2 | 0.001662753 |
| bones | 3 | 0.0928 | 2 | 0.001662753 |
| extent | 6 | 0.1855 | 5 | 0.001623995 |
| desire | 7 | 0.2165 | 6 | 0.001500664 |
| seven | 7 | 0.2165 | 6 | 0.001500664 |
| mindfulness | 11 | 0.3401 | 8 | 0.001378987 |
| enlarged | 4 | 0.1237 | 4 | 0.001358983 |
| delusion | 4 | 0.1237 | 4 | 0.001358983 |
| arising | 5 | 0.1546 | 5 | 0.001353475 |
| away | 15 | 0.4638 | 9 | 0.001334269 |
| fruits | 3 | 0.0928 | 3 | 0.001286481 |
| month | 3 | 0.0928 | 3 | 0.001286481 |
| external | 3 | 0.0928 | 3 | 0.001286481 |
| days | 3 | 0.0928 | 3 | 0.001286481 |
| return | 3 | 0.0928 | 3 | 0.001286481 |

Of course the first one is the *paritta* and the second constitutes the meditation instructions. In the same way that a human who peruses this list can immediately see that there are different foci in these different *suttas*, a computer would be able to detect similar themes in various *suttas* and group them together along thematic lines. Therefore it is very clear that there is something going on here that is of use to humanities scholars, even if only to use computers to effect an initial sorting of a mass of unknown texts based on the terms that are most prominent in each one. We can see in *sutta one* that the focus on various supernatural beings is consistent with the tenor of the *parittas* that are aimed at enlisting what we might call magical power against the malevolent forces of the supernatural. We also see that laypeople are prominent in this list. In the second text, we see that breathing is mentioned prominently, as is discerning, focusing and other elements that are key features of meditation practice.

The text parsing engine that I used (http://www.online-utility.org/text/analyzer.jsp) also produces a list of the most common longer phrases in the text, and here again we can learn a lot. Here are some of the most common phrases in the *Mahāsatipaṭṭhāna:*

| | |
|---|---|
| in this way he remains focused internally on | 13 occurrences |
| monk remains focused on mental qualities | 10 |
| a monk remains focused on the body in | 7 |
| by not clinging to anything in the world | 7 |

And here from the *Āṭānāṭiya Sutta:*

| | |
|---|---|
| they too say 'we reverence gotama the conqueror | 4 occurrences |
| to pay homage to gotama the conqueror the | 4 |
| request the yakkhas to pay homage to gotama | 4 |
| even the non humans pay reverence to thee | 4 |
| of this quarter is a great king named | 4 |
| yakkhas to pay homage to gotama the conqueror | 4 |
| who has a retinue of attendants and is | 4 |
| laywomen may live at ease guarded protected and | 3 |

So, again, we can see that these lists are very helpful in determining the basic contours of the *sutta.*

A particularly useful deployment of word-frequency analysis, beyond getting the basic gist of a text, is for authorship attribution. Authors have distinctive phrases that they tend to use to express certain ideas, and each person has their own lexical "signature" expressed through their particular choice of words that is different from that of other people. This can sometimes be effectively used to ascertain the authorship of texts when this is in dispute. In Buddhist studies, this kind of analysis can be very useful, as there is particularly little known about the authorship of various texts. For example, did Buddhaghosa really write the commentaries attributed to him along with the *Visuddhimagga?* Of course, in this case it is not so easy, because even the tradition does not hold that he wrote the commentaries from scratch, but rather that he translated them from Elu into Pali. Even so, studies have shown that translators can also be identified in this way, as the word choices are so strong that they come through even in translations. There is also an important question about whether Nāgārjuna authored all the texts attributed to him. In fact, this question can be put to many authors of many Buddhist texts and it is possible that computationally aided stylometric analysis can help us to answer these questions.

A religious text that has been subject to a considerable amount of computational analysis is the *Book of Mormon*, because a lot rides upon whether it can be shown to have been written by one or several people; the founder of Mormonism Joseph Smith claims to have translated the text from golden plates that were written by various prophets in ancient times, whereas skeptics believe that he or some other individual associated with him fabricated the text themselves. Some of the work that has been done in this context can be used by Buddhologists as well. A comprehensive examination of previous studies of word usage in the *Book of Mormon*, followed by a new multivariate approach to measuring the richness of the vocabulary in different sections of the Mormon holy texts can be found in Holmes (1990).

## Collocation Analysis

Much can be learned by looking at which words appear in the vicinity of other words in sentences, known as collocation analysis. Many data mining techniques treat text as a "bag of words," meaning that the word order is not considered when preparing statistical representations of the word occurrences. While this is very useful for many tasks, such as document classification, sometimes word order needs to be taken into consideration. Collocation analysis uses at least some aspects of word order as it looks at which words tend to occur in close proximity to which other words. It is also very useful for word sense disambiguation, because it highlights the context in which a word is used, although, of course, there are many different ways of approaching it, some of which are too complicated to go over here (Bouma 2009). Therefore, if there are various occurrences of the word "leaves" for example, this method will help the computer understand which of these refers to a person exiting and which to parts of a tree based on the other words occurring around it. I performed a relatively simple query that manages to display a great deal of information about the uses of words and concepts in the text under study. First, I designed a program to find all the occurrences in a document of an input word and then assign a score to the five words that occur before and after the word in the text. The closer to the main word the collocated word is, the higher the score. In this case I assigned a score of 5 to the words immediately adjacent to the keyword, then 4, 3, 2 and 1 for the other words respectively.

For example, let's look at the sentence "I will declare the law to the multitudes for the continual increase of *good* and blessings to them and to make them vigilant in their life." If the key term in which we are interested is "good", then "of" would score 5, "increase" 4, "continual" 3, "the" 2 and "for" 1. Likewise for the subsequent words, "and" scores 5, "blessings" scores 4, etc... Evidently, most of the words that are scored in this particular example are stopwords – words, that is, that are so common that they do not really provide a lot of extra meaning. A better way to run this program would be not to count the stopwords, so "increase" would score 5, "continual" 4, "multitudes" 3, "law" 2, "declare" 1. Once this is done, I then loaded this data into a relational database built in MS-Access and wrote a query that added up all of the location-based scores and multiplied this by the total amount of occurrences that each collocated word had, regardless of its exact proximity to the keyword, in order to arrive at yet another score. This second score takes into consideration both the overall amount of co-occurrences of the words as well as the position of the co-occurring word relative to the keyword. In the above example, let us say that there were 30 occurrences in the text under study of the word "good." Let us further say that in those 30 sentences, there were 5 occurrences of the word "blessings" and in 2 of these "blessings" was right next to "good," in 2 others it was three words away, and in 1 it was five words away. So the total score would be: (5+5+3+3+1) * 5 = 85. This way of scoring allows both the frequency of the co-occurring word and its position to be taken into account. There are no doubt a number of different and more sophisticated ways of scoring this kind of co-occurrence, but they will all take these basic factors into consideration and apply some transformations of these numbers – perhaps normalizing it to a score between 0 and 1. Next, I added one more parameter to the score, and that is the global frequency of the co-occurring term in the corpus under study. This was used as in TF-IDF to offset the more popular terms. Arranging the words by this final score gave some very interesting results that surely can tell us something about the usage of the keyword, and it is a good and simple way to analyze how word usages might have changed over time. If one were to perform this kind of analysis for various corpora separated by some period in time, say perhaps the root canonical texts and the commentaries or sub-commentaries of the Pali canon, it might display some very informative results.

I here present some examples of collocation analysis, some of which may be obvious, but that is good – it shows that the system does produce results that concur with insights that scholars have gained through close readings of the texts. In fact, this is so important that it is common to use pre-existing notions of word relationships in order to ascertain the usefulness of different scoring techniques. There are, as I have said, many different ways to score these kinds of analyses, and therefore not only it is not "cheating," but it is actually wise to do something that on the surface appears to go against the tenor of scientific investigation, which is to tweak the data until it gives an answer that you are looking for. However, in this case, one should pick an uncontroversial word relationship and assure that the scoring system that you use can at least reproduce that relationship. One may then use that same scoring system with the other words that one is not sure about. In the current example, one of the words that I searched for was "conquer" and I saw that "desire" was a common co-occurring word. I then used a scoring system that pushed the collocation score between conquer and desire up to a high number, and then looked to see how this kind of scoring system would affect the other words.

For example, these are collocated words with high scores that emerge from an analysis of the *Dīgha Nikāya* as found at Sacred-Texts.org. The main keyword is in bold and the collocates are in plain text in descending order of their closeness score.

**Tab. 2**

| **Conquer** | **Evil** | **Good** | **Senses** | **Soul** | **Suffering** | **Worship** |
|---|---|---|---|---|---|---|
| Mara | dispositions | works | controlled | completely | escape | worshipping |
| Crossed | consequences | age-enduring | guarded | describe | end | sun-worship |
| thrice | translucent | heaping | doors | annihilated | desire | worshipped |
| hast | cultured | efficacy | door | maintain | | worshipper |
| Understanding | courses | crop | regards | distinct | | fire-god |
| desire | deeds | goodness | composed | Sir | | clasped |
| death | states | deeds | five | theory | | enlightened |
| Can | evil-doing | charity | objects | sworn | | revered |
| pain | lust | accumulating | pleasures | soul | | fire |
| | avert | cheer | guard | plane | | bo-tree |
| | plight | wise | well | grounded | | Buddhists |
| | devoid | persevered | beauty | eternal | | turning |
| | Shunning | gentlemen | through | souls | | dhamma |
| | deed | goodwill | gone | potthapada | | offerings |
| | enters | | | ways | | paid |
| | | | | healthy | | perfumes |
| | | | | conscious | | |

For those who might say that this is nothing new, that one knows this already, that is good. At this point I am not trying to do anything new, but rather to show that computers can recreate insights that learned people already have about the texts in question. With that confidence, we can then move in future to using the computers to help us with more advanced and innovative lines of questioning. For example, one might find that amidst the expected terms, some unexpected ones are strongly associated with the main word. It may then be that the word has some valences that were not previously noticed and one could re-examine what is known using conventional methods about this term which might lead us to rethink some issues salient to Buddhist studies. A very fruitful line of investigation might be to examine the profiles of various words in different strata of texts, for example one might look at the uses of a word in the root canonical texts, then examine it in the commentaries and sub-commentaries, to see if its semantic field has changed over time. We would then examine how the uses of certain key – but highly contested – ideas such as *kamma* (moral actions and their consequences), *cetanā* (mental volition), and *nibbāna* (the ultimate state of bliss), or problematic compounds such as *anattā*, have changed from the canonical period to the commentarial periods by looking at signals such as what words tend to be used in similar contexts in different texts and how (or whether) these contexts change over time. This kind of analysis could highlight connections between ideas and their subsequent evolution at a deeper and more significant level than what has been attempted previously, and could reveal much about the lived Buddhism of the periods under study.

## Semantic Vector Space Mapping

A Semantic Vector Space Map involves the use of a neural net to process a corpus in such a way as to provide a multi-dimensional mathematical representation of the relationships between the words. It

> "presents (embeds) words in a continuous vector space where semantically similar words are mapped to nearby points ('are embedded nearby each other'). Vector Space Models have a long, rich history in Natural Language Programming, but all methods depend in some way or another on the Distributional Hypothesis, which states that words that appear in the same contexts share semantic meaning" (https://www.tensorflow.org/tutorials/word2vec/).

Essentially it is a way of reducing the mass of words in a corpus, and all the relationships between them, to a set of vectors in a vector space that can account for the various ways that words are used and manifest the relationships between them. These vectors are essentially strings of numbers with each number representing an occurrence of some word in a text. Thus words used in similar ways will have similar vector scores – that is to say similar positions in the vector space – and we can therefore learn about which words are analogous to which. In a sense this is similar to the creation of a thesaurus, except the words here are not limited to ones with the same approximate semantic space – that is to say the same meaning – but can extend to words that are used in more broadly similar ways. As such it can be seen as a transformation of a text from one format into another, in this case one that reduces the complex of words into distinct mathematically describable vectors that can be used to highlight the similarities or differences between the words, their semantic meaning and their usages. As Ben Schmidt says, embedding words in these vector spaces reduces words into a field where they are purely defined by their relations:

> Such a space allows us to do two things. The first, much like topic models, is to think in terms of similarity: what words are like other words? How can we learn from those relations? How do unexpected closenesses extend our understanding of a field?... Word embedding models try to reflect similarities in usage between words to distances in space... Word embedding models try to reflect similar relationships between words with similar paths in space (http://bookworm.benschmidt.org/posts/2015-10-25-Word-Embeddings.html#fn14).

The space that is used for this kind of transformation is known as a vector space, which is a linear space that is constituted by vectors or entities that are abstract mathematical concepts and which can be added or subtracted from each other or upon which various mathematical procedures can be executed.

In terms of how this actually works when applied to language, a simple example should be able to show the key ideas. If we have a two dimensional grid with the x axis representing some semantic value, such as weight, and the y axis representing size, for example, we can map words into this space to represent their semantic value as seen in figure 1. The higher the score for each dimension, the stronger that feature is associated with the word. So a low score on the "size" axis would mean the item is small and a high score would mean it is big. Here we can see that a beach ball would be large but light, a gold bar would be small but heavy, a car big and heavy and an airplane bigger and heavier.[3]

I built a rudimentary neural net in the R statistical programming language based on the word2vec system described by Tomas Mikolov and his associates (2013) and trained it with all the Theravāda texts found on Sacred-Texts.org. Here is an example of the top five words that score the closest to Savatthi,

3 For a detailed yet accessible description of word vectors, see https://blog.acolyer.org/2016/04/21/the-amazing-power-of-word-vectors/ .

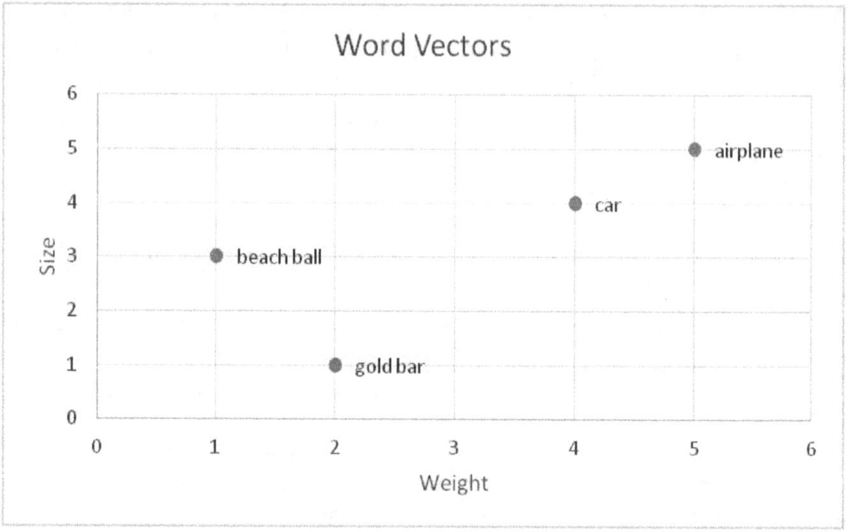


Fig. 1

which was a major city during the Buddha's time and capital of the Kosala kingdom. These should be words that are found in similar contexts and are used in similar ways: 1) rajagaha 2) kosambi 3) vesali 4) nobleman 5) anathapindika. We can see that the first three words are also major cities that were frequented by the Buddha. The next two words are strongly associated with Savatthi because Anathapindika was a major donor who supported the Buddha, and all of these cities, as major capitals of Indian kingdoms, had many noblemen living within them.

If we look at some other words with close vector scores, we can also see interesting relationships between the words:

Tab. 3

| City | Caravan | Mindfulness |
|---|---|---|
| Gates | Journeying | Concentration |
| Decorated | Robbers | Aspirations |
| Palace | Carts | Impermanence |
| Tower | Leader | Experiences |
| Town | Merchandise | Samadhi |

These related words can tell us a lot about the concerns of the texts in regards to the keyword. For example, if in the earlier strata of texts we find "robbers" closely associated with "caravan" as above, but in later texts we do not, that suggests that perhaps stronger rulers were able to consolidate their power and assure the safety of travelers more effectively later on.

## Conclusion

There are many different ways to use computers to analyze a text, pursuant to different research goals. While a close reading of one text by a human is still the best way to pick up all the nuances, allusions, ideas and arguments found within it, computational approaches open up a whole new world of analytical possibilities, especially for large amounts of text that a human reader could never digest. These methods leverage the power of statistics to analyze the distribution of words and phrases throughout a text and corpus, and can note patterns and assess the significance of co-occurring words, of words used in similar contexts and of repeated phrases, or rare phrases and other linguistic features. While the algorithm may not be able to understand the nuances of a single word taken in isolation as a human does, taken together, the information it gathers as it skims over millions of words tells a story that we would do well to hear. Of course, for those who are skeptical about the ability of a computer program to achieve any level of real comprehension just by looking at the placement of words in a text, we must remember that words do not have intrinsic meaning, but rather acquire their meaning even for the human reader through the web of relations with other words; each word can exist only in an interdependent relationship with other words that delimit and shape its meaning (Saussure 2013). The methods that I have presented in this chapter are a good way to start taking advantage of these structures.

## References

Bouma, Gerlof. 2009. "Normalized pointwise mutual information in collocation extraction." In *Proceedings of the Biennial GSCL Conference 2009*, 31–40. Tübingen: Gunter Narr Verlag.

Burrows, John. 2004. "Textual Analysis." In *A Companion to Digital Humanities*, edited by Susan Schreibman, Ray Siemens and John Unsworth, 323–349. Malden, MA: Blackwell Publishing.

Froehlich H. 2015. "Corpus Analysis with Antconc," Programming Historian. http://programminghistorian.org/lessons/corpus-analysis-with-antconc

Holmes, D. 1992. "A Stylometric Analysis of Mormon Scripture and Related Texts." *Journal of the Royal Statistical Society* 155(1): 91–120.
Mikolov, Tomas, Kai Chen, Greg Corrado, and Jeffrey Dean. 2013. "Efficient Estimations of Word Representations in Vector Space" http://arxiv.org/pdf/1301.3781.pdf
Miner, Gary, John Elder and Andrew Fast. 2012. *Practical Text Mining and Statistical Analysis for Non-structured Text Data Applications.* Saint Louis: Academic Press.
Pew Foundation. 2001. *Cyberfaith: How Americans Pursue Religion Online.* http://www.pewinternet.org/2001/12/23/cyberfaith-how-americans-pursue-religion-online/ Accessed January 23, 2017.
Saussure, Ferdinand de. 2013. *Course in General Linguistics*, edited by Roy Harris. London: Bloomsbury.

Gregory Price Grieve

# An Ethnographic Method for the Digital Humanistic Study of Buddhism

## Introduction

Ethnography refers to a qualitative method for making implicit social phenomena explicit. For instance, on the evening of December 12, 2008, I was running late as I arrived at the home of Hope Long, the avatar hosting the ABG (Agnostic Buddhist Group) Friday night open discussion.[1] My encounter with Hope did not happen in the actual world but rather online, in the digital environment of the virtual world of *Second Life*. Launched in 2003 by the Linden Lab, and coming to the focus of mainstream media in late 2007, *Second Life* is an online three-dimensional interactive virtual social space almost entirely built and influenced by the people who use it. Housed in cyberspace, this virtual world can be accessed via the Internet from any networked computer on the globe. My study focused on the Hoben Mountain Zen Retreat. Often labeled Western, nightstand, or convert Buddhists, the inhabitants of Hoben typically came from North America, Europe, or other parts of the developed world but could also be found in many cosmopolitan centers of developing nations. Convert Zen Buddhism is a diverse and flexible religion, but its practitioners tend to focus on several facets of the tradition: the therapeutic, the nonhierarchical, the nonviolent, the ecological, and, most importantly, the meditative (Grieve 2017). When I entered the room, Hope walked over and said, "Clint. love your robes ; ) [an emoticon for winking]." Hope Long was the founding member of ABG and held much authority in the group, often directing the flow of conversation with just a few well-chosen words, or, in this case, a single emoticon. I was logged on as my research avatar Clint Clavenham, who is a tall imposing male figure, with a stern face, shaved head, bookish glasses, and full Buddhist monastic robes.

1 Whether to use an informant's real name or to use a pseudonym is one of the most challenging choices ethnography has to make. There is no universal rule, and it needs to be decided on a case-by-case basis. This choice becomes even more problematic when you are doing research in virtual worlds where the people already have pseudonyms. When data were gathered from published documents such as websites, groups, or note cards, I used the actual avatar's name (but not their real-life name) and the actual name of the groups. When the data were gathered from interviews, surveys, or participant observation, I used pseudonyms for avatars' names, regions, and groups.

https://doi.org/10.1515/9783110519082-004

**Fig. 1:** Gregory Grieve's research Avatar Clint Clavenham at Convert Zen Buddhist Second Life Location ( Photography by Gregory Grieve)

I looked around and noticed to my surprise that none of the sixteen other avatars were wearing vestments. Instead, they were dressed in fairly typical everyday *Second Life* attire—short sparkly skirts, ball gowns, faded jeans, and t-shirts, and someone was in a Native American costume (Grieve 2015; Grieve 2017; Grieve and Heston 2011).

A digital humanistic method can display either Buddhism online, or online Buddhism (Helland 2000, 2005). A "method online" uses digital media to archive, arrange, and organize actual world Buddhist practice, while an "online method" focuses on Buddhist practices that take place in digital environments. Digital ethnography studies online Buddhism, and differs from other digital humanistic methods because it focuses on participant observation of media practices that it conveys through thick description. Participant observation is a qualitative method of data collection in which a researcher gains intimate familiarity with a group's ethos, or lived world, by living for an extended period of time with that group. Thick description is a method that describes both a practice and the social context that gives that practice meaning. In this chapter I will proceed in three stages. First, I outline a digital humanistic ethnographic method for online Buddhism by describing the concepts of virtual field, participant observation, and thick description, as well as touching briefly upon ethics. Second,

I use *Second Life*'s Zen community as a case study and illustrate the importance of objects, places, avatars, groups, and events, as well as outlining the study's timeline. Finally, I discuss the outcomes of using ethnography to represent what it means to be human online so as to understand why Hope was winking at me and my virtual robes.

## Method

Rather than using digital media to analyze the Buddhism that takes place in the actual world, a digital humanistic ethnographic method collects and organizes the Buddhist media practices that take place in digital environments. When I asked residents to describe *Second Life*, most replied, as a survey respondent did in 2010, "I usually just tell people it's an online social/educational/ roleplaying game. But that misses the point." To record the lived reality of such online Buddhist practices, my method extends the classic ethnographic notions of the field from the observation of actual collocated, face-to-face physicality to digitally mediated social environments. Using an avatar, my research team and I engaged in a conventional ethnography using participant observation and thick description of *Second Life*'s Zen Buddhist community between November 2007 and October 2011. Concretely, our findings were recorded in shared field notes, screen shots, written documents, and material culture.

**Fig. 2:** Virtual Research Team. Principle investigator and five assistants Sabrina Epps, Rebecca Davis, Kevin Heston, Michelle Lampley and Jayme Mallindine (Photograph by Gregory Grieve).

## A virtual field

The concept of "field" has long proved problematic for ethnography, particularly when describing online environments (Bainbridge 2000; Benedikt 1991; 1996; Appadurai 1996). The myth of the ethnographic field as a discreet, bounded geographic locale is proving to be increasingly outdated and untenable as globalization blurs the boundary between "here" and "there" (Fox 1991; Gupta and Ferguson 1997; Kohn 1995). Like the magic circle of a playground, an ethnographic field consists of a shard of the social world that is artificially demarcated in time and space (Huizinga 1950). While probably always true, with the rise of digital media, a "field site" can no longer be seen merely as a physical location of face-to-face collocated individuals but rather must be viewed as an intersecting net between people, practices, and shifting terrains, both physical and virtual (Orgad 2008).

Fields proceed not from objective reality but from the interests of the researcher in dialogue with the subject under study. Buddhist social fields could be described as actual, hybrid, online, and virtual. One could focus the field on actual-world practices, such as on worship, pilgrimage and the reading of scripture. One could also imagine a hybrid field, which takes into account a community composed of both the actual world and online communication (Amichai-Hamburger 2005; Cheong, Huang, and Poon 2011; Jenkins 2006; Satwicz 2006). The interpretation of hybrid environments could also include an online field component, which uses the interactivity of blogs and chatrooms as the focus of study (Mitra and Cohen 1998).

While many ethnographers trace out the connections between online and offline social fields (Hine 2008; Kendal 2002; Markham 1998), this method focuses on an online Buddhism which limits the field to virtual spaces using avatars (Boellstorff et al. 2012; Grieve 2017). The mid-1990s saw the first emergence of such virtual studies (Dibble 1998; Grieve 1995; Markham 1998). Virtual environments include worlds such as *Second Life*, as well as early Multi-User Dungeons (MUDs) and the Massive Multiplayer Online Role Playing Games (MMORPGs), such as *The Elder Scrolls Online* (ZeniMax Online Studios, 2014). I argue that virtual sites constitute a distinct conventional social space, filled with innovative Buddhist practices, which offer new social fields with differing social positions, lifestyles, values, and dispositions. The difficultly with digital environments is that their social reality is often doubted, and the communication that takes place there is frequently deemed inauthentic. I found that the virtual data collected in game environments were real and authentic and, while distinct from other digital and actual locations, were not dichotomized from them (Grieve and Heston 2011).

## *Participant observation*

While a Buddhist digital humanistic ethnographic study may employ textual analysis, interviews, and surveys, its essential methodological tool is participant observation, which usually employs digital tools and emerges organically from the Internet's digital affordances (Boellstorff 2013; Ducheneaut, Yee and Bellotti 2010; Hine 2000). Pioneered in the first half of the twentieth century by anthropologists such as Bronisław Malinowski (1929; 1961; 1992), E.E. Evans-Pritchard (1940), and Margaret Mead (1928), participant observation is a qualitative method in which researchers take part in the daily activities of the group under study and record what they observe. Following the work of Tom Boellstorff (2008) and Julian Dibble (1998), the social space my research team explored was a virtual site, and we conducted our study almost entirely from within *Second Life* using research avatars. What makes participant observation a scientific research method (as opposed to just "hanging out") is the fact that the researcher is observing as well as taking part in a group's activities. As one inhabits a group's social world, one also needs to stand back and observe by watching and listening, while taking both physical and mental notes. Observation means logging concrete documentation of social structures, examples of everyday life, and everyday utterances. Concretely, we took "scratch notes" during our time inworld and then after logging off would spend almost as much time writing more detailed descriptions in our shared field notes, incorporating and describing snapshots, objects, and conversations.

## *Thick description*

Because it blurs the distinction between the objective language of the scientist and the subjective language of the novelist, however, ethnographic writing – not to mention virtual ethnographic writing – can be challenging (Clifford and Marcus 1986; Geertz 1983, 19–35; Miller & Slattter 2000; Morningstar & Farmer 1991; Murthy 2008, 2011). Still, while ethnographies can properly be called fictions in the sense of "something manufactured," because they are grounded in the "immersion of the field," ethnography remains a proven method for understanding religious worldviews (Gupta and Ferguson 1997). The goal of all this documentation is to create thick description. As the American anthropologist Clifford Geertz defines the term, a thick description describes both a social practice and also the context in order for that practice to become meaningful to an outsider. Geertz uses the example of a wink (1973, 5–7). If someone winks it could mean that they are expressing sexual desire or trying to communicate a secret, or they might "actually have been fake-winking, say, to mislead outsiders into imagining there was a conspiracy afoot" (Geertz 1973, 7). Without knowing the context, we reduce the wink to the thin description that the person is merely "rapidly contracting his right eyelid" (1973, 7). In a similar fashion, in the context of *Second Life*, one could accurately describe the emoticon "; )" as a semicolon and a bracket, and one could note that it can be found at the end of approximately .0078 percent of *Second Life* Chat and Instant Message utterances. Yet such a "thin description" does not explain what this sign means to an insider. In Geertz's words, it does "not uncover the conceptual structures that inform our subject's acts," and allow us to ". . . construct a system of analysis" (1973, 27).

## *Life cycle of an ethnographic method*

A prolonged life cycle is crucial for any ethnographic project because it allows the researchers to become part of the group's everyday routines and to inhabit the insider's world, and it gives them the flexibility to follow alternative hypotheses as they arise during the study. Looking back over our time inworld, the research followed a life cycle similar to that of an avatar – from noobie, to middie, to elder. In the first, or noob stage, we lumbered through the virtual world, and our main aims were identification through exploration, engagement in low-level participant observation, and collection of material culture. The second, or middie, stage lasted from June 2008 through October 2009 and was the most intense period of fieldwork. This period marked a change from exploration and discovery to reporting, and the research became more systematic and routinized. In the middie stage we concentrated on description and engaged in participant observation and the collection of material culture. In June 2009, we ceased participant observation and engaged in a month of inworld open interviews, during which my research team spoke with sixty-nine residents.

The third, or elder, stage lasted from November 2009 to October 2011 and concentrated on confirmation, control, and fact-checking. As the game researcher best known for being the cocreator of MUD1, Richard Bartle, writes in *Designing Virtual Worlds*, "There comes a point when players have advanced so far that they feel they have achieved everything that they set out to achieve. They are no longer interested in activities that used to occupy their time: they feel they have 'made it.' The question then arises: What can they do instead?" (Bartle 2004, 451). By the end of 2009, I felt as if no new data were being generated by our participant observation or inworld exploration. The research thus moved from concentrating on participant observation to structured interviews and surveys.

With the key informants, I conducted a series of long, out-of-world, open interviews using Skype or the telephone ($n$=13). I also conducted three surveys in 2010. First, with the help of IDC Herzliya's Advanced Reality Lab, I used an animated avatar bot to conduct a broad survey of randomly selected residents that asked about religious affiliation ($n$=1,227). Second, with the assistance of Kevin Heston, a graduate student, I used the web-based tool SurveyMonkey to administer a 100-question survey to *Second Life* religious practitioners ($n$=86); and third, we gave a similar survey to Buddhist Residents ($n$=108). Finally, between 2011 and 2013, I used the qualitative data analysis program, Atlas.ti, to catalogue and code the team's field notes, 9,339 note cards and objects, as well as data mine over 23,200 groupchat posts.

### *Ethics*

Because virtual ethnographers' first and foremost responsibility is to those they study, ethnographic research must consider ethics from the very beginning. For digital humanistic ethnographers, this means that they must never forget that there are real users behind the on-screen avatars. I identified three chief elements of ethical research: informed consent, anonymity, and transparency. First, following the practices of the American Anthropological Association, I understood informed consent as being composed of the communication and comprehension of the study's goals and voluntary participation (American Anthropological Association 2004). The second concern was anonymity, and I felt that each bit of data had to be carefully judged for an appropriate response. In addition to my own moral diligence, both my university's Institutional Review Board document, which monitored my research ethics and was based on a mix of institutional and national guidelines, and *Second Life*'s terms of service, required that informants' identities and what they told me be kept confidential (Boellstorff et al. 2012). Third, ethics was maintained through transparency, by rejecting such deceptive practices as being a "fly on the wall" and going "undercover" in the guise of an alternative identity.

## Case Study

The case study concerns convert Zen Buddhist groups that practiced in the virtual world of *Second Life* between November 2007 and October 2011. Using mouse and keyboard instructions, one can explore *Second Life*, which includes three-dimensional builds and environmental sounds. One can communicate with other residents via voice and built-in public chat and instant messaging. Residents can buy and make clothes, objects, and buildings as well as buy and rent property. One can conduct businesses using the inworld currency, run nonprofit and educational groups, role-play, and socialize in any number of ways with others (Au 2008).

Buddhist practices are expressed through avatars, objects, places, groups, and events. After logging on through the *Second Life* viewer, users assume an identity by creating an online character called an avatar. In computing, an avatar is the on-screen representation of the user, which can be a three-dimensional model such as in *Second Life*, a two-dimensional icon as used in many chat forums, or a textual description as used in MUDS. Avatars differ from other digital media practices because of bodies. Unlike film, which shows bodies, or print and radio that tell about bodies, virtual worlds afford a virtual embodiment (Grieve 2015). As such, avatars are not simply game tokens but embody highly personal manifestations of Buddhist practice. In *Second Life*, the default avatar shape is humanoid, and one can choose to be either male or female, but one's avatar can be customized through a graphical user interface to modify gender, body shape, skin, hairstyle, and clothes

The dressing up of avatars played a key role in *Second Life* convert Zen Buddhism. This may come as no surprise, for monk robes have always played a crucial role in Buddhist practice (Faure 1995). Consider the free robes handed out at Hoben by the talented builder Ryusho Ort, which were based on popular Soto So-Fuku robes that he described as "Japanese Soto monk kesa (robes). Also applicable for Chinese and Korean Traditions." Following some twenty-five centuries of custom, which had traveled from India and been adapted as Buddhism spread through Asia, Ryusho's robes consisted of the "triple robe" style: a lower covering (*antarvasa*) made of a skirt and pants, an upper covering (*uttarasaṇga*) made of a shirt, and an outer robe (*saṃghati*).

Avatars interact with objects, which makes *Second Life* distinct from nonvirtual world digital media practices such as the World Wide Web and email. Obviously in the end there really is no difference between a game environment and the web. Both are merely pixels on the screen that are controlled by users through keystrokes and mouse clicks. On the conventional level of lived media practice, however, virtual objects have a "materiality," a term that refers not only to the concrete physical world but also to the fact that objects are pragmatic as well as semantic. In *Second Life* objects can be such things as cars, houses, jewelry, and even less obvious things like hair and clothing. All religious practice requires material culture, and it is through interaction with it that practitioners become entangled with a tradition. Online Buddhism does not differ. The central object in Zen Buddhist practice is virtual meditation cushions, or *zafus*. In real

**Fig. 3:** Free Buddhist monk Robes from Hoben Hoben Mountain Zen retreat (Photograph by Gregory Grieve).

life, a *zafu*, often translated in English as a "sewn seat," is a meditation cushion used for *zazen*, or Zen meditation. A *zafu* is typically round in shape, roughly fifteen inches across, and packed tight with *kapok*, a silky fiber obtained from the fruit of the silk-cotton tree. My research revealed that, while modeled after real life, *Second Life* meditation cushions were modified to fit the virtual site. For example, the simple *zafu* was ubiquitous throughout *Second Life*'s Buddhist community and can be traced back to the original Japanese sit pillow, which was created by the well-known builder CrystalShard. CrystalShard initially created the Japanese sit pillow as a freebie, to be included with one of the first items she designed, a sushi table created in 2004. Because the cushion was full perm (i.e., free to copy, modify, and transfer), the Japanese sit pillow has since become a meme, iterations of which have been customized and modified, and can now be found all over *Second Life.*

The interaction of objects and avatars creates places. Virtual Buddhist spaces differ from flat digital media because they are social spaces to which users go and through which they navigate. On *Second Life*, "places" are the virtual environments built by residents in which avatars dwell and consist of an almost unimaginable variety of venues. Building on *Second Life* allowed residents to express their imaginations. Using the platform's building tools, the *Second Life* Zen community built spiritual places that focused on zendos. In Japanese, *zen-dō* translates as the "place of Zen" and is where *zazen* (sitting meditation) is practiced. *Hoben's zendo was at the center of the region and also at the center of the community's practice.* It sat in the middle of a forested island that was surrounded by rough seas and modeled on an Asian mountain retreat. During my research, the region's other buildings included three meditation halls, two temples, a monks' retreat, rental cabins, a gift shop, a lounge, spaces for Tai Chi and concerts, as well as a wisdom publication library, HIV Awareness Center, and an Addiction Recovery Center.

Groups were at the center of *Second Life*'s Buddhist community. Being inexpensive and hard to disband, they tended to be quite stable and were the backbone of different social clouds. While many residents initially logged on out of curiosity, those who continued to come back were almost always integrated into some type of group. On September 1, 2009, *Second Life*'s Zen Buddhist cloud consisted of five core groups: Bodhi Center, Gekkou Buddhist Group, Hoben Mountain Zen Retreat, Zen Center Retreat, and the Zen Sitting Group. Four of the groups were formed nearly at the same time in late 2007 or early 2008. The remaining group, the Zen Sitting Group, was formed very early in *Second Life*'s history in 2003, and during 2008–2009 had no regular events and was mostly used for cross-posting for groupchat by the other Zen groups.

*Second Life* revolves around "events," which include activities related to arts, culture, charity, support groups, commerce, discussion, education, games, contests, nightlife, entertainment, pageants, and sports. As the *Second Life* webpage reads, "Looking for something to do in *Second Life?* Featured Events includes fun and interesting virtual world activities, such as fashion hunts, live music performances, conferences and more" ('Featured events' n.d.). Events at Hoben included campfire concerts, book discussions, Dharma talks and interviews, and more rarely weddings and memorials. By far the most prevalent and significant practice, however, was silent online meditation, which describes a media practice in which users rested their avatars for twenty to thirty minutes on virtual cushions while they meditated in real life in front of their computer screens

**Fig. 4:** Online Silent Meditation (Photograph by Gregory Grieve).

For the vast majority of Hoben community members, silent online meditation was seen as the central focus of their religious practice. As a survey respondent wrote on July 8, 2010, "It takes Practice to understand and engage in [the Buddha's teaching]."

# Conclusions

Focusing on Zen practice in *Second Life*, this chapter has analyzed an ethnographic method for the study of Buddhism that can be applied to the Digital Humanities more generally. It has outlined a qualitative method based on an online field, the methodological tool of participant observation, and the analytic instrument of thick description as well as briefly touching on ethics. The chapter illustrated a digital ethnographic method by examining *Second Life* Zen Buddhist objects, places, avatars, groups, and events as well as touching on the life cycle of the research project described. Still a question remains unanswered. Why was the *Second Life* user Hope Long winking at my monk robes and me?

One could give a translation, that in online postings "; )" signifies "happily winking," and simulating a real-life wink is often used at the end of an utterance to emote irony. One could also differentiate it from other emoticons such as ":-P" [sticking out tongue], and ": (" [unhappy face]. One could reference the first digital smiley used in 1982, an article on their humorous use in the March 30, 1881, issue of *Puck*, *The National Telegraphic Review Guide* from April 1957, and the use of the number 73 in Morse Code to signify "love and kisses." One could even give a possible genealogy of "; )" as originating in a speech by Abraham Lincoln (*New York Times* 2009). However, the historic, quantitative, and (possibly) genealogical definitions of the winking emoticon "; )" cannot replace the rich depth of ethnographically contextualized thick description that generates an understanding that analyzes, synthesizes, and evaluates the imaginative play of game environments.

What was the thick description of the virtual robes? The five groups of the Zen Buddhist cloud formed a coherent community that differentiated itself from similar social units. I belonged to many groups that engaged with Buddhism, from the Agnostic Buddhist Group to Zen Temple at Mystical Mastery. At first sight there was no clear division between the convert Zen groups and the other communities that blended into the Zen Buddhist community such as the Tibetan, Theravada Buddhist, New Age, and to some degree Pagan and Liberal Christian Community groups. Yet my ethnography uncovered a clear distinction between these groups and the Zen community that could be gleaned through ethnography.

For most in *Second Life*, the robes do not have a great significance. For example, when I was not in a Buddhist region, people would inquire – as I was asked by a child avatar one time – "why are you wearing a dress?" However, for *Second Life*'s Buddhist community, the wearing of robes is a very important choice that displays much about how they imagine their Buddhist practice. For example, as a member of the Zen Buddhist Cloud said, defending why he did not wear robes, "personally I have all sorts of robes and such but do not wear them because I want to make it as clear as I can that I am not Real Life clergy." As I was later to realize, the Agnostic Buddhist Group tended not to wear robes because it fit into their basic belief that Agnostic Buddhism adopts the most basic tenets of Buddhism and leaves behind centuries of additions from other religions. Hope's wink was a not so subtle communication letting me know that my robes were not appropriate attire for such a gathering. Through ethnography, one finds that the "; )" while virtual, was a real and effective way to police community standards, and let me as a researcher know when I had stepped outside the accepted practices of the Zen Buddhist community.

## Further Reading

Boellstorff, Tom. 2008. *Coming of Age in Second Life: an anthropologist explores the virtually human*. Woodstock: Princeton University Press.
The first groundbreaking study of *Second Life*, it is still the benchmark for illustrating an ethnography of virtual social spaces.

Clifford, James, and Marcus, George. 1986. *Writing Culture: the poetics and politics of ethnography.* Berkeley: University of California Press.
This influential volume highlights the epistemic and political predicaments of the ethnographic method. Written during anthropology's crisis of representation and, it urged more nuanced and mediated responses to field work.

Grieve, Gregory. 2016. *Cyber Zen: imagining authentic Buddhist identity, community and religious practice in the virtual world of Second Life.* New York: Routledge.
This book details how *Second Life* Buddhist adherents form communities, identities, locations, and practices that are both a product of and authentic response to contemporary society. The investigation illustrates that to some extent all religion has always been virtual, makes conspicuous ideal forms of contemporary spirituality, and gives a glimpse of possible future alternative forms of religion.

Nardi, Bonnie. 2010. *My Life as a Night Elf Priest: an anthropological account of the* World of Warcraft. Ann Arbor: University of Michigan Press.
The monograph on *World of Warcraft* introduces readers to the history, structure, and culture of this massive video game environment. The book touches on issues of gender, culture, and addiction and illustrates why users are attracted to the game.

# References

American Anthropological Association. 2004. *American Anthropological Association Statement on Ethnography and Institutional Review Boards*, adopted by the AAA Executive Board June 4, 2004. Online. http://www.aaanet.org/stmts/irb.htm [Accessed May 10, 2016].

Amichai-Hamburger, Yair. (ed.). 2005. *The Social Net: Human Behavior in Cyberspace.* Oxford: Oxford University Press.

Appadurai, Arjun. 1996. *Modernity at Large.* Minneapolis: University of Minnesota Press.

Au, Wagner J. 2008. *The Making of Second Life: Notes from a New World.* New York: Harper Collins.

Bainbridge, William Sims. 2000. "Religious Ethnography on the World Wide Web." In *Religion on the Internet: Research Prospects and Promises*, edited by Jeffrey K. Hadden and Douglas E. Cowan, 55–80. London: JAI Press.

Bartle, Richard. 2004. *Designing Virtual Worlds.* Berkeley, CA: New Riders Publishing.

Benedikt, Michael. (ed.). 1991. *Cyberspace: First Steps.* London: MIT Press, 1991.

Boellstorff, Tom. 2008. *Coming of Age in Second Life: An Anthropologist Explores the Virtually Human.* Woodstock: Princeton University Press, 2008.

Boellstorff, Tom. 2013. "Rethinking Digital Anthropology." In *Digital Anthropology,* edited by H.A. Horst and D. Miller, 39–60. London: Bloomsbury Academic.

Boellstorff, Tom, Bonnie Nardi, C. Pearce, and T.L. Taylor. 2012. *Ethnography and Virtual Worlds: A Handbook of Method.* Princeton: Princeton University Press.

Bourdieu, Pierre. 1993. *The Field of Cultural Production.* Cambridge: Polity Press.

Bourdieu, Pierre. 1996. *The Rules of Art: Genesis and Structure of the Literary Field.* Cambridge: Polity Press.

Caillois, Roger. 2001. *Man and the Sacred.* Chicago: University of Illinois Press.

Campbell, Heidi, and Gregory Grieve (eds.). 2014. *Playing with Religion in Digital Games.* Bloomington: Indiana University Press.
Castronova, Edward. 2005. *Synthetic Worlds: The Business and Culture of Online Games.* London: University of Chicago Press.
Cheong, Pauline, S. Huang, and J. Poon. 2011. "Cultivating Online and Offline Pathways to Enlightenment." *Information, Communication and Society* 14(8): 1160–80.
Clifford, James., and George Marcus. 1986. *Writing Culture: The Poetics and Politics of Ethnography.* Berkeley: University of California Press.
Cowan, Douglas E. 2005. *Cyberhenge: Modern Pagans on the Internet.* New York: Routledge.
Dawson, Lorne. and D.E. Cowan. 2004. "Introduction." In *Religion Online: Finding Faith on the Internet*, edited by Lorne L. Dawson and Douglas E. Cowan, 1–16. London: Routledge.
Dibble, Julian. 1993. "A Rape in Cyberspace." *Village Voice* December 21: 36–43.
Dibble, Julian. 1998. *My Tiny Life: Crime and Passion in a Virtual World.* New York: Owl Books.
Ducheneaut, Nicolas, Nicholas Yee, and Victoria Bellotti. 2010. "The Best of Both (Virtual) Worlds: Using Ethnography and Computational Tools to Study Online Behavior." *Ethnographic Praxis in Industry Conference Proceedings* 1:136–48.
Erlandsson, Sven. 2000. *Spiritual but Not Religious: A Call to Religious Revolution in America.* Bloomington, IN: iUniverse.
Evans-Pritchard, Edward E. 1940. *The Nuer: A Description of the Modes of Livelihood and Political Institutions of a Nilotic People.* Oxford: Clarendon Press.
Faure, Bernard. 1995. "Quand l'Habit fait le Moine: The symbolism of the Kāsāya in Sōtō Zen." *Cahiers d'Extrême-Asie* 8(3):335.
"Featured events." Online. http://secondlife.com/destinations/events [Accessed November 11, 2015].
Fox, Richard. 1991. "Introduction: Working in the Present." In *Recapturing Anthropology: Working in the Present.* Santa Fe, NM: School of American Research Press.
Frasca, Gonzalo. 2003. "Ludologists Love Stories, Too: Notes from a Debate that Never Took Place." *Digital Games Research Conference 2003 Proceedings.* https://www.ludology.org/articles/Frasca_LevelUp2003.pdf [Accessed Nov 10, 2018].
Fuller, Robert. 2000. *Spiritual, but Not Religious.* Oxford: Oxford University Press, 2001.
Geertz, Clifford. 1973. *The Interpretation of Cultures.* New York: Basic Books.
Geertz, Clifford. 1983. *Local Knowledge: Further Essays in Interpretive Anthropology.* New York: Basic Books.
Golub, Alex. 2010. "Being in the World (of Warcraft): Raiding, Realism, and Knowledge Production in a Massively Multiplayer Online Game." *Anthropological Quarterly*, 83:17–46.
Grieve, Gregory. 1995. "Imagining a Virtual Religious Community: Neo-Pagans on the Internet." *Chicago Anthropology Exchange* 7:98–132.
Grieve, Gregory. 2015. "The Middle Way Method: A Buddhist Informed Ethnography of the Virtual World of Second Life." In *The Pixel in the Lotus: Buddhism, the Internet and Digital Media*, edited by Gregory Grieve and Daniel Veidlinger, 23–39. New York: Routledge.
Grieve, Gregory. 2016. Cyber Zen: Imagining Authentic Buddhist Identity, Community and Religious Practice in The Virtual World of Second Life. New York: Routledge.

Grieve Gregory, and Kevin. Heston. 2011. "Finding Liquid Salvation: Using the Cardean Ethnographic Method to Document *Second Life* Residents and Religious Cloud Communities." In *Virtual Worlds, Second Life, and Metaverse Platforms: New Communication and Identity Paradigms*, edited by Nelson Zagalo, Leonel Morgado, and Ana Boa-Ventura, 288–306. Hershey, PA: IGI Global.

Gupta, Akhil, and James Ferguson. 1997. *Anthropological Locations: Boundaries and Grounds of a Field Science.* Berkeley: University of California Press.

Hine, Christine. 2000. *Virtual Ethnography.* London: Sage Publications.

Hine, Christine. 2008. "Virtual Ethnography: Modes, Varieties, Affordances." In *The SAGE Handbook of Online Research Methods*, edited by N.G. Fielding, R.M. Lee, and G. Blank, 401–415. London: Sage.

Helland, Christopher. 2000. "Religion Online/Online Religion and Virtual Communitas." In *Religion on the Internet: Research Prospects and Promises*, edited by Jeffery K. Hadden and Douglas E. Cowan, 205–24. London: JAI Press/Elsevier.

Helland, Christopher. 2005. "Online Religion as Lived Religion. Methodological Issues in the Study of Religious Participation on the Internet." *Online—Heidelberg Journal of Religions on the Internet* 1, no.1, http://www.ub.uni-heidelberg.de/archiv/5823.

Huizinga, Johan. 1950. *Homo Ludens.* Boston: Beacon Press.

Iwamura, Jane. 2011. *Virtual Orientalism: Asian Religions and American Popular Culture.* Oxford: Oxford University Press.

Jenkins, Henry. 2006. *Convergence Culture: Where Old and New Media Collide.* New York: NYU Press.

Kendall, Lori. 2002. *Hanging Out in the Virtual Pub: Masculinities and Relationships Online.* Berkeley: University of California Press.

Kohn, Tamara. 1995. "She Came out of the Field and into my Home." In *Questions of Consciousness,* edited by Anthony P. Cohen and Nigel Rapport, 41–59. London: Routledge.

Lee, Donghun, and Linda J. Schoenstedt. 2011. "Comparison of eSports and Traditional Sports Consumption Motives." *ICHPER-SD Journal of Research in Health, Physical Education, Recreation, Sport and Dance* 6(2): 39–44.

Linden Lab. 2003. *Second Life.* Linden Research.

Malinowski, Bronislaw. 1929. *The Sexual Life of Savages in North-Western Melanesia: An Ethnographic Account of Courtship, Marriage and Family Life among the Natives of the Trobriand Islands, British New Guinea.* New York: Halcyon House.

Malinowski, Bronislaw. 1961. *Argonauts of the Western Pacific.* New York: E P. Dutton.

Malinowski, Bronislaw. 1992. *Magic, Science, and Religion.* Prospect Heights, IL: Waveland Press.

Markham, Annette N. 1998. *Life Online: Researching Real Experience in Virtual Space.* London: Sage Publications.

Mead, Margaret. 1928. *Coming of Age in Samoa: A Psychological Study of Primitive Youth for Western Civilization.* New York: William Morrow.

Miller, Daniel, and Don Slater. 2000. *The Internet: An Ethnographic Approach.* Oxford: Berg.

Mitra, Ananda and Eilsia Cohen. 1998. "Analyzing the web." In *Doing Internet Research. Critical Issues and Methods for Examining the Net,* edited by J. Steve, 179–202. London: Sage.

Morningstar, Chip, and F. Randall Farmer. 1991. "The Lessons of LucasFilms' Habitat." In *Cyberspace: First Steps*, edited by Michael Benedikt, 273–301. Cambridge, MA: MIT Press.
Murthy, Dhiraj. 2008. "Digital Ethnography: An Examination of the Use of New Technologies for Social Research." *Sociology*, 42(5): 837–55.
Murthy, Dhiraj. 2011. "Emergent Digital Ethnographic Methods for Social Research." In *Handbook of Emergent Technologies in Social Research,* edited by S. Hesse Biber, 158–179. Oxford: Oxford University Press.
Nardi, Bonnie. 2010. *My Life as a Night Elf Priest: An Anthropological Account of the* World of Warcraft. Ann Arbor: University of Michigan Press.
*New York Times.* 2009. "Is that an Emoticon in 1862?" January 19, 2009.
"Object." Online. http://wiki.secondlife.com/wiki/Object [Accessed May 2016].
Orgad, Shani. 2008. "How Can Researchers Make Sense of the Issues Involved in Collecting and Interpreting Online and Offline Data?" In *Internet Inquiry: Conversations about Method*, edited by Annette Markham and Nancy Baym, 33–53. San Francisco: Sage.
Pelling, Nick. 2011. "The (Short) Prehistory of 'Gamification.'" Online. https://nanodome.wordpress.com/2011/08/09/the-short-prehistory-of-gamification/ [Accessed May 10, 2016].
Pew Research Center. 2015a. 'Gaming and Gamers.' Online. http://www.pewinternet.org/2015/12/15/gaming-and-gamers/ [Accessed May 1, 2016]
Pew Research Center. 2015b. 'U.S. Public Becoming Less Religious.' Online. http://www.pewforum.org/2015/11/03/u-s-public-becoming-less-religious/ [Accessed May 1, 2016]
Russell, Steve. 1962. *SpaceWar!* Video Game.
Satwicz, Thomas. 2006. *Technology at Play: An Ethnographic Study of Young People's Video Gaming Practices.* Ph.D., diss., University of Washington.
*Second Life.* Online. http://secondlife.com/ [Accessed May 10, 2016].
Wagner, Rachel. 2012. *Godwired: Religion, Ritual and Virtual Reality.* New York: Routledge.
Wagner, Rachel. 2014. "The Importance of Playing in Earnest." In *Playing with Religion in Digital Games*, edited by Heidi Campbell and Gregory Price Grieve, 192–213. Bloomington: Indiana University Press.
Winnicott, Donald W. 1971. *Playing and Reality.* London: Tavistock.
ZeniMax Online Studios. 2014. *The Elder Scrolls Online.* Bethesda Softworks.

# Part Two: **Digital Conservation, Presentation and Archiving**

Kuo-Ming Tang and Shu-Kai Hsieh

# Ontologizing Buddhist Digital Archives: Two Case Studies

## Introduction

In philosophy, the field of ontology is the study of 'existence' in general, including asking questions about what *really* exists and how entities are related to each other. Such metaphysical inquiries help constitute our understanding and recognition of the world and seek to clarify the nature of reality. The term 'ontologies' (mostly in plural form), however, has recently begun to be used in computer science to refer to the *formal* and *declarative* description of a certain precise domain including "the glossary of the domain terms and the logical expressions describing the meanings and the relationships of these terms" (Gruber 1993).

Ontologies in this sense thus focus more on the relative organization of knowledge rather than concerns about existence and reality itself, and they therefore allow for structured sharing of knowledge related to the domain of the ontology. Ontologists and ontology engineers have developed different techniques of formal semantics for explicit conceptualization in any sort of information system, such as databases, catalogues, documents, Web pages, etc. In this way, ontologies can be used as shared semantic frameworks to make such information much more amenable to machine processing and interpretation yet still understandable for humans.

In recent years, there has been increasing interest in using ontologies in Digital Humanities to create shared knowledge frameworks that serve to lay out domains of knowledge more clearly and allow multiple parties to work within the same set of assumptions. In this chapter, we aim to highlight this line of thinking in the context of Buddhist Digital Archives in Chinese. Two case studies will be introduced in Sections Two and Three, followed by the Conclusion.

## The OntoLEX Approach: Constructing the OntoWordNet of CBETA

This section introduces our first case study on the lexicalized ontology for Buddhist Digital Archives.

https://doi.org/10.1515/9783110519082-005

In the current digital archives of Buddhist Sutras and writings, *lexicon, content* and *catalog* are three core elements of Buddhist knowledge. However, the close relationship among these three core elements has not been explicitly and systematically highlighted. This section introduces an *OntoLex* (Ontology-Lexicon) approach for the integration of cross-language Buddhist Scriptures and traditional Buddhist taxonomic knowledge structure. The approach originated from the Semantic Web community (Berners-Lee et al. 2003) and supports linguistic grounding of a given (reference) ontology by adding information about how ontology elements (classes, properties, individuals etc.) are realized in multiple languages, and thus is helpful for approximation to its target domain knowledge structure. The model we propose integrates the ontological-lexical resource known as WordNet and the Chinese Electronic Tripiṭaka Collection (CBETA) to establish the relationship of lexicon, content and catalog of cross-language Buddhist scriptures.

WordNet (Fellbaum 1998) is an online English lexical database developed by George A. Miller and Christiane Fellbaum at Princeton University, which has become an important lexical semantic resource in computational linguistics and English lexicology. English WordNet adopts the concept of a lexical matrix and is implemented as a lexical network. Word lemmata are clustered into sets of synonyms called synsets, which are interconnected with different kinds of lexical semantic paradigmatic relations such as hypernymy (higher order words that describe a class to which a word belongs) and meronymy (describing entities that are parts of a larger thing). For example, a hypernym of the word "tree" is "woody plant," as the set of woody plants is a higher order class that contains the word "tree," and a meronym of "tree" is "limb," as a limb is a part of a tree. One of the current developments of WordNet-related research is to rebuild the WordNet in an ontological framework (Huang et al. 2009) such as the *OntoWordNet* project (Gangemi et al. 2003), which aims to achieve a formal specification of WordNet as an axiomatic ontology that adheres to logical and ontological commitments.

The Chinese Buddhist Electronic Text Association (CBETA)[1] provides a large Chinese Buddhist Digital Archive containing more than 50 million character tokens that are freely accessible and the number keeps growing. It is noted that the complexity involved in the huge amount of CBETA data lies not only in their rich metadata such as genre, translators, and time of translation, but also in their temporal-geographic information revealing linguistic data that spans a millennium and was disseminated in different regions.

1 http://www.cbeta.org/unit.php

Our OntoLex approach starts with proposing an integrated framework for the ontological WordNet and the *Uni-Catalog* database in CBETA, which will help to establish the relationship of lexicon, content and catalog of cross-language Buddhist scriptures. For the part of ontological WordNet, we use the classification method of DLT (Domain Lexicon Taxonomy) proposed by Huang et al. (2004), and combine DLT with the traditional Buddhist knowledge-outlining and summarization system called "Ke-Pan" (科判) to build a Buddhist domain ontology. To put it simply, "Ke-Pan" can be understood as an authoritative and systematic way to achieve canonical text segmentation. With the classification structure of the linguistic resource, we can organize a comprehensive domain lexicon, and use the taxonomy nodes that link with the ontology to construct a Buddhist Ontological WordNet and we can use BibTEX (https://www.ctan.org/pkg/bibtex) reference management software to construct an ontological cross-language Buddhist catalog. This kind of ontological catalog established by BibTEX can easily retrieve data from large bibliographic data, and will be very convenient for information retrieval and services expansion (Tang and Hsieh 2012).

The construction steps consist of (1) The collection and preprocessing of Buddhist Scriptures, (2) The construction of an Ontological WordNet prototype, (3) The cross-lingual connection with the ontological catalog system, and finally (4) Integration and implementation on the Web. During the process, the interpretative alignment of the traditional scripture taxonomic knowledge structure ('Ke-Pan') was coupled with the Buddhist WordNet and catalog, which integrates lexicon, content and catalog of Buddhist Texts with WordNet and ontology technology. Figure 1 depicts the flowchart[2], and Figure 2 illustrates the constructed prototypical Buddhist Ontological Wordnet of *Yogācārabhūmiśāstra.*

Finally, an innovative attempt to import the concept of Ontology catalog in building a cross-language Buddhist Tripitaka catalog in different languages is constructed. In order to testify the corresponding relationship among Buddhist Scriptures cross-linguistically, the Buddhist Catalog functions as an important external evidence in the step. We use the word profile as the 'Internal evidence' to validate cross-language *Yogācārabhūmiśāstra*, then construct the connection of the catalog in Chinese, Sanskrit, Tibetan, and Pali. By way of the defined classes and properties of Buddhist Ontological WordNet and Catalog, the word sets of *Yogācārabhūmiśāstra* can correspond with the catalog of *Yogācārabhūmiśāstra*. In addition, other cross-language Buddhist Scriptures can now be corresponding with each other through the ontological WordNet and catalog as well. An integrated system can be made that links the constructed Buddhist On-

2 For detailed explanation please refer to Tang and Hsieh (2012).

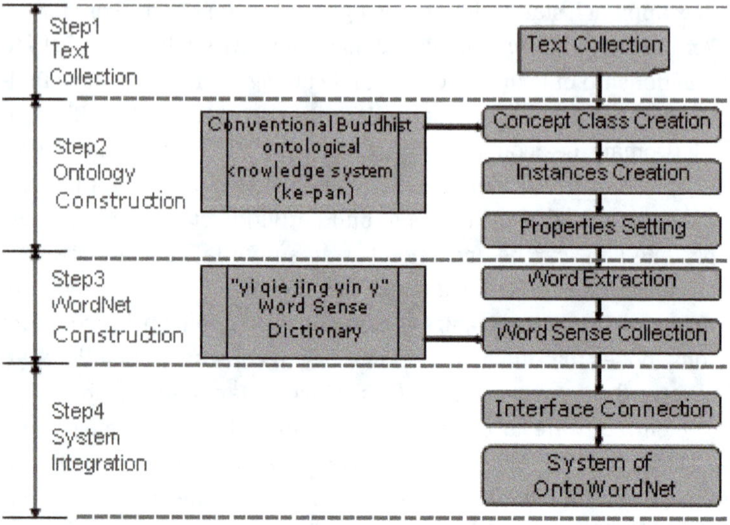


Fig. 1: Main Steps of Buddhist OntoWordNet construction

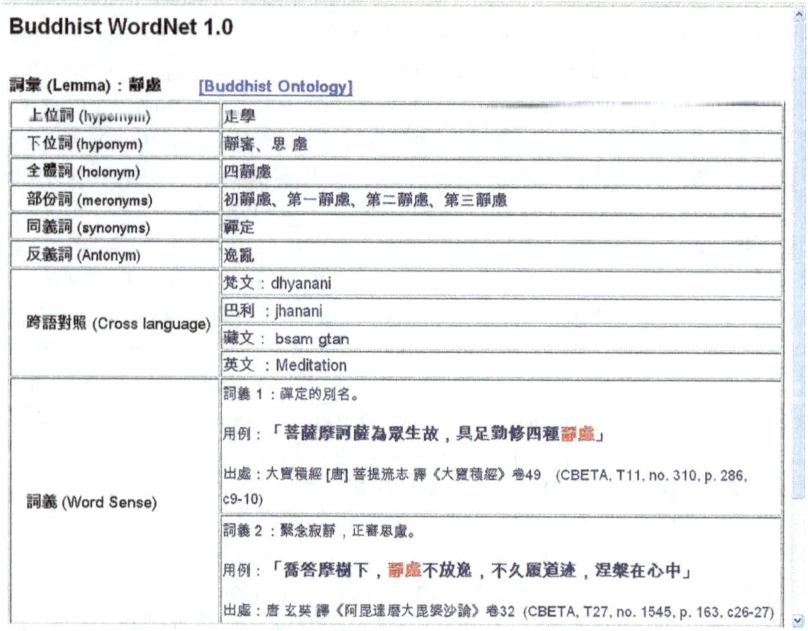

Buddhist WordNet 1.0

詞彙 (Lemma)：靜慮 [Buddhist Ontology]

| | |
|---|---|
| 上位詞 (hypernym) | 走學 |
| 下位詞 (hyponym) | 靜審、思 慮 |
| 全體詞 (holonym) | 四靜慮 |
| 部份詞 (meronyms) | 初靜慮、第一靜慮、第二靜慮、第三靜慮 |
| 同義詞 (synonyms) | 禪定 |
| 反義詞 (Antonym) | 逸亂 |
| 跨語對照 (Cross language) | 梵文：dhyanani |
| | 巴利 ：jhanani |
| | 藏文： bsam gtan |
| | 英文 ：Meditation |
| 詞義 (Word Sense) | 詞義 1：禪定的別名。<br>用例：「菩薩摩訶薩為眾生故，具足勤修四種靜慮」<br>出處：大寶積經 [唐] 菩提流志 譯《大寶積經》卷49 (CBETA, T11, no. 310, p. 286, c9-10) |
| | 詞義 2：繫念寂靜，正審思慮。<br>用例：「喬答摩樹下，靜慮不放逸，不久履道迹，涅槃在心中」<br>出處：唐 玄奘 譯《阿毘達磨大毘婆沙論》卷32 (CBETA, T27, no. 1545, p. 163, c26-27) |

Fig. 2: Buddhist Ontological WordNet

tology and Buddhist WordNet, with Buddhist Texts (scriptures), Catalog, and multi-language dictionary.

Through the lexicon, content and catalog of Buddhist Scriptures, a Buddhist knowledge platform can be built. Such assets will be very important for Buddhist Studies, because it can build up a cross-language Buddhist Tripitaka catalog in Chinese, Pali, Tibetan and Sanskrit. Our future goal is to establish a corresponding system for cross-language Tripitaka, capable of comparing lexicon and content between the scriptures of the Tripitaka in different languages. We believe that it will enhance our understanding of Buddhist thought interpreted in varied temporal and geographical contexts.

## The OntoTEXT Approach: Knowledge Path and Ontology Evolution of Buddhist Citation Content

This section introduces our second case study in applying ontologies to Buddhist Digital Archives.

There have been a large number of scriptures and texts accumulated over the history of Buddhism, which can be basically divided into the categories of canonical and non-canonical. The former, also called the Sutras (in Sanskrit) or Suttas (in Pali), are widely believed to be the actual sayings of the historical Buddha, while the latter are observations or commentaries on canonical texts by others. However, it is very often seen in Buddhist literature that the boundary between a quotation or exact copy of words or phrases and a paraphrase of the canonical texts is vague, which causes severe problems for both scholars and librarians who wish to conduct citation analysis. Determining whether the text in question is a direct quotation or paraphrase of the Sutras has great significance in the practice of the Buddhist community. However, it is a labor-intensive and time-consuming task to decide whether the text is in fact a genuine quote from within the huge amount of Buddhist canonical texts.

We use Natural Language Processing and text similarity techniques to handle the specific issue of Buddhist citation analysis. The motivation is two-fold: to make the genuine quotation behaviors explicit, and to trace the Buddhist knowledge path via the citation/quotation network. In general, Buddhist citations can be divided into three types: exact match, fuzzy match and unknown match. The example of exact match can be illustrated as when some scholar wrote: "E.g: ... 如經憶念不忘菩提心故 (As the sutra *said: Do not forget Bodhicitta*)." From the attribution content of *Daśabhūmikasūtraśāstra* vol.1: 《十地經》卷1：「憶念不忘菩提心故。教化成就一切眾生界故。得通達分別一切處法故。」 (*Do not for-*

*get Bodhicitta.* Educate and grow up all living beings. Have access to all the dharma.) (CBETA T26, no. 1522, p. 124). Here we can see that the text of the quotation matches the original exactly, but in practice examples of fuzzy matches are more likely to be found. For example, we often see the proverb "華嚴經云不忘初心，方得始終" (*Avataṃsaka Sūtra said:* keeping to your original aspiration leads you to success). It is often assumed that this proverb does indeed come from the *Avataṃsaka Sūtra*, which is an important Buddhist text. However, we cannot actually find the same sentence in the *Avataṃsaka Sūtra*. The quotation content may only be referencing the idea or rewriting some sentences of the *Avataṃsaka Sūtra*. The closest paragraph is:《大方廣佛華嚴經》(*Avataṃsaka Sūtra*)卷76：「如是一切諸所作事，從初發心乃至法盡，我皆明憶，無有遺餘，常現在前，念持不忘。」(From the beginning of the mind to the end of world, I can remember everything that I have done. It often appears in front and never forget.) (CBETA, T10, no. 279, p. 417, b28–29). The unknown matching type in contrast, refers to the cases where the quotation source is mentioned but cannot be identified in the existing Sutra (translations).

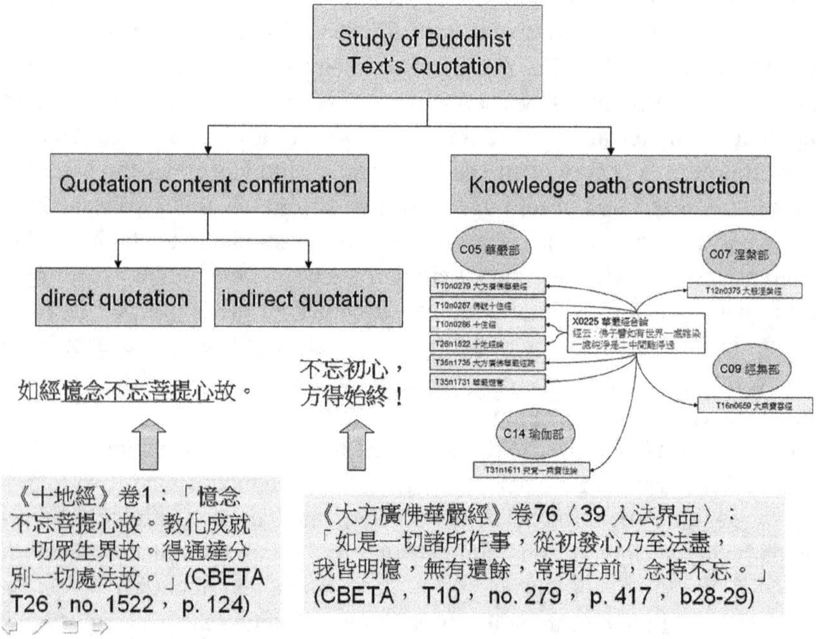


**Fig. 3:** A canon backtracking reference framework

We propose a 'canon backtracking reference' framework (shown in Figure 3), which can be used to (1) confirm quotation content and (2) construct a knowledge path. Recent citation content analysis (Zhang et al. 2013) has demonstrated that citations reflect a citer's intellectual process, cognitive interaction, attitude and sentiments toward the subject item in question. Under the lens of deeper semantic analysis, collective citation behavior can be used to detect scientific breakthroughs and other important information. In the context of Buddhist studies, we believe that citation content also reveals the Buddhist ontological knowledge path. With the aggregation of information with connections to the canon, meta-data as well as the temporal index, patterns and flows of knowledge evolution could be explicitly traced and 'Buddhist citation ontologies' could possibly be built.

The proposed system consists of three modules: (1) data pre-processing and indexing, (2) full-text query and retrieval, and (3) citation content analysis. The data are adopted from CBETA.org which is developed and maintained by the Chinese Buddhist Electronic Text Association. The first module handles the encoding, missing Chinese characters and segmentation issues, n-gram indexing and citation content extraction. We employ the proposed 'canon backtracking reference' method to perform the citation content extraction part. This method utilizes the following information as cues and conducts interactive correlation analysis:

(1) quotation strings (Q): A sentence of quotation content that is used to indicate where the reference has occurred.
(2) quotation length (L): The number of words contained in the reference content.
(3) quotation text (D): The quotation content which is identified by the text number.
(4) citation text (R): The attribution content which is identified by the text number.
(5) context (T): The context of citation text.

Take《華嚴經合論》(An Integrated Exegesis of *Avataṃsaka-sūtra*) as an example. Such as "經云：一一世界滿十方。十方入一亦無餘。世界不增亦不減 (Sutra said: every single world is full of ten worlds. Ten worlds fit into one world, the world itself does not increase or diminish.). The information cues used for the system are as follows:

(1) quotation strings (Q): "一一世界滿十方。十方入一亦無餘。世界不增亦不減",
(2) quotation length (L) = 21 characters,

(3) quotation text (D): X0225《華嚴經合論》(An Integrated Exegesis of *Avatamsaka-sūtra*),
(4) citation text (R): T0279《華嚴經》(*Avatamsaka Sūtra*),
(5) context (T): The context of *Avataṃsaka Sūtra* .

Table 1 gives a snapshot of the extraction of quotation texts of "An Integrated Exegesis of *Avataṃsaka Sūtra*" in the preprocessing stage, where phrases followed by '經云' (Sutra said...) are extracted (as marked in red).

**Tab. 1:** Quotation extraction of "An Integrated Exegesis of *Avataṃsaka Sūtra*"

| | | |
|---|---|---|
| 。一一世界互相含入。經云。 | 一一世界滿十方。十方入一亦無餘。世界不增亦不減。無比功 | X0225_001.txt |
| 故。為說第一義法空。經云。 | 一乘者令小人大。更無餘乘故。又理無二故。亦名一 相。瑜伽 | X0221_010.txt |
| 為無形之形無色之色。經云。 | 一切處普賢菩薩。一切處金色世界。一切處文殊師利。一切處 | X0225_002.txt |
| 生即死皆不移時。是故經云。 | 一念普觀無量劫。無去無來亦無住。如是徧知三世事。超諸方 | X0225_003.txt |
| 從八地方具無功。瓔珞經云。 | 三賢菩薩。法流水中任運至佛。初水後水一性水者。因佛果佛 | X0225_002.txt |
| 。要穿身過出在外。舊經云。 | 下入至金剛際乃住。二何以故徵。意云。何以至彼方住耶。三 | X0221_013.txt |
| 三昧諸智慧門為體。如經云。 | 世界海漩無不隨入者。海者廣大義。漩者甚深義。明此三昧體 | X0225_003.txt |
| 。未明發一切智心故。經云。 | 乘一切智乘。直至道場。以乘普光明大智之乘。還不出普光明 | X0225_004.txt |
| 那等。剎那等者。仁王經云。 | 九百生滅為一剎那。九十剎那為一念。按俱舍等。謂時之最少 | X0221_015.txt |
| 大乘。非名佛乘。法華經云。 | 佛乘唯有一。無二亦無三。即引彼三乘。總歸一乘。小乘雖有 | X0225_001.txt |
| 。何況此行不出海中。經云。 | 佛子。譬如有世界。一處雜染。一處純淨。是二中間。難得過 | X0225_004.txt |
| 覺不知。別求佛見。故經云。 | 佛子設有菩薩。於無量百千億那由他劫。行六波羅蜜。修習種 | X0225_001.txt |
| 不滯。悉皆無作涅槃。經云。 | 佛性非是作法。但為客塵煩惱所覆故。是故今從十住初位。以 | X0225_001.txt |

| | | |
|---|---|---|
| 利。一切處不動智佛。經云。 | 佛身充滿於法界。普現一切眾生前。應受化器悉充滿。佛故處 | X0225_002.txt |
| 樂。如修慈經說。又如經云。 | 修慈定者。臥安覺安。天護人愛。不毒。不兵。水火不喪。眠 | X0221_010.txt |
| 入他等是上行。若依論經云。 | 入出於地。是上下行也。四履水下是涉水不沒。五身出下是熾 | X0221_010.txt |
| 二種。所以者何。善戒經云。 | 受菩薩戒。要先具前三戒。方得與授。問遮難中先問此事。廣 | X0221_005.txt |

In the module of full-text query and retrieval, we use Solr[3], an open-source search platform built on Apache Lucene, and provides web APIs for different programming languages via http protocol and extensible plug-in architecture on demand. Figure 4 shows the architecture of full-text index and search module. The full-text and citation contents are indexed at the same time and returned in JSON format.

Once indexed, the third module provides in-depth search tools for further exploration of the citation content. Quotation analytic tools are implemented as shown in Figure 4. If a user queries the quotation strings (Q): "一一世界滿十方。十方入一亦無餘。世界不增亦不減 (every single world is full of ten worlds. Ten worlds fit into a world, the world does not increase neither diminish.)" in 《華嚴經合論》 (An Integrated Exegesis of *Avataṃsaka-sūtra*), this tool can perform a deep search of all of the sutras in order to find the citation text (R) and its context (T) as shown in Figure 5.

Quotation content information can also be used further to study the evolution of knowledge. We propose the OntoText approach in tracing knowledge evolution in Buddhist studies. From the relevance information of the quotation, it can reveal which sentences were inherited and developed by other sutras in Buddhist texts. If we join the temporal and categorical information, this can more clearly analyze the evolutionary path of the topic, and construct a quotation knowledge ontology as shown in Figure 6.

[quotation text] X0225_004.txt
經云：佛子！譬如有世界，一處雜染，一處純淨 (Sutra said: Buddha disciples! For example, there is a world of filth and there is a world of cleanliness as well)
[citation texts] total: 7757 results

3 http://lucene.apache.org/solr/

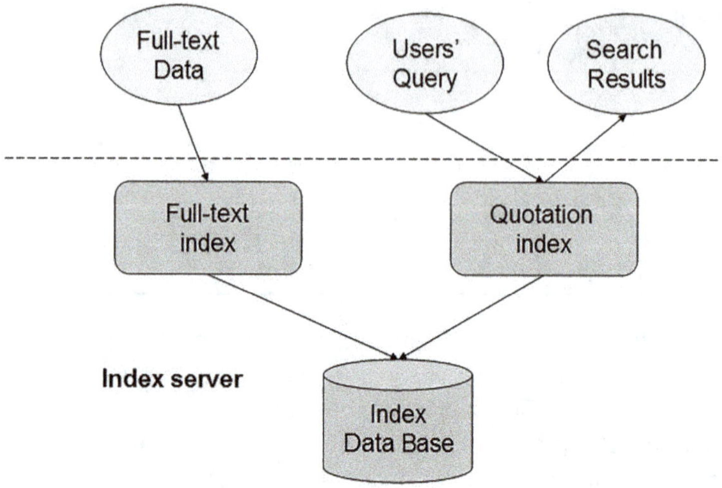


**Fig. 4:** Architecture of full-text index and search module

**Fig. 5:** Quotation analysis tool

Using the quotation analysis tool, the relevance of the quotation for other sutras can be found, including *Avataṃsakasūtra* (T10n0279 大方廣佛華嚴經), *Daśabhūmikasūtra* (T10n0286 十住經), *Daśabhūmikasūtraśāstra* (T26n1522 十地經論) in the *Avataṃsakasūtra* Collection (C05 華嚴部), *Mahāparinirvāṇasūtra* (T12n0375 大般涅槃經) in the *Mahāparinirvāṇasūtra* collection (C07涅槃部), *Mahāyāna Ratnameghasūtra* (T16n0659 大乘寶雲經) in the Miscellaneous sūtra collection (C09

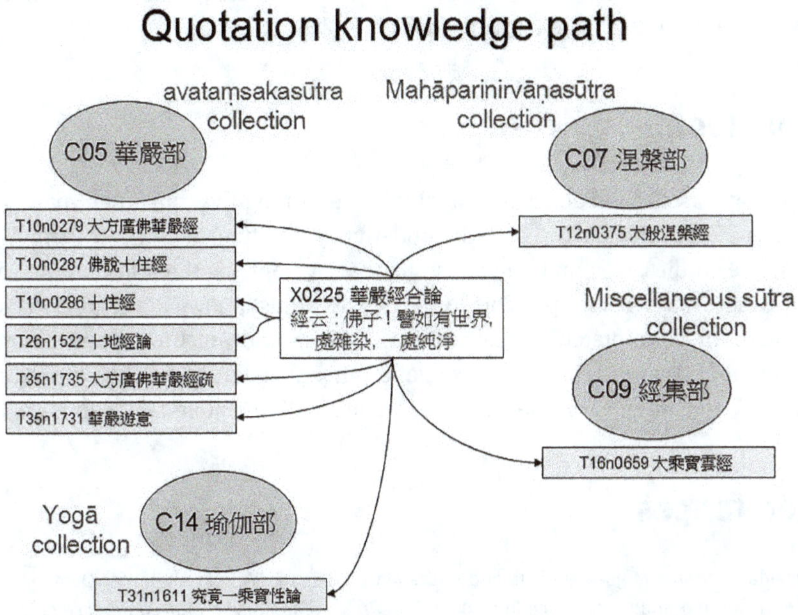


**Fig. 6:** Buddhist Knowledge Evolution via quotation relevance

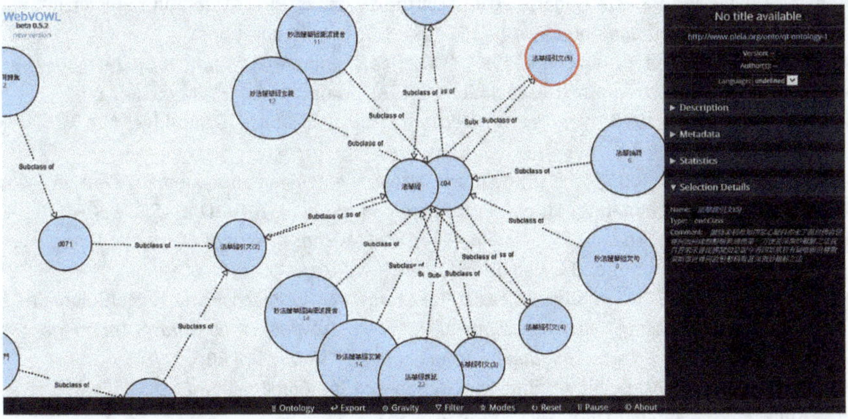


**Fig. 7:** Visualization of quotation knowledge path

經集部), and *Mahāyānottaratantraśāstra* (T31n1611 究竟一乘寶性論) in Yogā collection (C14 瑜伽部). It can be concatenated and gradually constructed as a network of quotation knowledge paths or quotation ontology. The visualization of the quotation knowledge network looks like Figure 7.

## Conclusion

Ontology-based approaches are capable of describing the constituent parts and processes of entities, as well as the underlying structures that affect them. With two case studies, we aim to demonstrate that by applying them to Buddhist digital archives, it becomes possible to see how Buddhist knowledge is diffused, circulated, and interpreted among various scholars and practitioners in different temporal and geographical contexts, and our understanding of knowledge and cultural transmission within Buddhist studies will be empirically supported.

## References


Almeida, Mariana, Miguel Almeida and Andre Martins. 2016. “A Joint Model for Quotation Attribution and Coreference Resolution.” In *Proceedings of the 14th Conference of the European Chapter of the Association for Computational Linguistics, Gothenburg, Sweden.* N.p., 39–48.

Berners-Lee, Tim, et al. 2001. *The Semantic Web.* Scientific American Magazine.

Bonami, Olivier and Daniele Godard. 2016. “On the Syntax of Direct Quotation in French.” In *15th International Conference on HPSG,* 358–377. CSLI Publications.

Cappelen, Herman and Ernie Lepore. 1997. “Varieties of Quotation.” *Mind* 106:429–450.

Chinese Buddhist Electronic Text Association (CBETA). Available: http://www.cbeta.org/

Fellbaum, Christiane. 1998. *WordNet: An electronic lexical database.* Cambridge, MA: MIT press.

Gangemi, Aldo. et al. 2003. “The OntoWordNet Project: extension and axiomatization of conceptual relations in WordNet.” In *Proceedings of CoopIS/DOA/ODBASE* , 820–838.

Huang, Churen, et al. (eds.). 2009. *Ontology and the Lexicon: A Natural Language Processing Perspective.* Cambridge, UK: Cambridge University Press.

Huang, Churen, et al. 2004. “Domain Lexico-Taxonomy: An Approach Towards Multi-domain Language Processing.” In *Proceedings of the Asian Symposium on Natural Language Processing to Overcome Language Barriers, Hainan Island.* 54–60.

Hyland, Ken. 1999. “Academic Attribution: Citation and the Construction of Disciplinary Knowledge.” *Applied Linguistics* 20(3):341–367.

Pareti, Silvia, et al. 2013. “Automatically Detecting and Attributing Indirect Quotations.” EMNLP. N.p., 989–999.

Pouliquen, Bruno, Ralf Steinberger and Clive Best. 2007. “Automatic Detection of Quotations in Multilingual News.” In *Proceedings of Recent Advances in Natural Language Processing,* 487–492.

Quintão, Marta. 2014. “Quotation Attribution for Portuguese News Corpora.” Master’s Thesis Tecnica Lisboa.

Sundar, S. Shyam. 1998. "Effect of Source Attribution on Perception of Online News Stories." *Journalism & Mass Communication Quarterly* 75(1): 55–68.

Tang, Kuo-Ming and Shu-Kai Hsieh. 2012. "Toward an Integrated Framework of Lexicalized Ontology for Buddhist Digital Archives." *International Journal of Computer Processing of Oriental Languages* 24(1):103–112.

Yan, Erjia. 2014. "Finding Knowledge Paths among Scientific Disciplines." *Journal of the Association for Information Science and Technology* 65(11): 2331–2347.

Zhang, Guo, Ying Ding and Stasa Milosevic. 2013. "Citation content analysis (cca): A framework for syntactic and semantic analysis of citation content." *Journal of the American Society for Information Science and Technology* 64(7): 1490–1503.

Paul G. Hackett

# Digital Encoding, Preservation, Translation, and Research for Tibetan Buddhist Texts

## Introduction and Overview of Needs

The transmission of knowledge—in one form or another—lies at the core of every religious tradition from the meaning of a textual corpus to the techniques of guiding novitiates through a series of orchestrated physical and psychological experiences. The Buddhist tradition is no exception. As part of the religious heritage of India, the Buddhist tradition grew out of the same cultural matrix of languages and methods as the many other religious traditions of the subcontinent, a central aspect of which was the intertwined transmission of textual and oral knowledge. Although the original transmission of Buddhist knowledge appears to have been entirely oral in the early years of the tradition, even with the advent of a written corpus, the oral component never disappeared and in many sub-domains remained indispensible to the proper understanding of the literary strains of what would come to comprise the textual canon.

When Buddhism began to filter into Tibet in the seventh century (C.E.), the proximity of Tibet to India offered both a unique opportunity and a unique challenge to Tibetans as they attempted to take-up these two parallel sources of knowledge transmission. Unlike works in the Chinese canon, in which commentary was embedded in and surrounded the translations themselves, the Tibetans maintained a strict division between text and oral commentary, although often relying on the latter in their translation of the former and only, if ever, committing that oral tradition to writing in separate commentarial works—a pattern of documentation seen in Indian Buddhism as well. Consequently, when attempting to work with a text in Tibetan, the first and foremost concern is recognizing (and benefitting from) the commentarial context in which it is embedded.

Part and parcel of this intertwined textual and oral tradition is the revelation of narrative combined with an on-going theme of narrative loss and the decline of the tradition. Such is seen in the Indian sources, in the revelation traditions in general (such as the “Perfection of Wisdom” scriptures), and in particular with the restricted transmission lineages of Tantra. For example, in one of his works, the eighth century siddha-scholar Buddhaśrījñānapada claimed to be committing to writing an oral tradition in danger of being lost:

https://doi.org/10.1515/9783110519082-006

> This meaning was to be passed on in the ears [of a disciple]. Now, living in such times, even these precious teachings of the Buddha need to be thoroughly explained in order to remain. This level of the transmission having been severed, all should understand [this] as the disappearance of the teachings of the Buddha.[1]

Writing some six hundred years later, Bu-ston Rin-chen-grub, in his *Direct Instructions on [Nāgārjuna's] "Five Stages"* (*rim lnga dmar khrid*), reported that he too, was committing to writing an oral tradition for the sake of preserving it, though related a dire warning given to him by his teacher Dharmasvāmin Bsod-nams-rgyal-mtshan-dpal-bzang-po that he had in turn, received from his teacher Grags-chen-pa:

> The writing down of oral precepts is, in general, similar to the dethronement of a king, or to a king roaming aimlessly through a village. There are many objections to it. The effectiveness of the precepts will vanish. When a man will find this book, he will think that it was not necessary for him to obtain the oral precepts, and that he could obtain them through reading [the book]. In the end, the exposition of oral precepts would become a mere recitation. In short, it would cause the disappearance of the oral precepts.[2]

This tension between the desire to preserve the teachings and the danger of adulterating them through committing them to writing is a theme that reappears throughout the tantric tradition, and is the "double-edged sword" that characterizes all oral traditions.

Even for the contemporary scholar of the Tibetan traditions who is fortunate enough to be in contact with the oral tradition of a text of interest, not all words and their meanings are always clear. Since textual corruption through copying and the natural degradation of the oral tradition inevitably lead to the loss of meaning with regard to a text, one need not say more about those texts for which the oral tradition has been lost.

Situations such as those just described are by no means new or limited to the recent past. Working with textual data in the absence of an oral commentarial tradition was a challenge that was faced even in pre-modern Tibet. Bu-ston Rin-chen-grub, for example, discovered an untranslated Sanskrit manuscript in the library of Reting monastery that he attempted to translate. In approaching

---

**1** Buddhaśrījñānapāda, *The Oral Instructions of Mañjuśrī* (*mañjuśrī-mukhāgama; 'jam dpal [dbyangs gyi] zhal lung*) D 1853.

**2** Bu-ston, *Advice on the Direct Instructions on the "Five Stages" of the Glorious Guhyasamāja, the Wish-fulfilling Jewel, the Precious Flower* (*dpal gsang ba 'dus pa'i rdzogs rim rim lnga'i dmar khrid kyi man ngag yid bzhin gyi nor bu rin po che'i za ma tog*), p. 65 / fol.21a; Roerich, *Blue Annals*, pp.424–425.

the *Tāra-mūla-kalpa*, however, he was presented with a text that had no written commentaries and for which the oral tradition had apparently disappeared. What Bu-ston was forced to do instead was compose a highly literal word-by-word translation of the text, in full knowledge of the limitations placed upon him by circumstances. He wrote:

> Because I [Bu-ston] neither met with a *paṇḍita* [i. e., someone learned about this book], nor obtained a commentary bearing witness on the book, I pray that learned persons correct it.[3]

What Bu-ston would have benefitted from was being able to identify parallel passages in the *Mañjuśrī-mūla-kalpa*, of which there are numerous instances.[4] This need for large text data sets for comparative research and exegesis is in fact the focus of the vast majority of digital humanities research efforts—both at the beginning of the Tibetan digital humanities efforts, and down to the present time.

## The Early History of Tibetan E-text

The history of Tibetan digital humanities begins with the attempt to display Tibetan in script on computers. In this regard, 1983 appears to have been a watershed year in the history of Tibetan computing.

One of the earliest attempts to display Tibetan script on computers was done in 1983 on an Apple II computer by Ronald Schwartz at the University of Newfoundland. The program—called "Barkhang"—took keyboard input, used a Wylie parser, and produced output on an Okidata dot matrix printer. With the assistance of Richard "Skip" Martin, Curator of the University of Virginia Tibetan Collection, the system was announced and demonstrated at the Annual Meeting of the Association for Asian Studies in San Francisco that same year.[5] The next year, Schwartz acquired a typesetter's sheet that included samples of all the characters used for printing Tibetan with movable lead type. They were photographically enlarged, digitized, and used to generate a font that included standard Tibetan characters and punctuation, as well as retroflex characters and a few Sanskritic stacks. With a small grant from Memorial University, Schwartz

3 Bu-ston reports on his experiences attempting to translate the *Tāra-mūla-tantra* in the colophon to the *Tāra-mūla-kalpa* (cited in "Introduction," Landesman, forthcoming).

4 Noted in Landesman, forthcoming.

5 "A Program to Produce Tibetan Script Using the Wylie System." Paper presented in the session on Computers in South Asian Studies, Annual Meeting of the Association for Asian Studies, San Francisco (March 1983).

hired Jeff Sparkes to develop a pre-processor for LaTeX ("tfilt") written in the C programming language that took text in Wylie roman transcription and prepared it for producing text in the Tibetan script. That original Unix program was then ported to MS-DOS by William Magee at the University of Virginia. Although that program released in 1987 was effectively a beta, lacking a full complement of characters and punctuation, it nonetheless brought elegant Tibetan script typesetting into public reach.[6]

Shortly after the release of the Apple Macintosh with its graphical interface, a number of people seized the opportunity to create Tibetan script fonts. The first of these was Pierre Robillard in Toronto who, in 1985, released his first set of dot-matrix bitmap fonts called "Tibetan" and "Mantra." With the development of laserprinting technology, Robillard updated his fonts to Postscript versions for laserprinters and dubbed them LTibetan and LMantra. The resulting system released in 1988 called *Tibetan on the Macintosh* featured both fonts and a romanization-to/from-script conversion program (Tibetan Editor) combined with a Wylie transcription parser written by Chet Wood (Wylie Editor) that allowed for the conversion of entire documents from Wylie transcription to the LTibetan font. The advantage of Robillard's *LTibetan* font encoding was that it presented the entirety of normative Tibetan and minimal Sanskrit/mantra support in a single font and, together with a "Desk Accessory" that provided sorting functionality for the font, constituted a complete system for working with Tibetan script e-text. Shortly thereafter, Marvin Moser ported the font to Windows (released as *Tibetan for Windows*). Both systems soon gained popularity at American universities and among the Tibetan exile community.

Several other fonts for Tibetan for the Macintosh were released in the late-1980s from John Rockwell ("Tibetan 11/3"), Mark Giacone and Philip Payne ("LASERTibetan"), and Peter Lofting ("Thimbu" and "Punaka" for Dzongkha), though none of them gained the broad acceptance of Robillard's system.

On the x86 PC side of computing, Tony Duff and Gary Weiner of the Tibetan Computer Company of Colorado designed a system of bitmap fonts for use within the "WordPerfect" word processing program, which were released in 1986. Following a similar strategy, Peter Ebbatson in Oxford developed the Atisha Word

6 Since that time, the font and Wylie pre-processor have been maintained and modified by Robert Knight of Princeton University, Sam Sirlin, Beat Steiner, Oliver Corff, and others. The original program for Latex, and implementations by Sirlin and Steiner remain available at http://ctan.org. The digitized font from the typesetter's sheet has been preserved throughout these implementations together with additional stacked Sanskritic characters and punctuation modelled on the original font.

Processing system in 1989 for use with the ChiWriter word processing program with support for both dot-matrix and laserprinters.

Later in the 1990s, Weiner devised the Sambhota system of fonts, which split pre-composed glyphs across several fonts. Duff, on the other hand, revisited his typeface and with input from a noted Tibetan calligrapher, developed a series of highly refined vector graphic fonts (most notable among them being "Tibetan Machine") which served as the basis (officially and unofficially) for many subsequent font developers. In addition, he went on to create a number of resources including keyboards for Tibetan input optimized for speed (a DVORAK-style Tibetan keyboard) and ease of memorization.

Meanwhile in China, given the already large font sets created for Chinese, separate Tibetan fonts were not created, but rather standards proposed to fit Tibetan character sets into pre-existing Chinese fonts. In the mid-1990s proposals for Tibetan encoding standards were put forward for the inclusion of Tibetan as part of the larger Chinese government standard, GB 18030–2000.

## Localization of Operating Systems for Tibetan

While many operating systems had been localized by the early 2000s, Tibetan lagged behind. In an attempt to overcome this deficit, in 2004 researchers in the PRC began working on a project to establish a set of standard terms for information technology in Tibetan. In May of 2005, a research project for a "China National Standard for Tibetan Computer Terminologies"[7] was established with government funding under the supervision of the China Tibetology Research Center. Concluding in late 2006, the project produced a trilingual dictionary of information technology terms in Tibetan, Chinese, and English, published at the end of that year.[8]

All these efforts were combined with attempts to devise a Tibetan keyboard entry system. In addition to the various keyboards developed as part of font packages, several attempts were made to utilize and/or modify the Wylie transcription system. Although Wylie's original presentation of a transcription scheme utilized normative English letter combinations to represent Tibetan, he nonetheless continued to use diacritic characters for Sanskrit morphemes represented in Tibetan characters. In the mid-1990s, scholars in Japan devised the

7 That is, a project to create a vocabulary set equivalent to the ISO/IEC 2382–1~34 standard (and the Chinese standard, GB/T 5271.1~34).
8 Tashi Tsering (2007).

"Extended Wylie" system for the purpose of reducing all the letter combinations to a non-diacritic input scheme; a decade later a similar thing was attempted by staff members at the University of Virginia proposing an H-K-style[9] keyboard input method of similar name, a.k.a. "Extended Wylie Transcription Scheme" (EWTS), with the latter unsuccessfully attempting to promote it as a transcription scheme for data storage and representation. In this latter regard, EWTS as well as the Library of Congress's own diacritic transcription scheme were eventually dismissed, and in 2015, the U.S. Library of Congress finally adopted the most common academic standard for romanization of Tibetan known simply as "Wylie" with diacritic support for Sanskrit represented in Tibetan letters.

Although all these issues may be deemed technical and pedestrian from one perspective, these efforts nonetheless were crucial in the advancement of the field and truly marked the start of the era of Tibetan digital humanities.

## Tibetan Text Digitization, Tools, and Research Environments

### *Text initiatives*

#### E-text

In 1987, as the first diverse set of Tibetan script systems were being propagated, the foundations of the first public e-text archive—the ACIP data set—were being laid in India, where the Asian Classics Input Project (ACIP) began establishing computer centers in India staffed by Tibetan refugees who were receiving training, equipment, and modest wages in order to input Tibetan Buddhist texts.[10] Taking the *Thesaurus Linguae Graecae* (TLG) project as a model, the project staff focused on producing flat-ASCII text that could be distributed on CD-ROM. After devising a Romanization scheme that would include a variety of

**9** The H-K or "Harvard-Kyoto" transcription scheme was a romanization scheme for Sanskrit designed to avoid the use of diacritic marks that had been the academic standard in use for over a hundred years (the International Alphabet of Sanskrit Transcription or IAST). With the widespread usage of Unicode in both email and mobile devices, and the effective extinction of typewriters, the utility of such schemes has greatly decreased.

**10** Part of the preparatory work for this project was the construction of a custom word processor for the x86 PC platform by Steven Bruzgulis under the guidance of Geshe Lobsang Tharchin in New Jersey. The TTPS system was designed specifically for working with the e-texts that were to be produced by ACIP.

punctuation marks and a minimal form of mark-up tags, monks in South India were trained and equipped with computers, and data input was begun. In the spring of 1990, ACIP released its first set of 12 CD-ROMs of data and its reception marked the project as an unqualified success with over 5,000 individual requests for copies of the data set.

At the present time, the ACIP data set—having seen six official releases—remains the largest publicly available Tibetan e-text archive. Other groups and organizations affiliated with individual monasteries and religious sects,[11] as well as governmental organizations[12] have all publicly spoken of e-text archives that they have compiled, but to-date none have been made public.

The early 1990s also saw the advent of the Unicode Standard. Although Tibetan script was included in the 1.0 version, it was quickly deprecated and removed from the 1.1 standard and only reintroduced in 1996 as ver. 2.0 with substantial revision based on input from the Tibetan end-user community. While a few more characters have been added to the standard since ver. 2.0, the Tibetan Unicode encoding quickly became the *de facto* standard for encoding Tibetan e-text in Europe and America. In 2007, with the release by Microsoft of the Windows Vista operating system with full Unicode support for Tibetan, adoption of the Unicode standard began to gain wider acceptance in other countries.

Despite the growth of script encoding schemes, many of the text archives retained a romanization scheme for storage, processing, and scholastic annotation.

## Page images

Although commercial scanners for producing digital page images began to be commercially available in the mid-1980s, it wasn't until the mid-1990s that they were of sufficient quality to reach mass-market appeal. Nonetheless, given the unique page dimensions of Tibetan texts, for many years only hand-held portable scanners offered the possibility of scanning Tibetan texts, but remained inadequate for large-scale use. By the late 1990s, large-format flatbed and overhead scanners were becoming commercially available, coincidentally,

11 For example, many monasteries have been electronically typesetting their textbooks but have not released the underlying e-text. Similarly, the Kagyu, Sakya, and Nyingma sects have produced searchable e-text collections of many of their core writings, but retain them for internal use only.

12 Scholars in the PRC have published articles speaking of large corpora of Tibetan texts, though once again, none have been made public. See, for example, Lu Yajun et al. (2003).

just as E. Gene Smith, a former Field Director for the Library of Congress was retiring and setting up his private research library. After a short-lived project (HIAR —Himalayan and Inner Asian Resources), Smith eventually established the Tibetan Buddhist Resource Center (TBRC) and began the large-scale scanning and distribution of digital images of Tibetan texts. Although Smith passed away in 2010, his institution continues in partnership with Harvard University's Digital Repository Service (DRS) and remains the largest general repository of digital image files of Tibetan texts with an online minimally searchable file system (with some minimal bibliographic information) that has gone through several revisions.[13]

As this technology began to become more ubiquitous, many other projects and institutions began revisiting their manuscript and archival photographic collections. The Nepal-German Manuscript Preservation Project (NGMPP), active in Nepal since the 1970s microfilming Sanskrit and Tibetan manuscripts, began production of a comprehensive catalogue of their archive in 2002 making the resulting database available first on CD-ROM, and then online.[14]

Also in the late 1990s, a number of smaller individual collections began producing online archives and limited released digital products (CD-ROM, DVD-ROM). The International Dunhuang Project (IDP),[15] for example, founded in 1994 in an attempt to unify collections of Dunhuang materials held between disparate archives, began archival research on all aspects of Dunhuang. Although much of IDP's early work focused on conservation and cataloguing, they eventually began full digitization of manuscripts and other materials accessible online with full cataloguing and metadata information. This effort was supplemented in the 2000s by the "Old Tibetan Documents Online" (OTDO) archive,[16] which made searchable e-text of select documents available to the public through its website. Other notable endeavors include the projects of Kawachen,[17] who in 2007, together with the National Library of Mongolia (NLM) in Ulaanbaatar, Asian Classics Input Project (ACIP), and Yuishoji Buddhist Cultural Exchange Research Institute (YBCERI) produced digital image archives of the Tempangma

13 The most current interface can be found at http://www.tbrc.org/
14 Available at https://catalogue.ngmcp.uni-hamburg.de/content/index.xml
15 http://idp.bl.uk
16 http://otdo.aa-ken.jp/. The Old Tibetan Documents Online project was formed at the Research Institute for Languages and Cultures of Asia and Africa (ILCAA) of Tokyo University of Foreign Studies (TUFS) with Izumi Hoshi as coordinator and financial aid from the Japanese Ministry of Research and Education.
17 http://www.kawachen.org/

manuscript Kangyur and the Peking Kangyur, both held by the National Library of Mongolia.

## *Text access and manipulation environments*

By the late 1990s as the Internet offered an increasingly wider venue for the dissemination of Tibetan resources, many organizations and universities developed websites to host a variety of types of data from encyclopedic data to audio-video resources and GIS information on Tibet.[18] The idea of centralized comprehensive resources (and the websites and "link farms" that attempted such) was short-lived and by the 2000s, emphasis in digital humanities shifted to specialized websites of self-produced and curated data in the form of online databases and repositories of primary and secondary reference materials.

As noted, the Tibetan Buddhist Resource Center (TBRC) is currently the largest repository of digital images of Tibetan text. While initially accompanied by only the most minimal cataloging information, the staff at TBRC have been supplementing their file management system to include content information for some texts and authors, although even that information remains limited in scope. More detailed presentations of author biographies have been developed in the linked resource, "The Treasury of Lives" database[19]—a biographical encyclopedia of Tibet, Inner Asia, and the Himalayan region founded in 2007 as a project of the Shelley & Donald Rubin Foundation.

While for many years e-text searching was limited to full-text searching by individual users of their own downloaded data, in the late 2000s, a number of organizations attempted to create searchable archives of e-text. The most prominent and heavily accessed of these is the "Buddhist Canons Research Database" (BCRD),[20] which offers full-text searching on the Tibetan Buddhist canon together with detailed and cross-referenced primary and secondary bibliographic data together with active links to other repositories including TBRC, ACIP, SAT and CBETA, J-STOR, and other e-text and image archives of materials related to Buddhist canonical research.

Other research groups have focused on individual texts and text collections. One such project is the "Thesaurus Literaturae Buddhicae" (TLB) at the Univer-

---

**18** See, for example, Haig (2006).

**19** http://treasuryoflives.org/

**20** http://www.bcrdb.org/ (mirrored at http://databases.aibs.columbia.edu/).

sity of Oslo.[21] The TLB presents selected parallel texts aligned at the sentence level in Tibetan, Sanskrit, Chinese, Mongolian, French, and English manually curated by the faculty and staff of the University of Oslo's Norwegian Institute of Palaeography and Historical Philology under the directorship of Jens Braarvig. Other projects have attempted to provide collaborative research environments dedicated to specialized topics. In this regard, the "Wiki"-style collaborative environment became very popular in the mid-2000s with the rise to prominence of the "Wikipedia" project. A number of organizations implemented wiki-style websites for topics such as general information about an organization[22] to hosting entire dictionaries,[23] while others deployed the wiki model for subject-specific collaboration.[24]

## Research and Productivity Tools

Following the acceptance of the Tibetan Unicode standard, one of the biggest challenges facing the Tibetan end-user community was the conversion of legacy data. Fortunately, many of the original font designers created or distributed conversion programs for mapping between romanization and their font-specific encoding. For those systems that provided reverse conversion (script to romanization) however, either flat-text or RTF format was required and conversion to Unicode still required an intermediary of romanization.

In the early 2000s, Tashi Tsering developed the "Universal Tibetan Font Converter" (UTFC)[25] with funding from the Trace Foundation. The UTFC program covered seventeen different Tibetan encoding schemes including four Tibetan transliteration schemes (ACIP, ALA-LC, Wylie, "Extended Wylie"), Tibetan Unicode, and twelve legacy Tibetan fonts[26] in both RTF and HTML formats. Other solutions to the legacy font conversion problem were developed using Visual Basic macros

21 https://www2.hf.uio.no/polyglotta/index.php?page=library&bid=2 – one of the sections of the "Bibliotheca Polyglotta" https://www2.hf.uio.no/polyglotta/.
22 See, for example, the "Rigpa Shedra": http://www.rigpawiki.org/.
23 See, for example, the "Rangjung Yeshe" dictionary project: http://rywiki.tsadra.org/.
24 A good example of this is the international effort to document the "Tibet Mirror" (*me long*) newspaper at: http://www.tibetmirrorpress.org/
25 http://www.yalasoo.com/English/docs/yalasoo_en_utfc.html
26 The twelve are: Sambhota 1.0 (Sama), Sambhota 2.0 (Dedris), Bandrida, Tongyuan, Beida Founder, Huanguang, LTibetan, Jamyang, TCRC Bod-Yig, Tibetan Machine, Tibetan Machine Web, and National Standard Extended.

for execution within word processing programs to avoid complications with RTF round-trip conversions.[27]

Along with these developments, numerous Tibetan script fonts have been developed and made available to the public, in addition to stock system fonts now available with the major operating systems, others include the Xenotype fonts, Qomolangma fonts,[28] and Monlam fonts,[29] with the latter conveniently providing Roman character support to compensate for base-line adjustment issues.

A second challenge that confronted the legacy font community was the issue of sorting Tibetan in accepted dictionary sort-order. While writing computer programs to sort romanized Tibetan was relatively straightforward,[30] given the convoluted manner in which every custom Tibetan font encoded the script in combination with the particular rules for sorting syllables posed a challenge that most (other than the font's designers) considered too complicated to merit the effort required. During the end-user community's discussion in the post-1.0 Unicode Tibetan standard, the issue of ease of sorting was heavily debated. Although the Unicode standard provides a mechanism for specifying weights for sorting various scripts, the system was explicitly independent of the order and composition of the characters in the standard. Consequently, a separate series of weights were assigned to each Tibetan character in the standard. The process of devising and implementing a sorting routine at the operating system-level remained relatively complex.[31]

Despite these limitations, over the years attempts to produce a variety of electronic reference materials proceeded particularly in the area of electronic dictionaries. These early attempts at electronic dictionaries were either limited in scope by their textual basis[32] or were collaborative efforts guided by few if any lexicographic principles and procedures.[33] The only exceptions are electronic editions of previously published dictionaries and the Tibetan monolingual dic-

27 Hackett (2013).
28 http://www.yalasoo.com/English/docs/yalasoo_en_font.html
29 The Monlam "BodYig" fonts: http://monlamit.com
30 See Hackett, "Technical Note" to Hopkins et al (1992).
31 See Chilton (2003).
32 See Valby (1983).
33 These dictionaries appear to have no editorial or lexicographic oversight with numerous incomplete, incorrect, or highly contextual entries and equivalents. See, for example, "Rangjung Yeshe Dharma Dictionary": http://rywiki.tsadra.org/.

tionary currently being compiled under the direction of Geshe Lobsang Monlam.[34]

## Cutting-edge Research

Along with the other events previously mentioned, 1983 saw the first attempt at computer-assisted analysis of a Tibetan text.[35] During the decade that followed, progress in computational research on Tibetan language was slow. A notable exception to this was the project conducted at Bell Labs on a Tibetan Optical Character Recognition (OCR) system. Henry Baird, working with Kurt Keutzer and Reid Fossey, pioneered Tibetan OCR with moderate success on typeset Tibetan script though did not achieve their goal of processing woodblock prints—a goal that remains unattained at present. Several researchers in America and the PRC reported on similar attempts over the decades that followed and different aspects of the problem from measurements of morphological entropy[36] to syllable frequency in large corpora.[37]

It was not until Vladimir Danilov and Alexander Stroganov developed the "Yakpo" system[38] in the mid-2000s, that a successful system for machine typeset Tibetan became publically available. Since that time, Keutzer returned to the topic of Tibetan OCR and together with a young colleague, Zach Rowinski at the University of California at Berkeley, their collective efforts produced the "Namsel" OCR system.[39] Although the system itself is still not publically available, the preliminary textual output is being hosted by TBRC as an experimental e-text search system. Both systems, however, remain unevaluated in terms of efficiency in comparison to double-blind manual keying[40] in producing comparable levels of accurate e-text which some maintain still results in higher efficiency of e-text production.

**34** The "Monlam Grand Dictionary" (*smon lam tshig mdzod chen mo*) http://monlamit.com See also Monlam (2013).

**35** Valby (1983).

**36** Jiang (1998); Hackett (2003b); Lu et al. (2003), and others.

**37** Lu (2006).

**38** http://www.dharmabook.ru/ocr/

**39** Rowinski and Keutzer (2016).

**40** This was the procedure pioneered for Tibetan text input by ACIP which, together with morphological and statistical error-checking followed by manual proofing, has resulted in reasonably accurate e-text. Error rates for Tibetan OCR systems have been estimated between 95–99 per cent, although detailed error analysis remains to be performed.

The late 1990s saw the beginning of Tibetan Natural Language Processing (NLP) and Computational Linguistics. In 1997, Hackett designed and implemented a maximum-length word-segmentation system for Tibetan linked to full-dictionary look-up as part of a digital library interface for E. Gene Smith and the HIAR library.[41] Hackett subsequently revised the word segmentation algorithm incorporating full syntactic parsing coupled with a hybrid (rule-based/dictionary-based) system for automatic part-of-speech tagging[42] as part of his construction of the first documented Tibetan monolingual and cross-language search engine;[43] with its verb-based parsing system, the system also resulted in the first corpus-based Tibetan dictionary.[44] At roughly the same time, researchers in the PRC were similarly pursuing the topic of word-segmentation,[45] and in 2001, staff at the University of Virginia succeeded in replicating the maximum-length word-segmentation system for Tibetan making the system and its dictionary look-up publically available.[46] In 2005, researchers in the PRC likewise began pursuing a syntax-constrained verb-based parsing system as part of a larger machine translation initiative.[47]

Part-of-speech tagging remained an active subject for research throughout the 2000s. Researchers in the PRC pursued automatic part-of-speech tagging for Tibetan following a dictionary-based approach,[48] while a research project in the U.K. attempted to hand-tag training data for a rule-based approach, and although the project reported preliminary success at replicating tags for a small sample of training data, the project ended unfinished and far short of its target goal.[49]

Because success in machine translation has been shown to be dependent upon domain classification for translation equivalent disambiguation, semantic classification and topic identification remained two additional potential areas for exploratory research. In 2004, Qi Kunyu reported on semantic classification

41 Demonstrations of the system were given at HIAR (New York), the University of Maryland (College Park), and the University of Virginia (Charlottesville).

42 Hackett (2000b).

43 Reported in Hackett (2000a).

44 Hackett (2003a).

45 Tashi Tsering (1999); Chen et al. (2003), and others.

46 The system–essentially unchanged since that time–remains accessible as the "Tibetan-English Translation Tool" although the specific website address hosting it changes with unusual frequency.

47 Cai and Hua (2005).

48 Chen (2005); Tsering Gya and Dbangphyug Tsering (2010).

49 The project aimed at a one million word corpus, but at the end of funding only 200,000 words had been manually tagged. See: Garrett and Hill (2014).

as part of a support dictionary for Tibetan machine translation,[50] and in 2010, Hackett reported on topic-boundary detection using the constrained mutual information technique of lexical cohesion.[51]

## Audio-Visual and Mobile Resources

Recent years have seen rapid growth in mobile phone and mobile device (tablets, etc.) markets with a corresponding demand for applications and language resource support. Although there have been some developments for Tibetan in recent years including full script support on Apple and Windows platforms,[52] current mobile dictionaries remain simple application wrappers around web-browser data, although a few language primer and training tools are slowly being developed such as the applications from Kawachen in Tokyo.[53]

While speech-to-text has become a common element on many smart phones, development in this area for spoken Tibetan has lagged behind. This is due in no small part to the strong divergence between dialects of spoken Tibetan, and hence speech-to-text remains an unsolved problem. Scholars in China have attempted to approach the topic by distinguishing the three primary dialects of Tibetan: Central, Amdo, and Kham,[54] with the approach eventually expanded to thirteen dialects,[55] and researchers at Google have repeatedly expressed interest in all aspects of Tibetan language over the years with research positions advertised, although tangible results have yet to appear.

## Secondary Resources

As was indicated, the oral commentarial lineages associated with Buddhist literature are a vital component of Tibet's cultural legacy. Following the widespread destruction suffered by the Tibetan people and their cultural landscape under Chinese occupation during the "Cultural Revolution" (1965–1975) and since, these oral traditions have been brought to the brink of extinction.

---

**50** Qi (2004).
**51** Hackett (2010).
**52** The Android platform has lagged behind in providing support for Tibetan.
**53** The "Tibetan Reader" app being one such application. http://www.kawachen.org/app/tibetanreader_en.html
**54** Yang, Li, and Yu ( 2008).
**55** Li, Kong, and Yu (2008).

In an attempt to preserve and propagate this wealth of knowledge, in 2012 Robert Chilton and Graham Coleman under the auspices of the Orient Foundation for Arts and Culture (OFAC) launched the "Classical Tibetan Knowledge Archive and Multimedia Study Resource" as an archival and research resource for the study of the oral commentarial and ritual arts traditions of Tibet. Building on the initial groundwork of the Orient Foundation for Arts and Culture, who in 1993 established twenty-four multimedia documentation centers in the major Tibetan monastic universities and colleges of India and Nepal, the resulting archive of materials constitutes a unique and extensive collection of documentary materials including over 14,500 hours of detailed line-by-line oral commentaries to classical Buddhist and Bon texts, given by leading scholars and lineage holders and more than 600 hours of detailed video documentation of the classical dance, music, and ritual arts traditions.

Accessed locally, these multimedia documentary collections have been playing a significant day-to-day role in the education of the current generation of monks, nuns, scholars, artists, and students for more than twenty years. The multimedia archive, now accessible online at www.tibetan-knowledge.org, provides access to materials that can assist both indigenous scholars and international researchers in their study of Tibetan culture and especially the Tibetan literary heritage. In addition to opening up new areas of knowledge, the resource helps support:

- authoritative translation of classical textual sources through enhanced access to the oral commentarial explanation;
- reconciling of scribal errors and preparation of critically edited editions of texts by comparing differing textual editions in the context of the oral commentarial explanation;
- tracing the development of ideas and practices through analysis and comparison of oral commentarial explications handed down through diverse lineages of scholars;
- study of the ritual arts traditions in conjunction with detailed visual documentation.

The resource offers both Tibetan and English/roman script interfaces and can be searched using a traditional subject classification system, or by speaker/commentator name; by title of the corresponding text; by the author of the text; by the internal name given to the commentary; or by the place where the commentary or documentary video was recorded. A specially designed 'work area' of the resource enables simultaneous display and navigation of textual sources, oral commentaries, video documentation, and still images.

In addition, many lineages now maintain A/V archives of teachings by prominent figures in their lineages, such as www.dalailama.org, kagyuoffice.org, and others.

In addition to supporting the preservation of Tibetan monastic culture and oral traditions, the Orient Foundation has also supported direct access over the internet to the wide range of public services traditionally performed by monasteries for the lay community. In late 2014, "Gompa: Tibetan Monastary Services"[56] was released as part of a "soft launch," and since that time has facilitated access to ritual services for over fifty participating monasteries and temples.[57]

## Future Directions in Research and Development

As noted above, there has been rapid growth in recent decades in the field of Tibetan digital humanities. While audio and video capture and archiving has progressed, one of the key developments that still awaits is automated transcription using speech-to-text software. On the mobile front, more mobile native applications are expected to be produced as those platforms evolve beyond being mere portals to web-browser data.

On the text archive front, while image and e-text archives continue to expand, there remains a compelling need for annotation and analysis tools in order to perform advanced levels of analysis on these data sets. Rowinski and Keutzer have discussed the potential of large data sets for automatic semantic tagging using neural nets,[58] while Hackett has explored automatic parallel text alignment for canonical scriptures.[59] In general, while syntactic annotation of Tibetan seems well underway, semantic annotation remains a desideratum.

Semantic annotation—the process of augmenting e-text with concept-level information (i.e. standardized references to texts, people, places, organizations, etc.)—allows for higher precision and recall in searching, as well as the ability to correlate concepts and text passages between texts. This last function—textual interlinking—is of critical importance in research in Tibetan religious literature given the fact that as a complete body of work it is highly self-referential. While such an abstract reference system can be created for Tibetan canonical literature to divorce text citation from any individual print edition through refer-

56 https://www.gompaservices.com
57 Chilton (2016).
58 Rowinski and Keutzer (2016), 27–28.
59 Hackett (2016).

ence to sequential sentence numbering[60]—a system suitable for computational reference—it is somewhat less amenable to human citation for large texts. Consequently, no one has yet proposed such a reference system for Buddhist scriptures—that is, a system akin to the modern standard Judeo-Christian scriptural reference system devised in the 16th century. Although given the scale of the literature being dealt with, it is understandably a daunting challenge. Likewise, while image and e-text archives are becoming more and more developed, a system for automatically correlating the two remains incomplete, let alone correlating text and audio/video commentary, although once again, an abstracted and unified textual reference system could serve as a viable means of tagging and correlating the two.

In general, interoperability remains an unfulfilled goal between the various disparate endeavors described above, although collaborative agreements for data-sharing and partial cross-linking between projects like the Tibetan Buddhist Resource Center (TBRC), Treasury of Lives biographical database, Buddhist Canons Research Database (BCRD), and Asian Classics Input Project (ACIP) have been slowly moving the field forward towards a more seamless research environment. Such a treatment of text corpora as large data sets would finally offer one approach to compensating for the conceptual lacunae created by a broken oral commentarial tradition that typifies the Tibetan tradition at the start of the twenty-first century.

## Acknowledgements

Thanks to Ronald Schwartz for a detailed account of his activities, and likewise to William ("Bill") Magee, Robert Chilton, Tashi Tsering (Beijing), and Tony Duff (Kathmandu) who provided additional historical and bibliographic references.

**60** Hackett (2013). Although verse compositions are typically cited as chapter and verse, the citation of prose works are more difficult. For example, the passage in the *Heart Sūtra* giving the mantra "Oṃ gate gate pāragate pārasaṃgate bodhi svāhā" is typically cited in reference to the specific print edition of the Tibetan canon, e.g. D 21 fol. 45b line 5; N 26 fol. 63b lines 5–6; H 26 fol. 260b lines 3–4; etc. In all editions, it could be universally cited as: Tibetan Kangyur, Perfection of Wisdom division, sutra #14, sentence #86. When dealing with texts containing thousands of sentences, however, this citation system is of greater utility in a computational environment and less amenable to human citation.

# References


Baird, Henry S. 1992. “Document Image Defect Models.” In *Structured Document Image Analysis*, edited by Henry Baird, Horst Bunke, and Kazuhiko Yamamoto, 546 – 556. Berlin: Springer-Verlag.

Baird, Henry S., Reid Fossey, and Peter Lofting. 1990. “The typestyle jockey: Putting the horse out front in Devanagari and Tibetan.” *Nordic Institute of Asian Studies Report* 1990: 5 – 30.

Chen, Yu-Zhong (陈玉忠), et al. 2003. “基于格助词和连续特征的藏文自动分词方案.” 语言文字应用 [Language Application] 2003.

Chen, Yu-Zhong (陈玉忠) 2005. “信息处理用现代藏语词语的分类方案.” 第十届全国少数民族语言文字处理学术研讨会论文集 [Proceedings of the 10th National Symposium on Minority Language Processing] Xining, 2005.

Cai Cangtai (才藏太) and Hua Guanjia (华关加). 2005. “班智达汉藏公文翻译系统中基于二分法的句法分析方法研究.” 中文信息学报 [Chinese Journal of Information] 2005(19).

Chilton, Robert. 2003. “Sorting Unicode Tibetan using a Multi-Weight Collation Algorithm.” Paper presented at the Tenth International Association for Tibetan Studies (IATS-X) Seminar (Oxford).

Chilton, Robert. 2016. “Gompa – Tibetan Monastery Services.” Paper presented at the Fourteenth International Association for Tibetan Studies (IATS-XIV) Seminar (Bergen).

Garret, Edward, and Nathan Hill. 2014. “A Rule-based Part-of-speech Tagger for Classical Tibetan,” *Himalayan Linguistics* 13(2): 9 – 57.

Hackett, Paul. 2000a. “Approaches to Tibetan Information Retrieval: Segmentation vs. n-grams.” Master’s Thesis. University of Maryland at College Park. College of Library and Information Sciences.

Hackett, Paul. 2000b. “Automatic Segmentation and Part-of-Speech Tagging for Tibetan: A First Step Towards Machine Translation.” Paper presented at the Ninth International Association for Tibetan Studies (IATS-IX) Seminar (Leiden).

Hackett, Paul. 2003a. *A Tibetan Verb Lexicon*. Ithaca: Snow Lion Publications.

Hackett, Paul. 2003b. “An Entropy-based Assessment of the Unicode Encoding for Tibetan.” Paper presented at the Tenth International Association for Tibetan Studies (IATS-XIII) Seminar (Oxford).

Hackett, Paul. 2010. “The Use of yig-cha and chos-kyi-rnam-grangs in Computing Lexical Cohesion for Tibetan Topic Boundary Detection.” Paper presented at the Twelfth International Association for Tibetan Studies (IATS-XII) Seminar (Vancouver).

Hackett, Paul. 2013. “Digital Resources for Research and Translation of the Tibetan Buddhist Canon.” Paper presented at the Thirteenth International Association for Tibetan Studies (IATS-XIII) Seminar (Ulaanbaatar).

Hackett, Paul. 2016. “Automatic Parallel Text Alignment for Tibetan, Sanskrit, Chinese, and Pālī (and English) texts.” Paper presented at the Fourteenth International Association for Tibetan Studies (IATS-XIV) Seminar (Bergen, Norway).

Haig, Dan. 2006. “Towards the Grand Unification: transforming the THDL Gazetteer using XQuery, XForms, eXist, and XSLT.” Paper presented at the Eleventh International Association for Tibetan Studies (IATS-XI) Seminar (Königswinter).

Hopkins, Jeffrey et al. 1992. *Tibetan-Sanskrit-English Dictionary*. Dyke, VA: Tibetan Studies Institute.

Jiang Di (江狄). 1998. "书面藏语的熵值及相关问题," In 1998中文信息处理国际会议论文集. Beijing: Tsinghua University Press.
Li Yonghong (李永宏), Kong Jiangping (孔江平), Yu Hongzhi (于洪志). "藏语文-音自动规则转换及其实现," 清华大学学报(自然科学版) [Journal of Tsinghua University (Natural Science Edition)] 2008.
Landesman, Susan. Forthcoming. *The Tārā Tantra.* NY: AIBS.
Lu Yajun (卢亚军) et al. 2003. "基于大型藏文语料库的藏文字符、部件、音节、词汇频度与通用度统计及其应用研究," 西北民族大学学报 (自然科学版) [Journal of Northwest University for Nationalities (Natural Science Edition)] 2003.
Lu Yajun (卢亚军) and Luo Guang (罗广). 2006. "藏文词汇通用度统计研究." 图书与情报 [Books and Information] 2006.
Martin, Richard "Skip". 1983. "A Program to Produce Tibetan Script Using the Wylie System." Paper presented at the Annual Meeting of the Association for Asian Studies, San Francisco (March 1983).
Monlam, Geshe Lobsang. 2013. "On the Framework of the Complete Monlam Tibetan Dictionary." Paper presented at the Thirteenth International Association for Tibetan Studies (IATS-XIII) Seminar (Ulaanbaatar).
Qi Kun-yu (祁坤钰). 2004. "《机器翻译用现代藏语语义词典》的设计研究." 西北民族大学学报 (自然科学版) [Journal of Northwest University for Nationalities (Natural Science Edition)] 2004.
Roerich, George. 1949. The Blue Annals. Calcutta: Royal Asiatic Society of Bengal.
Rowinski, Zach, and Kurt Keutzer. 2016. "Namsel: An optical character recognition system for Tibetan text." *Himalayan Linguistics* 15(1): 12–30.
Tashi Tsering (扎西次仁). 1999. "一个人机互助的藏文分词和词登录系统的设计," In中国少数民族语言文字现代化文集. Beijing: Nationalities Publishing House.
Tashi Tsering. 2007. Tibetan-Chinese-English Information Technology Dictionary. Beijing: China Tibetology Publ.
Tsering Gya and Dbangphyug Tsering. 2010. "Research on a Standard for POS Tagging of Contemporary Tibetan for TIP." Paper presented at the Twelfth International Association for Tibetan Studies (IATS-XII) Seminar (Vancouver).
Valby, James. 1983. "The life and ideas of the 8th century A.D. Indian Buddhist mystic Vimalamitra : a computer-assisted approach to Tibetan texts." Ph.D. dissertation. University of Saskatchewan, Saskatoon, Dept. of Far Eastern Studies.
Yang Yangrui (杨阳蕊), Li Yonghong (李永宏), Yu Hongzhi (于洪志). "藏语安多方言的音联结构及统计分析," 西北民族大学学报 (自然科学版) [Journal of Northwest University for Nationalities (Natural Sciences)] 2008: 29.

Miroj Shakya

# The Digital Sanskrit Buddhist Canon Project: Problems and Possibilities

## Background

Sanskrit Buddhist works are of paramount importance for understanding the history of Buddhist literature. There are mere hundreds of Sanskrit Buddhist texts currently available throughout the world, although thousands are known to have existed in the past. Despite the disappearance of many Sanskrit Buddhist texts due to various reasons, some of their contents are preserved, to an extent, in Chinese and Tibetan translations. For the sake of preserving and disseminating the Sanskrit Buddhist texts remaining in the world, the University of the West, California, in cooperation with the Nagarjuna Institute of Exact Methods (NIEM) in Nepal, initiated the Digital Sanskrit Buddhist Canon project in 2003.

The Digital Sanskrit Buddhist Canon (DSBC) project was made possible through the shared vision of the late Min Bahadur Shakya, Director of NIEM, and Dr. Lewis Lancaster, Professor Emeritus, University of California, Berkeley, also a former President of the University of the West in Los Angeles. Shakya had been involved in the digitization of Sanskrit Buddhist texts since the year 2000 and, having gathered a large number of printed Sanskrit texts at NIEM, sought a partnership with the University of the West. Ven. Master Hsing Yun, founder of Fo Guang Shan, Kaohsiung, Taiwan and founder of the University of the West, kindly consented to be the sponsor of this worthy project under the joint leadership of Dr. Lancaster and Mr. Shakya. Master Hsing Yun's aim in sponsoring this project was to make available the original Sanskrit Buddhist texts online for all, free of cost. Ven. Master Hsing Yun has devoted his life to propagating a Humanistic Buddhism through education, cultural activities, charity and religious practices. This project was deemed wholly in line with his mission of spreading Humanistic Buddhism.

This project is not only a digitization effort, but at the same time an ambitious attempt to devise a Buddhist "canon" in Sanskrit. The project was named "Digital Sanskrit Buddhist Canon" even though the complete *tripiṭaka*s in Sanskrit, the "Sanskrit Canon" proper, had disappeared from the Buddhist world long ago. The goal of this project is to reconstitute a Sanskrit Buddhist Canon in the 21th Century by compiling all the Sanskrit Buddhist Texts extant in the world and making a new comprehensive structure for those texts. The project would create, in the United States, a comprehensive Sanskrit record whose

https://doi.org/10.1515/9783110519082-007

objectives would be (1) to unify all interpretations of Buddhism existing in Sanskrit, (2) to make available samples of the original manuscripts and (3) to encourage and facilitate feedback on the canon from all people interested in Buddhism across the world.

The main work of this project has been to transform the extant Sanskrit texts into e-texts, which are distributed both in Unicode Devanagari and in Unicode Roman with diacritics. In order to use digital text analysis and reference tools efficiently, it is desirable to have as many Sanskrit e-texts as possible for consultation. Likewise, the study of scriptures in Chinese and Tibetan translated from Sanskrit sources benefits from access to searchable Sanskrit texts. It helps us to interpret, edit and authenticate these translated texts. Since 2005, the DSBC e-texts have been downloadable at no cost to readers via the internet: http://www.dsbcproject.org. This site makes access very simple for potential users. It is a user-friendly site with searchable indexes to the Sanskrit texts, while the texts themselves are easy to cut and paste into various applications.

The source material to be input comprises the printed editions of the Sanskrit Buddhist texts published from the end of the nineteenth century onwards. Hundreds of Sanskrit Buddhist texts are available in print today. Now, for the first time in history, the primary texts of Indian Buddhism are becoming accessible to the whole world via the internet, not only as scanned images of book pages, but as e-texts produced by the DSBC. The DSBC is accelerating its work by broadening its bases and applying the latest computer technology. This project has so far digitized more than 545 titles, which amount to 48,056 printed pages. The DSBC seeks to complete the digitization of Sanskrit texts by the year 2020.

## Main Sources of DSBC Texts

After the Islamic invasion of India and the surrounding areas in the twelfth century, the rich heritage of Buddhism virtually disappeared in India, and the surviving teachings of the Buddha, as recorded in Sanskrit, had their meanings change in some ways by being translated through the years. At present, there is no complete Sanskrit Buddhist Canon, but Sanskrit Mahāyāna texts have been found in different areas of Nepal, India, Tibet (PRC), Gilgit (Pakistan), Sri Lanka and other regions (Hirakawa, 1990, 295). Many Sanskrit Manuscripts still housed in temples, monasteries and private collections in Nepal and Tibet are yet to be published or digitized. Among these collections, some are being cataloged and digitized on site by the National Archives and Asha Archives in Kathmandu, Nepal, as well as the Rare Sanskrit Buddhist Manuscript Preservation

**Fig. 1:** DSBC Homepage

Project in Lalitpur, Nepal, and others. But there are still many manuscripts not yet discovered, seen lying in a corner of some monastery. So the DSBC project is making an effort to preserve such manuscripts: the University of the West in collaboration with the Nagarjuna Institute of Exact Methods (A Center for Buddhist Studies) started a Rare Sanskrit Buddhist Manuscript Preservation Project in 2009. This project has so far digitized 400 manuscripts and is aiming to digitize one thousand manuscripts in the coming years.

## Nepalese Sanskrit Buddhist Texts

Nepal has by far the largest repository of Buddhist Sanskrit literature dealing with different aspects of Mahāyāna creeds and practices. It is the local monk scholars, as well as Vajracharya Pandits, who have contributed to producing and propagating these Buddhist manuscripts. As most of the important titles were discovered in the Kathmandu Valley, Nepal has historically played a central role in the preservation and subsequent dissemination of Sanskrit Buddhist literature.

As Kogen Mizuno (1982) reports, there were three main Indic languages used in the primitive Sūtras of Mahāyāna Buddhism. They are Classical Sanskrit, Sanskrit Derivative or Hybrid Sanskrit, and Gāndhārī Prakrit. The Sūtras of the Sarvāstivādin sect can be found in these languages, and other Mahāyāna Sūtras were mostly written down in these three languages. However, a lot of manuscripts discovered in Nepal are also in the Newar language and written in the *pracalita* and *rañjanā* scripts that are now only in regular use in the Kathmandu Valley. Mizuno pointed out that "Many of this sect's original Sanskrit texts have been discovered in India, Nepal and Central Asia, but most of them are incomplete" (Mizuno 1982, 33). In fact, many complete, reliable copies of the most important Mahāyāna Sūtras have also been preserved in Nepal.

After the downfall of the Pāla and Sena Dynasties in India in the twelfth and thirteenth centuries, Buddhism was overcome by the non-Buddhist sects in India; but in Nepal, many Buddhist Sūtras were well preserved along with other Mahāyāna texts written in Sanskrit (Vajracharya 1999, 52). Since in Kathmandu there was no tradition of maintaining lists of scripture, Buddhist Newars had no way to date the emergence of these scriptures or to maintain a comprehensive inventory. Newar Buddhists, however, have had a tradition of reading, reciting and copying these scriptures as a religious duty, which has preserved them from generation to generation (Vajracharya 1999, 42). Sponsoring such activities as copying, reciting and conducting discourses on them is considered to be merit-making (Vajracharya 1999, 43).

These Sanskrit Buddhist texts came to be known to the Western public after Brian Houghton Hodgson (Mitra 1971, xix) discovered them and made them available to scholars of the nineteenth century. The total volume of his discoveries, though still unknown, is estimated to be about 381 bundles, which includes two hundred copies of manuscripts distributed to scholars in Europe and the colonies (Mitra 1971, xxxv). By the end of the nineteenth century, printed editions of some Buddhist Sanskrit texts were produced using Nepalese manuscripts. Some of the first texts to be published were widespread in Nepal: the *Kāraṇḍavyūha* (1873), *Lalitavistara* (1877) and *Aṣṭasāhasrikā Prajñāpāramitā* (1888). They were published by the Asiatic Society of Bengal, the Buddhist Text Society of India, in the Russian Bibliotheca Buddhica series, and in various scholarly monographs and journals. Later, Parashuram Lakshman Vaidya republished many of these editions, often with arbitrary changes, in the Sanskrit Buddhist texts series at the Mithila Institute, Darbhanga (Hirakawa, 1990, 295). Vaidya's versions of the texts became much more widely distributed and used than the earlier editions. They were gathered at NIEM and were among the first printed texts input by the DSBC. Some of the major manuscript collections and preservation efforts in Nepal are as follows:

a) National Archives Collection
b) The Nepal German Manuscript Preservation Project (120,000 manuscripts with around 4,5000,00 folios were microfilmed, including the National Archives manuscripts) (Ehrhard 1991, 20)
c) Asha Archives Collection (7025 manuscripts)
d) Keshar Library Collection
e) Svayambhu Library Collection
f) Rare Sanskrit Buddhist Manuscript Preservation Project (400 Manuscripts)
g) Endangered Archives Programme (EAP 676), the British Library (surveyed 234 vulnerable Sanskrit manuscripts totaling 8734 folios in Lalitpur (Thapa, 2072 VS, 106–119)

In addition to the manual input of printed materials, the University of the West is making an effort to conserve the endangered literary heritage of the Kathmandu Valley of Nepal. The University started the Rare Buddhist Manuscript Preservation Project (RBMPP) in 2009, which aims to make manuscript images more widely available through digital photography. Sanskrit manuscripts are, as I have said elsewhere, "the primary means by which the ideas and traditions of pan-Indian Buddhism have been transmitted into the present day. Although many such manuscripts have been studied over the past two centuries, a great number of manuscripts, often containing unique information, remain inaccessible" (Shakya 2011, 16). One of the eventual goals is to use the DSBC e-texts alongside specimens of original manuscripts.

The RBMPP has now completed the scanning of four hundred manuscripts from private collections in the Kathmandu Valley. Several of these manuscripts are kept in the collections of individuals that have not been available to the institutional manuscript photography projects. Many of the scanned manuscripts belong to the collection of Akṣeśvara Mahāvihāra, located in Pulchowk, Lalitpur, Nepal. There is a biography of the Buddha in Sanskrit, which may be the largest so far found, variously titled *Sugatajanmaratnāvadānamālā*, or sometimes *Tathāgatajanmāvadānamālā*. Another text is a previously unknown Tantric Buddhist compilation called the *Guhyalokottaratantra*. The digitized collection contains much other valuable information on the South Asian Buddhist tradition transmitted in Nepal. Several texts belonging to the non-Buddhist Sanskritic tradition were also digitized.

## *Sanskrit Buddhist Texts from Central Asia*

Hundreds of Sanskrit Buddhist manuscripts or fragments have been unearthed from Central Asia, and more are likely to be found there. Recent explorations have shown that there are significant numbers of ancient Buddhist Texts written in Sanskrit and other Indic languages existing in Central Asia (Mizuno 1982, 42). Some were found near Gilgit in 1931. Most of these are kept in the National Archives at New Delhi. Nalinaksha Dutt and his colleagues published editions based on them from 1939 to 1954. Raghu Vira and Lokesh Chandra, Indian scholars, have published 10 volumes of facsimile editions of this collection (Dietz 1991, 129–130). Similarly, another collection found in Eastern Turkestan (in 1902, 1904, 1905, and 1913) (Dietz 1991, 162) by the German Turfan Expedition is kept in the Academy of Sciences in Berlin. These manuscripts were primarily from the Sarvāstivādin School. Some fragments came from Mūlasarvāstivāda and Dharmaguptaka School (Dietz 1991, 129–130).

The collection of Martin Schøyen has preserved Buddhist manuscripts and fragments which were found in a cave near Bāmiyān, in central Afghanistan. They date from the second to the eighth centuries CE (Braarvig 2010, xvii). Most Schøyen manuscripts dating from the second century were written in Kharoṣṭhī script (xviii).The Schøyen collection obtained these fragments of manuscripts from the London Bookseller San Fogg in the summer of 1996. Later they received more fragments between 1997 and 2000. This collection constitutes about 1000 manuscripts including 5000 leaves and fragments. These manuscripts were written on palm leaf, brick bark, leather and copper (xviii). Some of these manuscripts have been analyzed and transcribed by various scholars and published in the series *Buddhist Manuscripts in the Schoyen Collections* (xxiv). These printed editions are a potential source for the DSBC.

## *Sanskrit Buddhist Texts from Tibet*

Many Sanskrit manuscripts are kept in the Tibet Autonomous Region of the People's Republic of China, mainly in monasteries and in the Potala Palace in Lhasa (*The Encyclopedia of Religion* 1987). Some of the manuscripts are dated back to the 8$^{th}$ century CE. Rahula Sankrityayana, an Indian scholar, visited Tibet in the 1930s and found rare Sanskrit manuscripts in the monasteries of Tsang province in the Western part of Central Tibet (Kano 2016, 82).He successfully cataloged and photographed some of the manuscripts and published a list of them in the *Journal of the Bihar and Orissa Research Society* between 1935 and 1938. In January 2004, the People's Republic of China gave permission to the Institut für Kultur- und Geistesgeschichte Asiens (IKGA), Austria, to access photocopies of the manuscripts. Their joint research has been conducted mainly through the China Tibetology Research Center in Beijing and published in conjunction with the Austrian Academy of Sciences in the Sanskrit texts from the Tibetan Autonomous Region series. More critical editions of those manuscripts are scheduled to be published in addition to the following already published titles: (Documentation of Sanskrit 2014)

- Jinendrabuddhi's *Pramāṇasamuccayaṭīkā*
- Dharmakīrti's *Pramāṇaviniścaya*
- Dharmakīrti's *Hetubindu*
- 20 short Mahāyānasūtras
- Sthiramati's *Pañcaskandhakavibhāṣa*
- *Dharmadhātustava*
- *Saddharmasmṛtyupasthāna* etc.

These printed editions are another potential source for the DSBC.

## *Is the DSBC a* Tripiṭaka?

One of the primary goals of DSBC Project is to reconstruct the Sanskrit Buddhist Canon for the 21th Century. Much of the original content of the Sanskrit Tripiṭaka, the "three baskets" of *sūtra* (*āgama*), *vinaya* and *abhidharma*, has been lost. The history of Buddhism further mentions a Vaitulya-piṭaka, also known as the Vaipulya sūtras, which seems to have contained the Mahāyāna texts that are more common today. In 269 CE, a monk of the Abhayagiri sect of Sri Lanka seems to have embraced the Vaitulya-piṭaka. However, the Mahāvihāra sect rejected the Vaitulya-piṭaka because of its supposedly heretical doctrine and then later burned its texts with the support of the king (Dehigaspe 1958, 17–18). Some fragments of the oldest Buddhist Sanskrit texts relating to the *Udānavarga, Dharmapada, Ekottarikāgama*, and *Madhyamāgama* have been found in Eastern Turkestan (Nariman 1992, 7). Inscriptions of a few Sanskrit Buddhist sūtras were also found in the ruins of Gopalpur, Odisha, India dating back to 250 and 400 CE (8).The *Pratimokṣa Sūtra*, the main text of the Vinayapiṭaka written in Sanskrit, was found as fragments in Nepal by Bendall, and more completely in Central Asia.

In Nepal a core collection of nine Mahāyāna texts (the *navasūtra* or *navadharma*) is recognized. Nariman points out that "The principal texts of the canon of the Mūlasarvāstivādins – this is the designation of the Sanskrit canon according to tradition – were translated from Sanskrit into Chinese in

700 – 712 by the Chinese pilgrim I-tsing" (Nariman 1992, 8).The Chinese Tripiṭaka contains many non-canonical texts and philosophical or historical treatises which are not found in the Pali Tipiṭaka, and the same situation exists in the Tibetan Kanjur. So the Sanskrit Tripiṭaka which existed when translations were being made from it in the premodern era would not have been a carbon copy of the Pali Tipiṭaka. In the 21st century, a Sanskrit Tripiṭaka can instead be formulated with the incorporation of non-canonical texts and philosophical treaties along the lines of the translated Tripiṭakas. The effective core texts of the living Sanskrit tradition are the nine Mahāyāna scriptures (Nava Vaipulya Sūtras) which constitute the most important scriptural Buddhist texts in Newar Buddhism. It is referred to as the Nine Dharmas and is considered as a dharmamaṇḍala, the "circle of dharma", in Nepal. It can therefore be called a "Mahāyāna canon" containing the following titles:

1. *Aṣṭasāhasrikā Prajñāpāramitā*
2. *Gaṇḍavyūha*
3. *Daśabhūmīkā*
4. *Samādhirāja*
5. *Laṅkāvatāra*
6. *Saddharmapuṇḍarīka*
7. *Tathāgataguhyaka*
8. *Lalitavistara*
9. *Suvarṇaprabhāsa*

These nine Mahāyāna Buddhist texts are still being studied and worshipped in Nepal today. They are not considered to be the canon of a particular lineage or sect, but according to J. K. Nariman, their role is not less than that of a canon in Newar Buddhism (Nariman 1992, 64). Brian Hodgson conveyed the idea that "*Vaipulya*, treat of several sorts of *Dharma* and *Artha*, that is, of the several means of acquiring the goods of this world (*Artha*) and of the world to come (*Dharma*)"(Hodgson and Denwood 1972, 15). However, according to Nariman, "These so-called Nine dharmas are no canon of any sect, but a series of books which have been composed at different periods and belong to different persuasions, though all of them enjoy high veneration in Nepal today" (Nariman, 1992, 64).

Thus it is legitimate to claim that Newar Buddhism is a variety of Sanskrit Buddhism and its collections of Buddhist texts can together be called a Sanskrit Buddhist canon. Most of the Buddhist texts used by Newar Buddhists are in the original Sanskrit language, while the Newar language is used for translation, explanation or original material. Min Bahadur Shakya says: "Another peculiarity of Newar Buddhism is its ritual and its sacred literature which are written in the

Sanskrit language, because of which we can call Newar Buddhism a 'Sanskrit Buddhism' " (Shakya 2000, 2). Living Sanskritic Buddhism can at present be observed only in the Kathmandu Valley. From birth to death rituals, all the sacraments are being conducted according to the Buddhist manuals in Sanskrit. Many local Buddhist tales and legends are preserved in *purāṇa*s and *māhātmya*s written in Sanskrit. In this way Sanskrit is the medium that has traditionally united Buddhist Newars in the Kathmandu Valley. It is not necessary to maintain a sectarian identity in order to follow the Sanskrit tradition. Iain Sinclair points out that "Although Newar Buddhism does not see itself as part of a classical *nikāya* organization, some of its core processes can be identified with the Mūlasarvāstivādanikāya. The procedure for monastic ordination follows a Mūlasarvāstivādin handbook which was long ago absorbed into a tantric ritual digest created in Nepal" (Sinclair 2016, 14).

Hence, the DSBC is not trying to create a radically new form of Sanskrit Tripiṭaka, but rather is attempting to revive the old Sanskrit Tripiṭaka with the material available today. It is a painstaking task, because this material is so dispersed and fragmented, but the project assumes that further loss can be prevented by quick action.

## Content of the Digital Sanskrit Buddhist Canon

In the process of construction of a digital Sanskrit Tripiṭaka in the twenty-first century, the DSBC is in the process of categorizing all the Sanskrit texts which are available to us in printed form. DSBC has classified those texts into the three broad categories like the traditional Tripiṭaka: the first division, the word of the Buddha and his teachings, is the *sūtra-piṭaka*. A second division called the *vinaya-piṭaka* deals with the rules of conduct (*vinaya*) for those who lived by monastic discipline. Then the third is the *abhidharma-piṭaka*, reserved for exegetical literature.

In classifying the Sanskrit Buddhist literature, "there were alternate groupings, such as the twelve textual genres: *sūtra*, *geya*, *vyākaraṇa*, *gāthā*, *udāna*, *nidāna*, *itivṛttaka*, *jātaka*, *vaipulya*, *adbhutadharma*, *avadāna*, and *upadeśa*" (The Encyclopedia of religion 1987). Some of these groupings are named in the titles of Sanskrit texts. The DSBC also adopts these twelve textual genres for its classification scheme where appropriate. However, it is difficult to differentiate each of these types from others if a text does not state its own genre. In addition to the *abhidharma* genre commentaries, Mahāyāna Buddhists have their own commentaries on the Sūtras called *śāstra*, *vyākhyā*, *ṭīkā* and so on (The Encyclopedia of religion 1987). These are categorically not *abhidharma*. Thus, DSBC has classified those texts into three *piṭaka*, with the third tentatively called the *śāstra-piṭaka* ("basket of treatises") and provides subcategories for each genre as shown below:

*Bauddha-Samskrta-Tripitaka*

| *Sutrapiṭaka* | *Vinayapiṭaka* | *śāstrapiṭaka* |
| --- | --- | --- |
| *Avadāna* | | *Abhidharama* |
| *Dhāranī* | | *Stotra* |
| *Jātaka* | | *advayatantraṭīkā* |
| *Mahāyānasūtra* | | *darśana* |
| *Nirdeśa* | | *kāvya* |
| *Prajñāpāramitā* | | *Kośa* |
| *Pramāṇa* | | *lekha* |
| *Tantra* | | *madhyamaka* |
| *Yogācāra* | | *madhyamaka-yogācāra* |
| | | *nāṭaka* |
| | | *nīti* |
| | | *prajñāpāramitā* |
| | | *pramāṇa* |
| | | *sautrāntika* |
| | | *śilpaśāstra* |
| | | *vinaya* |
| | | *vividha* |
| | | *yogācāra* |
| | | *yoginītantraṭīkā* |
| | | *yogottaratantraṭīkā* |

**Fig. 2** The current structure of the digital Sanskrit *tripiṭaka*

Again, these classifications of the DSBC derive from categories given in individual texts. For example, if a text calls itself a *nirdeśa* or a *mahāyogatantra*, it is classified as such. This system does not try to be different than other classification systems. Rather, the DSBC gives priority to the original sources, and the classifications come out of those sources.

## Digitization Process

The digitization of Sanskrit texts had to wait until a compelling tool for converting Sanskrit material into a digital format arrived. In the year 2003, the DSBC started to use the "Itranslator 2003" software developed by Omkarananda Ashram Himalayas from Uttarakhand, India. Since then, the DSBC Project has been using it for transcribing Sanskrit Buddhist texts. This software allows us to convert texts into Unicode Devanagari and Unicode Roman Transliteration files (TXT, HTM, or RTF files mediated through the ITX (=ITRANS) encoding system). Itranslator 2003 software uses the Unicode 4.0 standard encoding (Stiehl 2003, 4–8). As a result, it is compatible with Unicode OpenType fonts such as "Mangal." But each page has to be typed through standard keyboard input. This input is currently done by the team led by Milan Shakya, Director, Nagarjuna Institute of Exact Methods in Nepal. At present proofreading is done by the coordinator of the project at University of the West in order to improve accuracy. Finally, both texts in Devanagari and Transliteration in Roman letters are uploaded to the Digital Sanskrit Buddhist Canon website. The DSBC Project Coordinator bears responsibility for selecting texts to be digitized, proofreading, design, and maintenance of the site.

## Sample DSBC Materials

Given below are screen shots of the current project and examples of the finished results of the digitized texts that users will be able to access on the DSBC website. Below is a screen shot of a digitized text in Roman transliteration with diacritics:

Parallel Devanāgarī version

प्रज्ञापारमिताहृदयसुत्रम् [विस्तरमातृका]

prajñāpāramitāhṛdayasutram|
[vistaramātṛkā]

|namaḥ sarvajñāya||

evaṃ mayā śrutam| ekasmin samaye bhagavān rājagṛhe viharati sma gṛdhrakūṭe parvate mahatā bhikṣusaṃghena sārdhaṃ mahatā ca bodhisattvasaṃghena| tena khalu samayena bhagavān gambhīrāvasaṃbodhaṃ nāma samādhiṃ samāpannaḥ| tena ca samayena āryāvalokiteśvaro bodhisattvo mahāsattvo gambhīrāyāṃ prajñāpāramitāyāṃ caryāṃ caramāṇaḥ evaṃ vyavalokayati sma| pañca skandhāṃstāṃśca svabhāvaśūnyaṃ vyavalokayati||

athāyuṣmān śāriputro buddhānubhāvena āryāvalokiteśvaraṃ bodhisattvametadavocat- yaḥ kaścit kulaputro [vā kuladuhitā vā asyāṃ] gambhīrāyāṃ prajñāpāramitāyāṃ caryāṃ cartukāmaḥ, kathaṃ śikṣitavyaḥ ? evamukte āryāvalokiteśvaro bodhisattvo mahāsattvaḥ āyuṣmantaṃ śāriputrametadavocat- yaḥ kaścicchāriputra kulaputro va kuladuhitā vā [asyāṃ] gambhīrāyāṃ prajñāpāramitāyāṃ caryāṃ cartukāmaḥ, tenaivaṃ vyavalokitavyam-pañca skandhāṃstāṃśca svabhāvaśūnyān samanupaśyati sma| rūpaṃ śūnyatā, śūnyataiva rūpam| rūpānna pṛthak śūnyatā, śūnyatāyā na pṛthag rūpam| yadrūpaṃ sā śūnyatā, yā śūnyatā tadrūpam| evaṃ vedanāsaṃjñāsaṃskāravijñānāni ca śūnyatā| evaṃ śāriputra sarvadharmāḥ śūnyatālakṣaṇā anutpannā aniruddhā amalā vimalā anūnā asaṃpūrṇāḥ| tasmāttarhi śāriputra śūnyatāyāṃ na rūpam, na vedanā, na saṃjñā, na saṃskārāḥ, na vijñānam, na cakṣurna śrotraṃ na ghrāṇaṃ na jihvā na kāyo na mano na rūpaṃ na śabdo na gandho na raso na spraṣṭavyaṃ na dharmaḥ| na cakṣurdhāturyāvanna manodhāturna dharmadhāturna manovijñānadhātuḥ| na vidyā nāvidyā na kṣayo yāvanna jarāmaraṇaṃ na jarāmaraṇakṣayaḥ, na duḥkhasamudayanirodhamārgā na jñānaṃ na prāptirnāprāptiḥ| tasmācchāriputra aprāptitvena bodhisattvānāṃ prajñāpāramitāmāśritya viharati cittāvaraṇaḥ| cittāvaraṇanāstitvādatrasto viparyāsātikrānto niṣṭhanirvāṇaḥ| tryadhvavyavasthitāḥ sarvabuddhāḥ prajñāpāramitāmāśritya anuttarāṃ samyaksaṃbodhimabhisaṃbuddhāḥ| tasmād jñātavyaḥ prajñāpāramitāmahāmantraḥ anuttaramantraḥ asamasamamantraḥ sarvaduḥkhapraśamanamantraḥ satyamamithyatvāt prajñāpāramitāyāmukto mantraḥ| tadyathā- gate gate pāragate pārasaṃgate bodhi svāhā| evaṃ śāriputra gambhīrāyāṃ prajñāpāramitāyāṃ caryāyāṃ śikṣitavyaṃ bodhisattvena||

atha khalu bhagavān tasmātsamādhervyutthāya āryāvalokiteśvarasya bodhisattvasya sādhukāramadāt- sādhu sādhu kulaputra| evametat kulaputra, evametad gambhīrāyāṃ prajñāpāramitāyāṃ caryaṃ cartavyaṃ yathā tvayā nirdiṣṭam| anumodyate tathāgatairarhadbhiḥ||

idamavocadbhagavān| ānandamanā āyuṣmān śāriputraḥ āryāvalokiteśvaraśca bodhisattvaḥ sā ca sarvāvatī pariṣat sadevamānuṣāsuragandharvaśca loko bhagavato bhāṣitamabhyanandan||

iti prajñāpāramitāhṛdayasūtraṃ samāptam|

**Fig. 3**

Below is a screenshot of the same text in Devanagari script:

Parallel Romanized version

Prajñāpāramitāhṛdayasutram [vistaramātṛkā]

प्रज्ञापारमिताहृदयसुत्रम्।
[विस्तरमातृका]

॥नमः सर्वज्ञाय॥

एवं मया श्रुतम्। एकस्मिन् समये भगवान् राजगृहे विहरति स्म गृध्रकूटे पर्वते महता भिक्षुसंघेन सार्धं महता च बोधिसत्त्वसंघेन। तेन खलु समयेन भगवान् गम्भीरावसंबोधं नाम समाधिं समापन्नः। तेन च समयेन आर्यावलोकितेश्वरो बोधिसत्त्वो महासत्त्वो गम्भीरायां प्रज्ञापारमितायां चर्यां चरमाणः एवं व्यवलोकयति स्म। पञ्च स्कन्धांस्तांश्च स्वभावशून्यं व्यवलोकयति॥

अथायुष्मान् शारिपुत्रो बुद्धानुभावेन आर्यावलोकितेश्वरं बोधिसत्त्वमेतदवोचत्- यः कश्चित् कुलपुत्रो [वा कुलदुहिता वा अस्यां] गम्भीरायां प्रज्ञापारमितायां चर्यां चर्तुकामः, कथं शिक्षितव्यः ? एवमुक्ते आर्यावलोकितेश्वरो बोधिसत्त्वो महासत्त्वः आयुष्मन्तं शारिपुत्रमेतदवोचत्- यः कश्चिच्छारिपुत्र कुलपुत्रो व कुलदुहिता वा [अस्यां] गम्भीरायां प्रज्ञापारमितायां चर्यां चर्तुकामः, तेनैवं व्यवलोकितव्यम्-पञ्च स्कन्धांस्तांश्च स्वभावशून्यान् समनुपश्यति स्म। रूपं शून्यता, शून्यतैव रूपम्। रूपान्न पृथक् शून्यता, शून्यताया न पृथग् रूपम्। यद्रूपं सा शून्यता, या शून्यता तद्रूपम्। एवं वेदनासंज्ञासंस्कारविज्ञानानि च शून्यता। एवं शारिपुत्र सर्वधर्माः शून्यतालक्षणा अनुत्पन्ना अनिरुद्धा अमला विमला अनूना असंपूर्णाः। तस्मात्तर्हि शारिपुत्र शून्यतायां न रूपम्, न वेदना, न संज्ञा, न संस्काराः, न विज्ञानम्, न चक्षुर्न श्रोत्रं न घ्राणं न जिह्वा न कायो न मनो न रूपं न शब्दो न गन्धो न रसो न स्प्रष्टव्यं न धर्मः। न चक्षुर्धातुर्यावन्न मनोधातुर्न धर्मधातुर्न मनोविज्ञानधातुः। न विद्या नाविद्या न क्षयो यावन्न जरामरणं न जरामरणक्षयः, न दुःखसमुदयनिरोधमार्गा न ज्ञानं न प्राप्तिर्नाप्राप्तिः। तस्माच्छारिपुत्र अप्राप्तित्वेन बोधिसत्त्वानां प्रज्ञापारमितामाश्रित्य विहरति चित्तावरणः। चित्तावरणनास्तित्वादत्रस्तो विपर्यासातिक्रान्तो निष्ठनिर्वाणः। त्र्यध्वव्यवस्थिताः सर्वबुद्धाः प्रज्ञापारमितामाश्रित्य अनुत्तरां सम्यक्संबोधिमभिसंबुद्धाः। तस्माद् ज्ञातव्यः प्रज्ञापारमितामहामन्त्रः अनुत्तरमन्त्रः असमसममन्त्रः सर्वदुःखप्रशमनमन्त्रः सत्यममिथ्यत्वात् प्रज्ञापारमितायामुक्तो मन्त्रः। तद्यथा- गते गते पारगते पारसंगते बोधि स्वाहा। एवं शारिपुत्र गम्भीरायां प्रज्ञापारमितायां चर्यायां शिक्षितव्यं बोधिसत्त्वेन॥

अथ खलु भगवान् तस्मात्समाधेर्व्युत्थाय आर्यावलोकितेश्वरस्य बोधिसत्त्वस्य साधुकारमदात्- साधु साधु कुलपुत्र। एवमेतत् कुलपुत्र, एवमेतद् गम्भीरायां प्रज्ञापारमितायां चर्यं चर्तव्यं यथा त्वया निर्दिष्टम्। अनुमोद्यते तथागतैरर्हद्भिः॥

इदमवोचद्भगवान्। आनन्दमना आयुष्मान् शारिपुत्रः आर्यावलोकितेश्वरश्च बोधिसत्त्वः सा च सर्वावती परिषत् सदेवमानुषासुरगन्धर्वश्च लोको भगवतो भाषितमभ्यनन्दन्॥

इति प्रज्ञापारमिताहृदयसूत्रं समाप्तम्।

**Fig. 4**

All the texts have some associated metadata which can be viewed at the top of the page for each digitized text under 'bibliographic details'.

## Evaluation and Dissemination

The Digital Sanskrit Buddhist Canon Project, as has been stated, has main two goals: (a) To preserve Sanskrit Buddhist texts; (b) To create, maintain and distribute a free electronic version of a Sanskrit Tripiṭaka. In order to achieve these goals, we are engaged in the digitization of published and unpublished Sanskrit texts and manuscripts and are making those materials available for open access by putting them online. The results will serve researchers who are in the field of Buddhist Studies or the humanities. In the future, new generations of Buddhist scholars and practitioners will continue to have access to texts which are now on the verge of disappearing from this world.

We have been using Google Analytics to collect quantitative data for evaluation. This quantitative data of Internet usage shows that we get thousands of hits a month on the DSBC website. It also showed where the users come from. In the seven-year period from 2009 to 2016, over half of the visitors were English speakers (57.26% from en-us, en-gb or en), followed by Chinese users (14.29% zh-cn or zh-tw), Japanese (5.42%), Russian (3.03%), Korean (2.47%) etc. It shows us that the impact of DSBC website is slowly growing in the world. For qualitative data, we gathered information through the social media such as DSBC Facebook page: https://www.facebook.com/Digital-Sanskrit-Buddhist-Canon-Project-165544636852716/ and the DSBC online blog. These quantitative and qualitative data are essential for determining the project's successfulness in achieving the desired long-term impacts.

The DSBC is continuously trying to disseminate the potential benefits to academic and non-academic communities around the world. We recently developed a new iPhone DSBC app compatible with iPad in 2015. The DSBC Website also hosts a blog which features new updates and activities of the project. The project is also regularly updating a DSBC page on the Facebook social networking site which disseminates the latest news regarding the project. The project has been utilizing more conventional ways of disseminating updates, such as participating in workshop and conference presentations. These conference presentations have been essential for building collaboration with other similar projects like Chinese Buddhist Electronic Text Association (CBETA) and others. Since coming online in 2005, the DSBC has been getting users from all over the world. Many online Buddhist text sites have been requesting DSBC to link up the Sanskrit texts on their site. Among them, Göttingen University in Germany- (GRETIL) – Electronic Texts in Indian Languages and related Indological materials from Central and Southeast Asia texts has requested and received permission to host a significant portion of the DBSC texts on its Internet servers. The response from users has been very encouraging and positive. It motivates us to engage in more initiatives for the preservation of Buddhist Sanskrit texts.

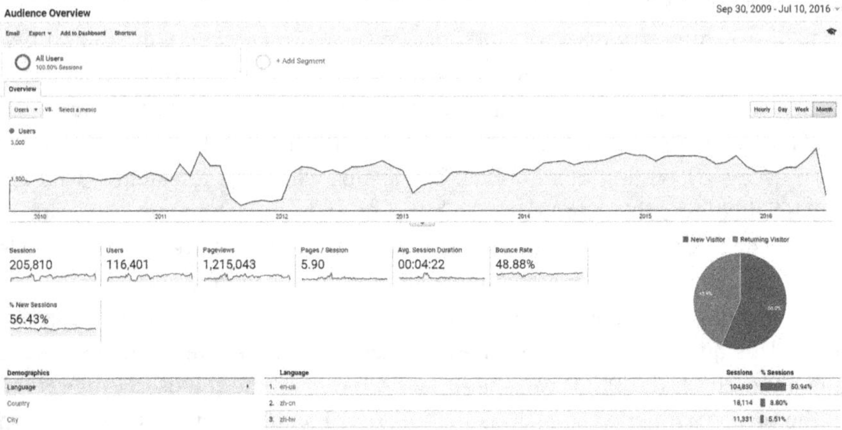


**Fig. 5:** Sample statistics chart of DSBC usage

# Future Goals

The DSBC project is gearing toward creating the whole Sanskrit Tripiṭaka, which will be the largest and most comprehensive corpus of this material created to date. We have envisioned incorporating all the texts that were composed by Buddhists. Some of these texts are not directly concerned with Buddhism, such as various works on grammar (*vyākaraṇa*), lexicography (*koṣa*), poetry (*kāvya*), poetics (*alaṁkāra*), and medicine (*Ayurveda*), etc. While these texts on 'secular' subjects do not necessarily assume acceptance of Buddhism, they were written in line with Buddhist principles. Historically, Buddhist institutions transmitted many 'secular' texts. It is evident that Buddhist communities in Nepal and Sri Lanka have preserved many such secular texts along with Buddhist texts. The DSBC is considering digitizing such secular texts as well.

After the completion of digitization, the DSBC hopes to produce a Sanskrit Buddhist Canon DVD in the year 2020. The availability of a complete set of Sanskrit Buddhist texts on digital media as well as in online browsing will be a significant milestone in Buddhist scholarship, and the inclusion of an offline version will be immensely useful, especially in places where internet usage is still not common. The DSBC hopes to develop various digital search tools and to mark up the texts in the future.

The DSBC will also be publishing a Sanskrit Tripiṭaka Series in the near future. In the digital age, hard copy is still important, as printed texts can last for centuries on good quality paper. The DSBC will keep hard-copy backups of the Sanskrit Tripiṭaka for the sake of preservation. There is still no up-to-date bibliography of all published Sanskrit texts. Even texts which appear in print are often very hard to find in libraries. There is no central repository of these texts. Most reliable editions were published in the West, and it is extremely hard to get copyright clearance for reprints. However, traditional custodians of these texts have not accepted that these texts should be covered by copyright in the first place. At present some editions can only be used through the goodwill of their editors or publishers.

## Conclusion

This Digital Sanskrit Buddhist Canon project fills a gap in digitizing and preserving the unique Sanskrit Buddhist textual heritage which had been gradually disappearing from the Buddhist world. The DSBC provides a stepping stone for the reconstitution of a Sanskrit Buddhist Tripitaka by its traditional users, having begun to collect the surviving Sanskrit Buddhist texts around the world. After the disappearance of Buddhist Sanskrit texts in India, there are still significant numbers of Buddhist Sanskrit texts preserved in various locations such as the Kathmandu Valley, Lhasa, Dunhuang, Western libraries and other places. The cataloging and printing of those Sanskrit texts is needed to complete the digitization of the corpus. Some reconstruction work can be done from Buddhist texts which are extant in Chinese and Tibetan translations.

## References


Braarvig, Jens. 2010. *Traces of Gandhāran Buddhism: an Exhibition of Ancient Buddhist Manuscripts in the Schøyen Collection.* Oslo: Hermes Publications.

Dietz, Siglinde. 1991. "The language of the Turfan and Gilgit Sanskrit Buddhist Texts." *Samyag Vag:* 129–161.

Ehrhard, Franz-Karl. 2016. "The Nepal German Manuscript Preservation Project." http://himalaya.socanth.cam.ac.uk/collections/journals/ebhr/pdf/EBHR_02_03.pdf [Accessed Dec 2, 2016].

*The Encyclopedia of religion* Vol 2. 1987. New York: Macmillan. sv. "Buddhist Literature: Canonization."

Hirakawa, Akira. 1990. *A History of Indian Buddhism from Śākyamuni to early Mahāyāna.* Honolulu: University of Hawaii Press.

Hodgson, Brian Houghton, and Philip Denwood. 1972. *Essays on the languages, literature, and religion of Nepal and Tibet.* New Delhi: Manjuśrī Pub. House.

Institut für Kultur- und Geistesgeschichte Asiens. 2014. "Documentation of Sanskrit manuscripts in Tibet." Austrian Academy of Sciences Institute for the Cultural and Intellectual History of Asia. http://www.ikga.oeaw.ac.at/Documentation_of_Sanskrit_manuscripts_in_Tibet [Accessed Dec 2, 2016].

Kano, Kazuo. 2016. "The Transmission of Sanskrit Manuscripts from India to Tibet: The Case of a Manuscript Collection in the Possession of Atiśa Dīpaṃkaraśrījñāna (980–1054)." In *Transfer of Buddhism Across Central Asian Networks (7th to 13th Centuries)*, edited by Carmen Meinert, 82–117. Leiden: Brill.

Mizuno, Kogen. 1982. *Buddhist Sūtras: Origin, Development, Transmission.* Tokyo: Kosei Publishing Co.

Mitra, Rajendralala. 1971. *The Sanskrit Buddhist Literature of Nepal.* Calcutta: Sanskrit Pustak Bhandar.

Nariman, Gushtaspshah Kaikhushro. 1992. *Literary History of Sanskrit Buddhism.* Delhi: Motilal Banarsidass Publishers Pvt. Ltd.

Pannasara, Dehigaspe. 1958. *Sanskrit Literature: Extant among the Sinhalese and the Influence of Sanskrit on Sinhalese.* Colombo: W.D. Hewavitarane Esq.

Shakya, Min Bahadur. 2000. "Preservation of Sanskrit Buddhist Manuscripts in the Kathmandu Valley: Its Importance and Future." Pacific Neighborhood Consortium." http://pnclink.org/annual/annual2000/2000pdf/6–4–2.pdf. [Accessed Nov 19, 2016].

Stiehl, Ulrich. 2003. "Technical Manual of Itranslator 2003." Sanskrit Web. http://www.sanskritweb.net/itrans/itmanual2003.pdf. [Accessed Dec 2, 2016.]

Shakya, Miroj ed. 2011. *The Catalog of Digitized Rare Sanskrit Buddhist Manuscripts.* Rosemead: University of the West.

Sinclair, Iain. 2016 "A Principled Asian Transnationalism: The Construct(ion) of Sanskrit Buddhism." Paper presented at 'Imagining Asia' Workshop, Nalanda-Sriwijaya Center, Singapore. September 30.

Thapa, Shanker. 2016. "Endangered Archives Programme and Digitisation of EAP-676 Manuscripts in Nepal." *Abhilekha* 33:106–119.

Vajracharya, Divya Vajra. 1999. *Nava Sūtra Samgraha*, Lalitpur: Bodhi Prakashan Kendra.

David Wharton

# Digital Libraries of Lao and Northern Thai Manuscripts

The Digital Library of Lao Manuscripts (DLLM) and the Digital Library of Northern Thai Manuscripts (DLNTM) went online in 2009 and 2016 respectively. These two closely-related collections contain images of over 18,000 manuscripts, making primary sources of over five centuries of literary heritage freely accessible for study.[1] The richness and variety of their contents bears testimony to the dedicated work of local sponsors, scribes and scholars who have copied and maintained the original texts throughout many generations, as well as to several large manuscript survey and preservation projects in recent decades and to the generosity of modern-day funders and the collaboration of many parties in implementing the digital library projects. This chapter provides an overview of the manuscript literature and of survey and preservation work to date, followed by an introduction to the digital libraries.[2]

## Traditional Literature of Laos and Northern Thailand

The manuscripts of Laos and Northern Thailand, or Lane Xang and Lan Na, have mostly been preserved through the continuous copying of palm-leaf manuscripts which are traditionally stored in wooden caskets in the libraries of Buddhist monasteries. The oldest extant manuscripts are monolingual Pali texts dating from the late 15$^{th}$ century CE when Chiang Mai was a regional centre for the study and dissemination of Buddhist literature, and the earliest known dated

1 Digital images of manuscripts (with the exception of those related to traditional medicine in the PNTMP collection) and other images and data are made freely available under a Creative Commons Attribution-NonCommercial 4.0 Unported (CC BY-NC 4.0) License. The names of the creators, attribution parties and copyright notices are included in the EXIF data for each image.
2 Several sections of this chapter are adapted from information available on the Digital Library of Lao Manuscripts website (http://www.laomanuscripts.net), the Digital Library of Northern Thai Manuscripts website (http:/lannamanuscripts.net), and from 'The Digital Library of Lao Manuscripts' in *Lao Studies Journal* Vol. 2, Issue 2. 2011: 67–74, written in collaboration with Harald Hundius and used with permission of the Centre for Lao Studies. The author was Technical Director of the two digital library projects.

https://doi.org/10.1515/9783110519082-008

manuscript, of the *Tiṁsati nipāta* section of the *Jātaka aṭṭhakathā vaṇṇanā*, was copied in CE 1471 (CS 833).[3] The earliest known dated manuscript in Laos, part of the *Parivāra*, a Vinaya text, was copied in CE 1520 (CS 882),[4] with the slightly later date possibly reflecting the transmission of the Tham script from Lan Na to Lane Xang during that period.[5] A smaller proportion of texts are written on other materials, such as mulberry or *sa* paper, which is much less durable than palm-leaf and the oldest examples found in these collections are a Lan Na *Ñattidutiyakammavācā* Vinaya text dated CE 1810 (CS 1172) and a Lan Na *Abhidhamma* chanting text dated CE 1817 (CS 1197),[6] while other Shan, Tai Lue and Tai Nuea *sa* paper texts date from the mid-19th century.

In Northern Thailand, there are relatively few manuscripts from the 17th and early 18th centuries, during the period of Burmese suzerainty over the region, but the following decades saw a resurgence in manuscript production. Many date from the early 19th century, when Khruba Kañcana, a charismatic scholar monk, developed Wat Sung Men, Phrae Province, as a centre of Pali and Buddhist studies, and initiated and mobilised support for the collection and copying of manuscripts in many parts of what is now Northern Thailand and in Luang Prabang, Laos. The entire library collection at Wat Sung Men, which contains over 1,700 manuscripts and is the largest in Northern Thailand, was microfilmed as part of the Preservation of Northern Thai Manuscripts Project (PNTMP), and is now available online.

Of the dated manuscripts (approximately half of the total), only 7 percent in Laos and 19 percent in Northern Thailand are from before CE 1800, and 43 percent and 59 percent respectively from the 19th century. In the Lao collection, 50 percent of dated manuscripts are from the 20th century, compared to only 22 percent in the Northern Thai collection. This significant difference stems from early 20th century centralised administrative and monastic reforms from Bangkok which effectively suppressed the use of the local Lan Na script and its related manuscript culture until the early 1960s when efforts to preserve the manuscript

3 This is in fact the oldest dated manuscript in Thailand, kept at Wat Lai Hin Luang, Ko Kha District, Lampang Province, PNTMP Code 030104030_02 (http://lannamanuscripts.net/en/manuscripts/3669). 'CS' denotes the Cunlasakkarat or 'Little Era,' beginning in CE 638.

4 Kept at the Provincial Museum in Luang Prabang (formerly the Royal Palace), PLMP Code 06018504078_00 (http://laomanuscripts.net/en/texts/6838).

5 Local conventions for transcription of Thai and Lao proper names are used in this chapter, which may differ from the systems used in the digital libraries.

6 The first of these texts is in the Lao collection (which contains a number of Lan Na texts), kept at Vat Siphonexai, Huayxai District, Bokeo Province (http://laomanuscripts.net/en/texts/549); the second is in the Northern Thai collection, kept at Wat Ban Luk Tai, Tha District, Lampang Province, PNTMP Code 030620121_02 (http://lannamanuscripts.net/en/manuscripts/5479).

tradition began. Manuscript production in Laos also suffered during the $20^{th}$ century, especially during the Second Indochina War and the years immediately following the proclamation of the Lao PDR in 1975, when the country met with extremely difficult conditions, with manuscript survey and preservation work reappearing in the mid-1980s. In Thailand (and also in Myanmar), the arrival of the printing press hastened the demise of the production and reading of handwritten texts, and the fact that the living manuscript tradition has survived better in Laos than in neighbouring countries may partly be a result of the country's comparatively undeveloped publishing industry. Throughout the region today, television, video and the Internet have more appeal than manuscript repositories, although there are ongoing efforts to keep stories from traditional literature alive amongst the younger generations. These take the form of the teaching of the scripts used in manuscripts, which differ significantly from the modern scripts in general use, and of the traditional methods of manuscript production and inscription, as well as adaptation of the contents of the manuscripts for presentation in a variety of media in modern Lao and Thai.

The vast majority of manuscripts in both collections are written in varieties of the Tham or Dhạmma script (i. e. Lan Na, Lao, Tai Lue and Tai Khuen) which is thought to have been first used for writing palm-leaf manuscripts during the latter part of the $15^{th}$ century, most probably in Chiang Mai, from where it spread to neighbouring Tai kingdoms including modern-day Laos. Others are in the Lao Buhan, Lik Tai Nuea, Shan, Khom, Central Thai, Thai Nithet, Burmese, and Tai Dam scripts. All of these scripts can be traced to South Indian writing systems which were adapted for writing Pali and vernacular languages in Southeast Asia. Texts are found in the Lao, Northern Thai (Lan Na), Tai Khuen, Tai Lue, Shan, Tai Nuea, Thai, Burmese, Tai Dam and Pali languages. The majority are from the Theravada Buddhist tradition, most commonly in bi-lingual versions with Pali and more or less elaborated translations or commentaries in vernacular languages, which shed light on the local interpretation of the Pali texts. One special genre is the huge number of extra-canonical works, especially narrative literature such as Jātaka stories, a considerable number of which are thought to originate from local Southeast Asian traditions. Many of these legends are among the most popular texts used by the monks in their recitations and sermons given to the lay people, and deserve special interest because they contain valuable information about social life and values in the Buddhist societies of the region. Other texts contain a wide range of works about history, traditional law and customs, astrology, magic, mythology and rituals, traditional medicine and healing, grammar and lexicography, as well as poetry and epic stories, folk tales, romances, etc. These rich manuscript collections have remained severely under-researched due to a lack of accessibility, despite an abundance of primary sources.

## Previous Surveys and Manuscript Preservation[7]

In Laos, almost all of the early surveys and registrations of manuscripts were undertaken by French scholars and their Lao assistants. Louis Finot's *Recherches sur la littérature laotienne*,[8] published in 1917 in the *Bulletin de l'École Française d'Extrême Orient*, still provides a useful overview of traditional Lao literature in a Western language. The *Liste générale des manuscrits laotiens* provided in the final part of his study is of two principal collections existing at the time: that of the Bibliothèque Royale de Luang Prabang (catalogued by M. Meiller, 1181 entries), and of the Bibliothèque de l'École française d'Extrême Orient (338 entries). Several other inventories of monastery or library holdings were undertaken during the period from 1900 to 1973, by both Lao and French scholars, listing a total of 3,678 manuscripts from 94 monasteries in nine provinces. A notable initiative is the work of the Chanthaboury Buddhist Council, under the leadership of Chao Phetsarat, which asked abbots throughout the country to submit lists of their manuscript holdings between 1934–36. Work on the EFEO inventory, plus research and analysis of manuscripts followed in 1950s and 1960s by Henri Deydier, Pierre-Bernard Lafont and Charles Archaimbault. An *Inventaire des Manuscrits des Pagodes du Laos*,[9] building on the previous work of French scholars, was conducted under the leadership of Pierre-Bernard Lafont in 1959 and covered altogether 83 monasteries: 13 in Luang Prabang, 25 in Vientiane, and 45 in Champasak. Other related catalogues during this period, while valuable tools in themselves, were of limited collections and not intended to be representative of Lao literature as a whole.

In March 1988, with the support of the Toyota Foundation, a conference was convened in Vientiane attended by monks as well as knowledgeable lay people from all over Laos who were invited to discuss the state of conservation of manuscripts in their home communities, and to exchange views on what should be

7 While this section focuses on projects beginning in the early 20$^{th}$ century often involving external funding and scholars, it is important to recognise the fact that the manuscripts have been maintained throughout the past five centuries by local monastic and lay communities.

8 Finot, Louis. 1917. 'Recherches sur la littérature laotienne' in *Bulletin de l'École française d'Extrême-Orient* (BEFEO 17.5: 1–128).

9 Lafont, Pierre-Bernard. 1965. 'Inventaire des manuscrits des pagodes du Laos' in *Bulletin de l'École française d'Extrême Orient* (BEFEO 52.2: 429–545).

done in order to safeguard the remaining manuscripts which were in danger of being forgotten in the monastic libraries. As a result of this meeting a project to set up a Lao-language *Inventory of Palm-leaf Manuscripts in Six Provinces of Laos*[10] was initiated by the Ministry of Information and Culture, again with the support of the Toyota Foundation. In the course of this project (1988 – 1994) altogether about 128,000 fascicles were inventoried from some 250 selected monasteries in Vientiane Capital and the provinces of Luang Prabang, Vientiane, Bolikhamxai, Khammuan, Savannakhet, and Champasak.

In Northern Thailand, the Siam Society supported a survey of manuscripts at Wat Lai Hin in Lampang Province, undertaken by Ajarn Singkha Wannasai, a leading local scholar of Lan Na literature and leader of local temple ceremonies, which was completed in 1966. Ajarn Singkha was also instrumental in the *Dokumentarische Erfassung literarischer Materialien in den Nordprovinzen Thailands* (DELMN) project, conducted by Harald Hundius from 1971 to 1974, funded by the German Research Foundation (DFG). This project was the first comprehensive survey of Lan Na manuscripts in the eight northernmost provinces of Thailand, with the scope of the research covering literary sources of Northern Thai as well as Buddhist and historical texts, law, astrology, medicine, etc. As part of this project over 1,000 texts were microfilmed at almost 100 locations throughout Northern Thailand, and almost 200 texts were copied into notebooks by local scribes in Lamphun Province, largely from manuscripts in the temples where they resided. These texts, which comprise over 21,000 pages, provide a valuable testament to the living scribal tradition at that time.

A separate project, taken over in 1981 by the newly established Social Research Institute (SRI) of Chiang Mai University, catalogued and microfilmed over 4,000 manuscripts, the majority of which cover secular fields of knowledge such as traditional law, customs, astrology, history and medicine. Since 2005, the École française d'Extrême-Orient (EFEO) has worked on the cataloguing and digitization of Northern Thai chronicles and other texts, which are available online on its Lanna Manuscripts website.[11] The Palm Leaf Studies Centre and Institute of Lanna Studies at Chiang Mai Rajabhat University has also done extensive work on the cataloguing and digitization of manuscripts in Northern Thailand and especially of the closely-related Tai Khuen (in Shan State, Myanmar) and Tai Lue (in Sipsongpanna, Yunnan Province, China).

---

**10** National Library of Laos. 1994. *Inventory of Palm-leaf Manuscripts in Six Provinces of Laos*. Vientiane: Ministry of Information and Culture.

**11** http://www.efeo.fr/base.php?code=807.

## *Preservation of Northern Thai Manuscripts Project*

Chiang Mai University's Center for the Promotion of Arts and Culture implemented the Preservation of Northern Thai Manuscripts Project (PNTMP) from 1987 to 1991, which included the largest survey of manuscripts to date in Northern Thailand. This project surveyed the holdings of over 100 temples throughout the eight northernmost provinces and selected over 6,000 important texts for microfilming, of which approximately 4,000 were microfilmed during the project due to time constraints. Copies of these microfilms are kept at the National Archives of Thailand, Chiang Mai University Library (CMUL), and at the Akademie der Wissenschaften und der Literatur, Mainz, Germany. The project was initiated by Harald Hundius while he was a guest lecturer and research adviser to help establish a Master's Degree program in Lan Na Language and Literature in the Thai Department of Chiang Mai University from 1983 to 1992, and was funded by the German Federal Foreign Office through its Cultural Assistance Program, with M.R. Rujaya Abhakorn as Project Leader.

The collection has a strong focus on indigenous (Southeast Asian) and secular traditions, in addition to containing a number of the oldest dated Pali manuscripts in Southeast Asia. Selection was done according to historical importance, cultural diversity and regional representation, and the age and quality of the manuscript. Microfilming, which was done at the suggestion of the German Federal Foreign Office, included the entire collection of over 1,700 manuscripts at Wat Sung Men in Phrae Province. However, due to time constraints, no microfilming was conducted in Chiang Rai and Lamphun provinces, and was conducted at only one temple in the whole of Chiang Mai Province (90 manuscripts at Wat Chiang Man). This major manuscript survey, preservation, and microfilming project was also the model for the Preservation of Lao Manuscripts Programme.

## *Preservation of Lao Manuscripts Programme*

The Preservation of Lao Manuscripts Programme (PLMP) of the Lao Ministry of Information and Culture was supported by the German Ministry of Foreign Affairs through its cultural assistance program from 1992 until 2004. The main objectives were to help the Lao PDR physically preserve its national literary heritage, to revitalize public awareness of its value and build local capacity for field preservation and for research and dissemination of these resources through the systematic survey and *in situ* preservation of manuscript holdings of over

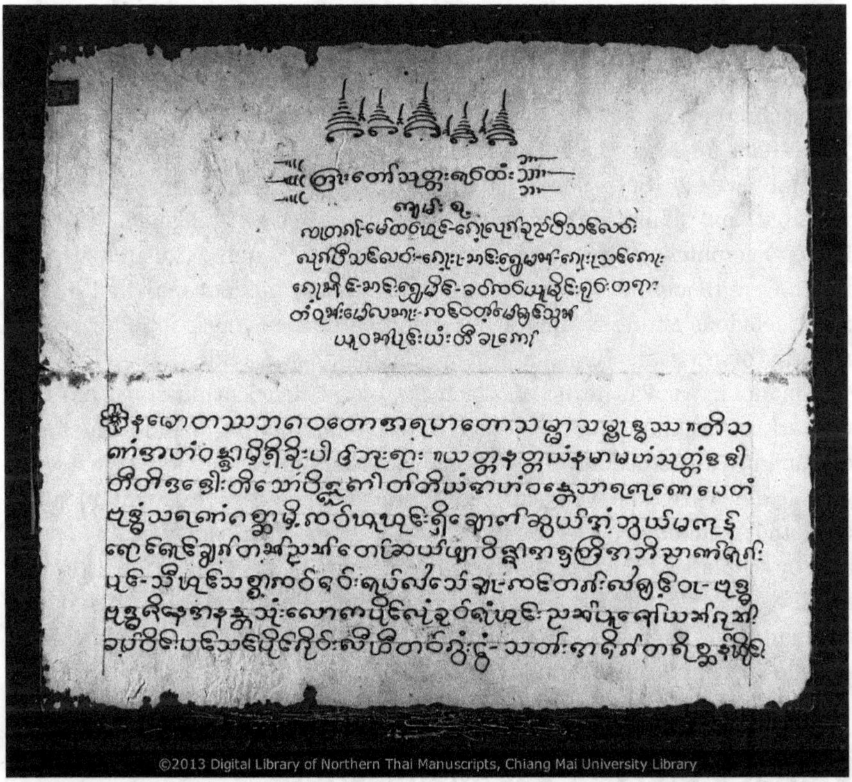


**Fig. 1:** Image of Shan manuscript (080102021_00) microfilmed during Chiang Mai University's *Preservation of Northern Thai Manuscripts Project* and later digitized and included in the Digital Library of Northern Thai Manuscripts.

800 selected Buddhist monasteries as well as state and private collections in all 17 provinces, or a total of some 86,000 manuscripts (368,000 fascicles).[12]

As a major product of the project, a collection of microfilm recordings of some 12,000 selected texts was made, including a large number of parallel versions or additional copies which are necessary for any serious study. The master copy is stored at the Lao National Film Archive and Video Centre, while a working copy is kept at the National Library of Laos, and a second copy at the Berlin State Library. Most important for the wider study of Lao culture, this collection is

**12** As in Northern Thailand, although this was far more extensive than any previous survey, it must be seen within the context of over 4,000 monasteries (*vat*) within the country. The selection of texts for microfilming further reduced the sample to only 380 locations.

by far the most extensive to date and can be seen as representative of the national literary heritage.[13] It comprises almost 500,000 frames, which on average contain about 6–8 palm-leaf pages, giving a total of some 3–4 million recorded manuscript pages.

Criteria for selection for microfilming were historico-cultural importance, cultural diversity or regional representation, age (all manuscripts over 150 years old) and quality of the manuscript. Within these general guidelines, priority for microfilming was given to extra-canonical literature, all manuscripts which were thought to represent indigenous literary traditions, and all texts of a non-religious nature whenever the condition of the manuscript allowed. The majority of texts are from the Theravada Buddhist tradition, including over 900 monolingual Pali texts, of which the oldest dated manuscripts are from the early 16th century. Almost 75 percent of the manuscripts are bi-lingual texts containing Pali-vernacular translations, glosses, and elaborations. Such bilingual texts, where the vernacular can provide important information about local understanding or interpretation of the Pali, are increasingly being appreciated by scholars for the insights they provide into the functions of the text in the real life of people, and as pedagogical tools. The collection also offers an opportunity to study a mass of extra-canonical Buddhist literature, which shows how societies used, practiced, and taught Buddhist values.

## Digital Library of Lao Manuscripts

Following the Preservation of Lao Manuscripts Programme, and in response to new possibilities available for the Internet presentation of digitized data, the National Library of Laos initiated the Digital Library of Lao Manuscripts project. This three-year project, which officially started in October 2007, was jointly implemented together with the University of Passau and the Berlin State Library, which hosts the server for the digital library. The aim of the digital library is to complement ongoing manuscript preservation work in Laos by making the extensive PLMP microfilm collection of primary sources more easily accessible

13 There also exist a number of literary traditions of the ethnic groups which form a large proportion of the total population of Laos. While the vast majority of these are oral traditions, notable examples of written literary traditions include the Hmong, Mien, and Lanten, and the Thai Dam, Thai Daeng and Thai Khao. These texts are generally more difficult to access and inventories of Lao literature have mostly focused on Lao and Tai texts stored in Buddhist monasteries. Given the remarkable ethnic and cultural diversity within Laos, much work remains to be done in recording and preserving its written and especially oral traditions.

**Fig. 2:** Local scholars identifying the date of a text for the PLMP manuscript survey, Wat Xiang Thong, Luang Prabang, 2004. Photograph by Harald Hundius © PLMP, National Library of Laos.

thereby facilitating the study of Lao literature and culture within Laos and overseas.

The entire PLMP microfilm collection was digitized by a professional company from a copy held in Germany, with batch settings adjusted for each microfilm roll. Image processing to improve legibility was limited, since it was not possible to make adjustments to individual images due to their huge number. While most images are clearly legible, there is considerable variation due to the condition of the original manuscript and also the quality of the microfilm images used for digitization. However, in some cases where downloaded images are difficult to read, significant improvements can be made using image enhancement tools such as those found in Adobe Photoshop, and a PDF guide is provided via the

DLLM website. Master copies of digital images, in 300 ppi TIFF format, are stored at separate locations in both the Lao PDR and Germany.

The website and all inventory data are mirrored in both Lao and English. The handling of titles was particularly challenging, since the actual titles appearing on the texts are complex in terms of orthographic variants, the common use of ancillary or supplementary terms indicating the genre of the text, etc., and the fact that a manuscript may contain several distinct works, each with its own title. Another common feature is that a single work may have more than one title, and alternative titles may sometimes be found within the same manuscript. For example, the extra-canonical Jātaka story with the Pali title *Tepadumā*, is found with the following titles: *Tepathumma*, *Lam tepathumma*, *Tepathumma kumman*, *Tepathumma bua hom*, *Bua hom*, *Lam thao bua hom*, *Lam thao bua hong*, *Bua hom bua hong*, *Bua hom bua hiao*, or *Thao bua hom bua hong bua hiao*.

The purpose of the inventory database is to enable users to access images of the primary sources, and the design of the user interface for searching the collection aims to make this process as straightforward as possible. The title search list was therefore simplified as much as possible, to contain a standardized main element of each title and also alternative titles, but not including orthographic variants or ancillary terms. An additional Ancillary Terms search option is provided for some 35 of these supplementary terms found in titles, including genres of text such as *salong*, *tamnan*, *jātaka/sadok*, translationary renderings such as *śabda/sap*, *nissaya/nisai*, *vohāra/vohan*, metric forms such as *khong*, *kham kon*, *samāsa/samat*, as well as titles and terms of address such as *kampha*, *cao*, *thao*, *nang*, *phanya*, etc.

The rendering of titles in modern Lao script and in Romanised form also aims to make the title search list as simple as possible for users, using the most common forms. The Lao title search list is therefore written according to the principles for Lao orthography in which the writing of Lao words follows their pronunciation, while orthographic variants and historical linguistic evidence found in the texts are preserved in the main inventory data (within the limitations of modern Lao orthography). Likewise, a simple Romanization system is used in preference to a linguistically more accurate system using diacritics or special symbols.

In deciding which data to include in the online inventory, the project had to strike a balance between what would be of most assistance to users of the digital library to access the images of primary sources and what was feasible during a three and a half year long project timeframe. This resulted in a relatively large number of options on the search page when compared to other digital libraries, mostly with lists to select from in order to keep users' typed input to a minimum and avoid difficulties due to orthographic variations and Romanization. However, other data, which might be expected in more detailed catalogues of limited numbers of texts (or produced over greater timeframes), such as summaries of the contents, cataloguing of locations and personal names, and details from colophons such as the names of sponsors and scribes, are omitted.

Since the official end of the project, some 1,800 manuscripts held at the National Library of Laos have been directly digitized to replace the greytone images digitized from microfilm, again with support of the German Federal Foreign Office, via the German Embassy in Vientiane.

Just as the PNTMP survey and preservation project in Northern Thailand provided a model for the subsequent PLMP project in Laos, the Digital Library of Lao Manuscripts was later used as a model for a similar digital library of several Northern Thai manuscript collections.

**Fig. 3:** Image of a Tai Lue manuscript directly digitized at the National Library of Laos and included in the Digital Library of Lao Manuscripts. Photograph © Digital Library of Lao Manuscripts.

## Digital Library of Northern Thai Manuscripts

The Digital Library of Northern Thai Manuscripts project, from 2013 to 2016, makes four manuscript collections available online, including a large number of directly digitized texts. The project was designed by Harald Hundius and David Wharton at the National Library of Laos, based on the Digital Library of Lao Manuscripts. The project was implemented by the National Library of Laos, in collaboration with the University of Pennsylvania and the Berlin State Library. The digital library was publicly launched in March 2016 and contains approximately 250,000 images of manuscripts.

The project was made possible through the kind permission and collaboration of Chiang Mai University Library for the digitization of the PNTMP microfilms (with the exception of medical treatises), which will comprise some 50–60 percent of the total number of manuscripts in the digital collection. A related collection of color images of manuscripts are being directly digitized in Northern Thailand beyond the project timeframe, the majority of which were selected during the previous PNTMP survey, but were not microfilmed at the time. The remaining two collections which form the digital library are digitized from the microfilms and handwritten notebooks produced during the *Dokumentarische Erfassung literarischer Materialien in den Nordprovinzen Thailands* (DELMN) project in the early 1970s. Once again, all digitization of existing microfilms and notebooks was undertaken in Germany, and the images were edited and renamed by the DLLM project at the National Library of Laos.

Although alike in basic structure and functions, the newer Digital Library of Northern Thai Manuscripts site benefited from advances in software since the Lao digital library. Considerable time was also spent on design and development during the Northern Thai project to ensure a more robust and quicker website, as well as to streamline user experience and the longevity of the site through ease of long-term maintenance. It can be viewed across a variety of formats, including tablets and smartphones, the Home page is a much-simplified navigational hub for the site, and the site allows full screen viewing of manuscript images.

Both websites also feature map interfaces showing the distribution of texts for any search criteria, which will display, for example, the locations of a selected text, or of selected languages or of dated manuscripts for a selected historical period. Another tool for researchers using the sites is an experimental 'image search' feature allowing online selection of part of an image (a word or any other feature), which can then be searched for within all images for that text.

**Fig. 4:** Digitization of manuscripts at Wat Cedi Luang in Chiang Mai during the DLNTM Project. Photograph by David Wharton © DLNTM.

## Preservation in the Digital Age

Through greatly increasing access to this large amount of primary sources, the aim of the digital libraries is to facilitate the study of Lao and Lan Na literature and culture. They also ensure the long-term safeguarding of these literary heritages in digital format, which is necessary given the ongoing loss of manuscripts in both regions due to neglect, and damage from improper storage, fire and rain, termites, rodents, and the sale of manuscripts. However, it should be emphasised that the main point of digitization is accessibility, and raising the profile of these traditional literatures, and that this is not to be confused with, or to displace or undermine, efforts to preserve the original manuscripts.

The best way to preserve the texts would ideally be to maintain their traditional use and copying, using the local palm-leaf technology which is well proven to last for over half a millennium. Today, while every effort should still be made to prevent the loss of these skills, it seems implausible to hope that the traditional copying methods might take place on a similar scale as in the past. Small-scale local promotion of the study of the traditional scripts still takes place, and it is to be hoped that this steady transmission from generation to generation will prevent its disappearance, but it appears unlikely to succeed on the scale required to preserve the manuscript corpus as a whole.

It is essential to see manuscript preservation as an ongoing task, rather than as an externally-funded project conducted over a limited time period, which is then 'completed.' However, in practice, projects will very likely continue to have an important role to play, since the results of efforts to encourage *in situ* local participation and ownership of the preservation process are mixed, with some excellent examples of local monks and lay communities taking responsibility for manuscript collections, but many more where they are seriously neglected.

Local institutions such as Chiang Mai University and Chiang Mai Rajabhat University in Northern Thailand, as well as the National Library of Laos, the Manuscript Conservation Association and Mahachulalongkornrajavidyalaya University (both in Thailand) and other institutions will also continue to play an important role in preservation, but the success of their efforts will ultimately depend upon an increased or perhaps more formalised commitment within local communities, and especially from the monastic communities which ideally act as custodians safeguarding the manuscripts stored in their temples from generation to generation.

While the traditional technology of palm-leaf manuscript production has changed little over the centuries, the format of digital copies of manuscripts, software innovation and the demands of 'active archiving' raise the related question of the need to preserve the digital data itself.[14] This applies not only to archiving, but also to the maintenance of the digital libraries.[15] By the time the Northern Thai site was completed in 2016, the older Lao site, which was designed in 2007, required a significant upgrade in terms of overall design and software used. The National Library of Laos also plans to expand the existing digital library to be a broader 'digital record of manuscript culture' which, while of intrinsic value in itself, is designed to complement the digital images of manuscripts in the existing Lao website. This surrounding manuscript culture is in fact even more endangered than the physical texts. Some of the data will be integrated in such a way as to allow users to listen to an audio recording while viewing digital images, which will greatly assist in the study of the texts and in learning to read the more complex scripts. Without doubt, these digital repositories, just as their counterparts in traditional temples, cannot be taken for granted, and will require considerably more resources for their maintenance. In fact, the best solution for long-term storage and retrieval of surrogate copies is not in digital format but most probably high-quality microfilm, which can be passively stored for very long periods and read in the future by simply shining a light through it without concern about changing digital formats. This solution, however, is for archival only, and lacks the accessibility of digital data.

## Conclusion

In providing online access to such a large number and variety of primary literary sources for the study of Buddhism and related local cultures, the two digital libraries are bridging the gap between the 'ancient' manuscript tradition and modern Internet technology. It is hoped that raising the profile of manuscript literature may also encourage preservation of the physical texts and their surrounding culture such as manuscript production, care and storage, and traditional use and recitation styles, which remain alive in Laos and Northern Thailand to this day. Increased commitment from local communities and monastics who are the custodians of the manuscript tradition will be essential to avoid

14 For these projects, edited images are archived at the Berlin State Library (which also hosts the servers for both digital libraries), Chiang Mai University Library, the University of Pennsylvania, and the National Library of Laos, providing best-practice data redundancy.

15 The technical creation of the two digital libraries was undertaken by Justin MacCarthy and Justin Reese using free and open-source software, implemented as Ruby on Rails web applications. The layout and formatting of the Thai website was greatly facilitated by Bootstrap.

their loss, as well as intervention from local and national institutions and the generosity of funding agencies who can perhaps be seen as modern-day 'sponsors' for the copying of texts in digital format, and for the construction of online manuscript repositories.

Following the tradition of recording the names of sponsors and scribes in manuscript colophons, the assistance of the German Federal Foreign Office over four decades was of particular importance, in funding both the Preservation of Northern Thai Manuscripts Programme and the Preservation of Lao Manuscripts project, as well as almost all digitization for the digital libraries.

The Digital Library of Lao Manuscripts Project was funded by the German Research Foundation (DFG) and the German Federal Ministry of Economic Cooperation and Development (BMZ), [16] and the principal funder of the Digital Library of Northern Thai Manuscripts was the Henry Luce Foundation, with further significant support from the Andrew W. Mellon Foundation, the University of Pennsylvania Libraries and the School of Arts and Sciences at the University of Pennsylvania. The University of Pennsylvania was instrumental in securing and administering US funding for the DLNTM project, with Justin McDaniel, Professor of Religious Studies, as Project Leader. Harald Hundius, Professor Emeritus of Thai and Lao Languages and Literatures at the University of Passau, Germany, has had a central role in the realization of these projects dating back to his initial work on Northern Thai manuscripts in the early 1970s, his participation in the Preservation of Northern Thai Manuscripts Project (PNTMP) in the 1980s, the Preservation of Lao Manuscripts Project (PLMP) in the 1990s, and as local Project Leader of both digital library projects from 2007 to 2016.

16 Deutsche Forschungsgemeinschaft (DFG) and Bundesministerium für wirtschaftliche Zusammenarbeit und Entwicklung (BMZ).

A. Charles Muller

# The Digital Dictionary of Buddhism and CJKV-English Dictionary: A Brief History

## Introduction

Sometimes it is hard to even remember what it was like to carry out academic research before the advent of the Web. I can still well recall, however, the atmosphere in the spring of 1995, as I was finishing up my first year at my first academic post, when the world of computing was suddenly abuzz about this new etheric realm called the World Wide Web, that few of my university colleagues had yet ventured into. Once I had my first peek into this new infinitude, I was smitten by the possibilities.

At the time, I had been working for several years on the compilation of a Chinese-English dictionary of Buddhist and classical Chinese philosophical terms, a project I had started in graduate school (in the fall of 1987), upon my coming to an awareness of the extreme dearth of comprehensive and reliable Chinese-Japanese-Korean-to-English dictionaries on classical texts. Several months earlier (mid–1994), I had sent this dictionary manuscript to a major academic publisher, and the publisher had recently responded with a cursory note explaining their lack of interest in publishing dictionaries (although they had actually published several dictionaries in the recent past). I understood at that point that they were not interested in gambling on publishing a dictionary compiled by a young, unknown scholar.

It then dawned on me that the Web might be the perfect place to release this work-in-progress. How else could one offer a compilation of this type so quickly to such a wide audience, which could, at the same time, offer an entirely new set of options for collaboration-based compilation and editing? Such collaboration has become commonplace nowadays (although there are still few *scholarly* projects that demonstrate the same level of collaboration of the DDB project), long since defined by the term "crowd-sourcing." But at this point in time, no one in the fields of the Humanities—not to mention Asian or Buddhist studies—had ever attempted such a thing. While from the present-day perspective this might seem like a no-brainer, at that time the notion of being able to make such reference materials available more freely, more quickly, and more cheaply, to a wider range of people than one could have ever imagined was unthinkable—such a huge leap from the print reference works that were the standard option at the time, and quite far beyond the CDs which were in vogue during the 90's. The

https://doi.org/10.1515/9783110519082-009

Web had the potential of enabling the kind of collaboration not conceivable in the age of paper publication. All I had to do was figure out how to convert the data into an HTML document and upload it to a web site.

Still, it was a bit of a gamble for a young academic. The Web was seen by many in academia as an unknown specter, rapidly being populated by quasi-academic data produced by all kinds of people, few possessing specialist credentials, and virtually all escaping peer evaluation. There was, in fact, widespread disdain for web publication in the academic world, with it taking at least a full decade for academia to begin to take the web seriously, especially in the Humanities. During the first decade of the web, information sources were often developed in a non-academic manner, and such sources filled the Web. By 2005, it was almost too late for the development of new web reference works, as the open space had already been fully occupied by Wikipedia and Google.[1] But this was way before the appearance of these technologies, and I was convinced that it would work. First, the compilation that I had in hand (some 2,800 entries) was already bigger than anything else available (in terms of modern, scholarly CJK-English works), which meant that if I put what I had on the web, it was already going to be the best reference work in the field online. And if I could keep at it, and gain collaboration, I thought, it would only be a matter of time before it gained critical mass.

All these things would come to pass. Within a few weeks of my placing of this compilation on the web in a simple hard-linked HTML format, it was discovered by web-aware scholars, the first being Christian Wittern.[2] Christian suggested that I convert the data to SGML (Standard Generalized Markup Language) format, and I was over time able to learn enough about SGML such that I could continue to develop the content of the dictionary on my own, using this markup framework. I was also contacted by Jim Breen (founder of the WWWJIC project[3]) with whom I had extensive discussions about online resource development. Early the next year, this *Dictionary of East Asian Buddhist Terms* [DEABT] was positively mentioned in the first JIABS article on Buddhist Studies and the Internet, written by Jamie Hubbard,[4] who subsequently became one of the first con-

---

[1] On the central role played by Wikipedia in washing away incipient individual online reference projects, see Jaron Lanier's *You Are Not a Gadget* and *Who Owns the Future?*
[2] Now of Kyoto University (http://www.zinbun.kyoto-u.ac.jp/zinbun/members/wittern.htm), a scholar of Chinese Chan Buddhism, who also happened to be one of the most advanced theorists and practitioners of digital technology in the Humanities fields and who was collaborating with Urs App at Hanazono University in digitizing Zen texts and reference sources.
[3] Now located at http://www.edrdg.org/cgi-bin/wwwjdic/wwwjdic?1C, still a thriving project.
[4] Hubbard, 1995. https://www.smith.edu/academics/faculty/jamie-hubbard

tributors, and a long-time supporter of the project. After this, a few of the other early content contributors, including Gene Reeves,[5] Charles Patton,[6] Iain Sinclair[7] and Dan Lusthaus contacted me to offer their own digitized glossaries to the DEABT.

My initial naming of the work as the *Dictionary of East Asian Buddhist Terms* was based on the fact that my basic area of interest was in the East Asian Buddhist canon, and therefore the orientation was toward Asian sources. But since I, and several early collaborators were working on Abhidharma, Madhyamaka, and Yogācāra Buddhism, a large portion of the content actually dealt with Indian Buddhist schools, figures, and concepts. Furthermore, during the process of developing this compilation in the late 90's, two distinct areas of content became apparent: (1) content related directly to Buddhism, and (2) Confucian-Daoist content, historical information, and other non-Buddhist content. For the purpose of organization, acknowledging contributors and their contributions, as well as for grant application purposes, it became increasingly apparent that it would be better to separate the two types of data into two separately identifiable compilations. These were renamed as: (1) The *Digital Dictionary of Buddhism* [DDB], focusing on terms, texts, temple, schools, persons, etc. found in Buddhist canonical sources; (2) the *Chinese-Japanese-Korean-Vietnamese/English Dictionary* [CJKV-E], which compiles detailed information on Chinese ideographs, as well as ideograph-comprised compound words, text names, person names, etc., found primarily in the Confucian and Daoist classics. It also includes vocabulary from many Neo-Confucian texts, as well as other philosophical and historical sources. Its information on individual ideographs is intended to be comprehensive, containing pronunciations and meanings from ancient and modern sources from the Sinitic cultural sphere including China, Korea, Japan, and Vietnam. Modern-day meanings of single ideographs and modern compound words are included incidentally, but the coverage of modern materials is not intended to be comprehensive.

During the earliest phase of the development of the project—from 1995 to around 2000, much was happening in terms of creating connections in the world of digital Buddhist Studies. Early pioneers of the digitization of Buddhist Studies began to connect with each other, and began to gather for academic meetings. One of the main venues for these early meetings was the Electronic Buddhist Text Initiative [EBTI][8] with the main impetus and leadership coming

5 http://www.wisdompubs.org/author/gene-reeves.
6 http://www.buddhism-dict.net/credits/patton.html.
7 http://buddhism-dict.net/credits/sinclair.html.
8 http://www.buddhism-dict.net/ebti.

from Lewis Lancaster of UC Berkeley. The rapidity of the digitization of all of the Buddhist canons, and especially the East Asian versions, can be in great part attributed to the prodding and encouragement from Prof. Lancaster, who strongly encouraged Korean, Taiwanese, and Japanese groups to pursue the digitization of their respective canons. Through the EBTI Lancaster also worked to bring together scholars working in all facets of the digitization of Buddhist Studies. At early EBTI meetings of the EBTI held in Taipei, I was able to meet Lancaster, Christian Wittern, Urs App (Hanazono/IRIZ), Ven. Chongnim (Tripiṭaka Koreana), Ven. Huimin (CBETA), Masahiro Shimoda (SAT), Jamie Hubbard (Smith College), Robert Chilton (ACIP), C.C. Hsieh (Academia Sinica), Susan Whitfield (IDP), John and Susan Huntington (OSU), and many others who would become influential figures in the digitization of Buddhist studies. Such meetings provided a fertile environment for collaboration and exchange of ideas that greatly influenced the course of my own project and the others.

Another important spinoff of the development of the DDB and my involvement with other digital projects through the EBTI, was H-Buddhism.[9] The present H-Buddhism network, the Web's central hub of information for the academic study of Buddhism, has its roots in a personal list that I began to maintain from 1996 to let people in the field know about ongoing developments in digital resources. I eventually put this list on a listserv under the name BudSchol, which in August 2001 moved to H-Net under its present name.[10]

# Using XML

## What is XML?

During the late 90's, around the same time as the advent of Unicode, the SGML (Standard Generalized Markup Language) world turned to the emerging XML (eXtensible Markup Language) standard,[11] and the DDB/CJKV-E project followed, taking best advantage of the strong points of XML. No doubt, most readers of a volume on Digital Humanities already know what XML is, but it might be worthwhile to briefly clarify its distinctive aspects, and our reasons for choosing

9 https://networks.h-net.org/h-buddhism.

10 The history of the development of H-Buddhism is recounted briefly at https://networks.h-net.org/node/6060/pages/23146/about-h-buddhism, and a more detailed account of the birth of early online Buddhist discussion fora is given at http://www.acmuller.net/articles/buddhist_listserves.html.

11 http://www.w3.org/XML.

it as our data format (since, in fact, the vast majority of web-based reference works do not use XML, opting instead for traditional database platforms).

The "ML" of XML stands for "markup language," and it is a term that comes from the world of book printing, where, for decades, typesetters have made handwritten marks on manuscripts to indicate format. For example <H1> is a top-level header, <P> indicates a paragraph, etc. The language that underlies the Web—HTML is also a markup language, in this case, a language, like in typesetting, that indicates style and formatting. SGML and XML build on this, and not only mark up format and style, but most importantly *content*. For example, in HTML, we might have something like <italic>Moby Dick</italic> to mark up a book title, whereas in SGML/XML, this would be done as <title>Moby Dick</title>. When one saves something like a dictionary in a database format and needs to include that data into one's prose writing, the data must be exported from the database into a text-compatible format. With XML, one can leave the structure of one's textual project as it is, and just place tags around the data where it sits. If the tags are removed, one still has the data, intact. If the author is using the same general tag set (such as, for example the TEI tag set introduced below) for the rest of his projects (books, articles, bibliographies, etc.), the data, along with the tags, can be copied in and out of these other projects, and still function the same way.

## The Text Encoding Initiative [TEI]

Because textual scholars in the West have been using markup since the 1980's, a de facto standard for tag sets has emerged through the work of the members of the Text Encoding Initiative [TEI],[12] and the tag sets for the DDB/CJKV-E dictionaries are based on TEI, which, in its guidelines, has a module that treats lexicographical works. Throughout the TEI in general, there are also recommendations for usage of what are known as "attributes"—metadata about metadata. The usage of attributes, along with the main XML tags (called "elements" or "nodes") gives great flexibility in fine-tuning information about data. Indicating, for example, not only that a certain word is a title, but that it is a Chinese title of a text with Indian provenance. Please see the following example:

Here, the reader can see the range of application of attributes. For example, lang="zh" system="py", means that the language of the term wrapped in the tags is Chinese, and the romanization system is Pinyin. Other attributes indicate

12 http://www.tei-c.org

```xml
<entry ID="b4e00-..." added_by="Iain Sinclair" add_date="2001-09-08" update="2018-10-13" rad="一" radval="01" radno="001" strokes="00">
<hdwd>一切功德莊嚴王經</hdwd>
<pron_list>
<pron lang="zh" system="py" resp="Iain Sinclair">Yīqiè gōngdé zhuāngyánwáng jīng</pron>
<pron lang="ko" system="mc" resp="Charles Muller">Ilche gongdeok jang-eom wang gyeong</pron>
<pron lang="ja" system="hb" resp="Iain Sinclair">Issai kudoku shōgonnō kyō</pron>
<pron lang="vi" system="qn" resp="daouyen">Nhất thiết công đức trang nghiêm vương kinh</pron>
</pron_list>
<sense_area>
<trans resp="Charles Muller" rend="hide"><title level="entry" lang="en" prov="ind">Sutra of the Kingly Arrangement of All Dharmas and Merits</title></trans>
<sense resp="Iain Sinclair" ref="Hirakawa, YBh-Ind">Skt. <title level="entry" lang="sa" prov="ind">Sarvadharmaguṇavyūharāja-sūtra</title>; Ch. <title level="entry" lang="zh" prov="ind">Yiqie gongde zhuangyanwang jing</title>; Tib. <title level="entry" lang="bo" prov="ind">chos thams cad kyi yon tan bkod pa'i rgyal po</title> [To.114/527]. 1 fasc. (<xref canonref="http://21dzk.l.u-tokyo.ac.jp/SAT/T1374.html">T 1374</xref>.21.890–894). trans.
```

Fig. 1: Text Encoding Example

the names of those responsible for distinct units of data. Other attributes encode dating information, character information, provenance, and so forth. The extent to which markup is applied is dependent on the needs of the project. Depth of markup at both the level of node and attribute can be increased or decreased, according to necessity. Tags and their attributes can be created however one likes, but we have found it helpful to follow the TEI guidelines as much as possible, and thus the dictionary is based mainly on TEI.[13]

## *Michael Beddow and other technical help*

I was active on a wide range of technical forums at the time, including for Linux, TEI, XML, XSLT, and so forth, and continually posted notices of both technical

13 Some of the minor differences in the DDB/CJKV-E structure and the tags recommended by TEI are due to my early inability to fully understand the TEI guidelines. Thus some differences were embedded during the early period, but all new tagging done after 2005 or so, including everything in the <sense> fields of the DDB/CJKV-E follows TEI. It would be possible to now make the dataset fully compliant with the present TEI P5 module for lexicons, but this would entail a bit too much rewriting of the transformation/output processes of XSLT, CSS, and Perl to make it worthwhile.

and content upgrades to the DDB, and the publicized shift in the format of the DDB and CJKV-E attracted the attention of XML aficionados such as Louis-Dominique Dubeau,[14] who wrote the first proper DTD (Document Type Definition) for both works. At this time, however, while the local data was saved in XML, the online version was still published in static HTML every few months or so, since I was not able to apply XSLT transformations dynamically, and lacked the technical knowledge to construct a search engine. At the same time, the DDB/CJKV-E data set was unique in the world at the time, being the only substantial polyglot data project on the web in XML format. Because of this, I was contacted by XML developers at Microsoft, XMetal, XMLSpy, and others for the usage of this data set for their test purposes. But none of these companies were interested in helping to implement the XML data on the Web in a dynamic manner.

Then, in 2001, the most important event in the history of the project (other than the invention of HTML) occurred. Through my participation on the Mulberry XSLT support listserv, I was able to enter into a conversation with Michael Beddow[15] (formerly of Leeds University and Kings College London), a specialist in German literature who also happened to be an amazing web programmer. Michael was already developing a set of tools to deliver the TEI-XML-based Anglo-Norman Dictionary[16] with a search engine and XSLT. With consummate skill, care, and generosity, Michael took the DDB/CJKV-E XML data and created a search engine using XPath/XLinking, along with Perl—a search engine which was, to the best of our knowledge, the first at the time that would search mixed Latin and double-byte East Asian text in XML/Utf-8 encoding. Michael's search mechanism was a novel creation which still serves its purpose quite well (albeit in an occasionally-updated and enhanced manner).[17] Michael has continued to provide primary support to the DDB and CJKV-E project up to the present, adding various enhancements, periodically updating the system, providing web site security—and even proofreading entries in the dictionary. Most recently, in October of 2016, he enhanced the search algorithm of the DDB to allow for search via modern simplified Chinese characters. The level of technical support Michael

14 https://github.com/lddubeau

15 https://en.wikipedia.org/wiki/Michael_Beddow.

16 http://www.anglo-norman.net.

17 Soon after the completion of this framework, Michael and I were asked to submit an article to the online *Journal of Digital Information.* That article, entitled "Moving into XML Functionality: The Combined Digital Dictionaries of Buddhism and East Asian Literary Terms," can be read at *http://journals.tdl.org/jodi/article/view/jodi-65/82.* (*Journal of Digital Information: Special Issue on Chinese Collections in the Digital Library*, Volume 3, issue 2, October 2002).

has provided to the project is far beyond the services that could have ever been gained by contracting a web development company, and the project would never have achieved anything close to its present level of success without his support.

## Middle Period: Heading for Critical Mass

### *Digitization and assimilation of older materials*

With the new implementation of Michael's search engine, usage of the DDB, jumped drastically. Seeing this, I was encouraged to invest even more time and energy into rapidly expanding its coverage. Based on funding from a JSPS grant-in-aid and with the help of my students,[18] I digitized the Soothill-Hodous *Dictionary of Chinese Buddhist Terms*, a major copyright-expired reference work on Buddhism. The digitization being finished in 2002, I gradually added much of this data to the DDB, judiciously editing in the process.[19] But this data, along with my own steady input (I was constantly adding terminology while translating texts) raised the DDB content to around 15,000 entries, thus creating a respectable basic range of coverage. The same JSPS grant also enabled us to digitize Lewis Lancaster's landmark work, *The Korean Buddhist Canon: A Descriptive Catalogue*.[20] Using the data from this compilation whenever we created a new entry on a text from the Chinese canon, we were able to quickly gain all the basic information of dating, provenance, translation, variant versions, and so forth. To this we were able to add content information for the given text from other sources. And of course, we could at the same time include corrections based on interim research. Around the same time, in collaboration with researchers at IRIZ, Tripiṭaka Koreana, and Dharma Drum University, we completed the main part of the construction of a master index of the major East Asian Buddhist lexicons and encyclopedias (including 300,000 terms, an ongoing project),[21] which we set into place as a supplementary digital concordance for our work. All these enhancements led to a steady increase in the number of users of the dictionaries.

---

**18** The DDB and CJKV-E have benefited from several JSPS grants, listed in full at http://www.acmuller.net/grants.html.

**19** The Soothill-Hodous dictionary was published in the 1930's and much of the information was incorrect and outdated, so we needed to be careful in the way we added it.

**20** http://www.acmuller.net/descriptive_catalogue/index.html.

**21** http://www.buddhism-dict.net/ddb/allindex-intro.html.

## What? No contributions?

But there were also disappointing moments. Despite the extensive volunteer efforts of our team to offer all this material for free with the hope of stimulating collaboration, as of 2002, despite our strongly-expressed requests for contributions from users, except for a very small handful of generous, forward-thinking scholars, we were receiving almost no contributions, despite our clear explanation that it was intended to be a collaborative project. On the other hand, we had clear numerical data and anecdotal information to confirm that this resource was now being used extensively for teaching and research by large numbers of scholars and students in our field, receiving tens of thousands of accesses each month.

We thus began to experiment with leveraging the password policy (which had originally been set up only for security purposes, to be discussed just below) to establish a two-tiered access structure of member/guest. We started out by allowing guests fifty searches a day. Users seemed quite happy with this, but very few felt motivated to contribute. We then gradually decreased the number in increments of ten until we reached the number of ten. At this point users began to scream—and then we knew we had the right number. And so, we began to tell them . . . "If you want full access, you have to contribute, one way or another." We set the bar low in terms of size of contribution: For qualified scholars, one A4 (letter) page of data for two years of full access. Actually, quite small, but the aim, which has been successful, was to give our users the experience of being a *collaborator* rather than a simple "user."

It worked. Before long, a surprising number of highly-respected scholars began to operate in a way that they never had before, and some even began to display a sense of pride and belonging in being part of the project. We made further adjustments as we went along. For example, we responded to the suggestion made by a representative of Starr Library at Columbia University to allow institutions pay for access, setting a fee of $300 per year (a fee that is about 1/10th the cost of the average rate for such a resource, I am told by many librarians). UC Berkeley, UCLA, Harvard, Princeton, and others soon followed, and within a year, more than twenty more institutions were subscribed. The present number of subscribing libraries fluctuates between fifty-five and sixty.[22] Thinking along the same lines, to meet the demand for non-scholars who wanted access, we offered the option of individual subscriptions at $30 per year. From these two sources, we secured a small, but steady income that we used for pay-

---

22 http://www.buddhism-dict.net/ddb/subscribing_libraries.html

ing graduate student assistants to input new data, and thus the size of the database continued to grow faster and faster, and this continues to be the case up to the present moment.

## *Massive contributions*

The above series of transformations resulted in a situation where contributions, large and small, began to flood in. Most important were the massive contributions by scholars who had compiled, or were compiling their own reference materials. These consisted of either thousands of small entries or hundreds of pages of longer entries, often coupled with extensive voluntary proofreading of other entries in the dictionary. These scholars, listed in order of the approximate size of their contributions are: Ockbae Chun, Paul Swanson, Michael Radich, Jeffrey Kotyk, Griffith Foulk, John Powers, Dan Lusthaus, Gene Reeves, Seishi Karashima, Iain Sinclair, Stephen Hodge, and Ven. Ñāṇatusita.[23] In addition to this, more than three hundred individuals have made contributions, the more prolific of which are listed on our credits page in approximate order of the significance of their contributions.[24] There are also a number of people who, when reading through the dictionaries, carefully record and report errors, an indispensable dimension of the project.[25] The overall result of these combined large and small contributions have made the DDB/CJKV-E dictionaries into one of the most successful and enduring *responsible* and *scholarly* "crowd-sourced" projects in the entire history of the Web.[26]

Based on these collaborative developments, the coverage of both dictionaries has leaped dramatically, such that the combined coverage of both compilations is presently (in November 2016) more than 106,000 entries. By 2005, many, if not most graduate programs in Buddhist Studies in North America and Europe were using the DDB/CJKV-E in their classes, and this trend has

**23** Details of the contributions of these scholars are provided at http://www.buddhism-dict.net/credits/credits-ddb.html.

**24** Ibid.

**25** A few of the more steady contributors of this category include Wolfgang Waletzki, Gene Reeves, Robert Kritzer, Dan Lusthaus, Jeffrey Kotyk, Charles Jones, Ven. Ñāṇatusita, Achim Bayer, Jimmy Yu, Charles Patton, Ockbae Chun, Michael Beddow, and Pierce Salguero.

**26** The caveat of "responsible and scholarly" distinguishes the project from anonymous works such as Wikipedia. It is my feeling that no matter how extensive the coverage of Wikipedia becomes, it will always suffer from the weakness of lack of clear providing of credit and responsibility for its entries.

grown stronger over time. The DDB has become a basic reference work for the field of Buddhist studies. It is used in the teaching of courses on Buddhism, and is regularly cited in scholarly research articles and monographs. Many DDB authors are acknowledged as leading authorities in their sub-areas of Buddhist Studies.

## Dealing with Copyright

The Web, as we look out on it today—being forced into some kind of order by the tech giants for purposes of profit—and by governments trying to fight off monopolizing trends, is already under much tighter control than it was at the beginning. Conventions have been established regarding copying, and the Creative Commons Licenses have been well-used for more than a decade. But in the beginning, nobody knew what to do. People like me tended to be naïve and idealistic, thinking only "build it, and they will come." Well, come they did, and take, they did; it was indeed, the Wild West. Since the DDB/CJKV-E were, in the beginning, simply maintained in a static HTML format, it was a simple task for anyone with a modicum of web skills to download the entire data set. We had also given permission to CBETA to include a copy on their CD, which made the data conveniently portable in a single directory. It didn't take long before copies of the DDB were popping up all over the Web, sometimes with due attribution attached, sometimes with it stripped out and relabeled as "Such-and-such Buddhist Organization Dictionary of Buddhism." This had to stop.

During the early 2000's the issue of copying and copyright came to be one of the principal topics of discussion on the Net. Larry Lessig, author of such books as the *Future of Ideas* [27] was coming up with the idea of the Creative Commons license,[28] and during his stay at the University of Tokyo as a visiting professor, he got me on board. I applied it to everything on my site, along with my dictionaries. Unfortunately, during the early period of the CC licenses, people tended not to read the fine print, and just took it as license to do whatever they wanted with the data. I had applied a fairly strict CC license to the Soothill-Hodous dictionary that I had put online, but people just copied it at will, posted on their sites, and claimed credit for it, often stripping out the name of even Soothill and Hodous, and usually removing my name from the header as digitizer.

---

**27** See my review at http://www.acmuller.net/reviews/future_of_ideas.html.
**28** https://creativecommons.org/licenses

And then Wikipedia came. At first I thought it was a great thing, and added some Buddhist terminology. But after too many occasions finding my writing dumbed-down, deleted, or contorted, and not being able to readily do anything about it, I gave up. But things got much worse when colleagues began to report to me that content from DDB entries was appearing in Wikipedia without attribution. From this, I had a brief go-around with Jimmy Wales' minions, which ended in a decidedly unsatisfactory manner for me, with Wikipedia's legal team informing me that Wikipedia entries were "third-party" data, over which they had no control. They treated me like an insect.[29]

So I gave up on the Creative Commons, and returned to the practice of just adding a copyright notice at the bottom of each entry. The problem of wholesale copying of the site (done mostly by Buddhist organizations) was largely taken care of through Michael Beddow's efforts at web security and our implementation of the password access system described above.

## DDB/CJKV-E Applications

The size and reliability of the DDB/CJKV-E dataset, along with its readily-accessible XML format made it attractive as a lookup tool and as an add-on supplement for textual databases, as well as for the building of other stand-alone applications. In 2008, based on the expert programming work of Kiyonori Nagasaki of the International Institute of Digital Humanities,[30] the DDB was linked in an interoperative manner with the online SAT Taishō Text Database,[31] set up in a way wherein when one opens up a scripture from the online Taishō canon and selects a portion of text with one's mouse, the words in the DDB contained in that text will be displayed in the right-hand window with short definitions and links into the DDB entries themselves. Soon after, Jean Soulat, a Windows specialist based in France created a standalone parsing/lookup application called DDB Access,[32] which allows one to parse and look up words from Buddhist and non-Buddhist Sinitic texts in a powerful manner using both the DDB and CJKV-E data. The dictionaries are also integrated into Jean Soulat's web-based Smarthanzi[33] Chinese lookup and parsing tool. Sutta Central[34] also has Chinese

29 For my feelings about Wikipedia, see http://www.acmuller.net/wikipedia.html. I'm still not a fan.

30 http://www.dhii.jp/index-e.html.

31 http://21dzk.l.u-tokyo.ac.jp/SAT/ddb-bdk-sat2.php.

32 http://download.smarthanzi.net/ddbaccess.

33 http://www.smarthanzi.net.

versions of the Āgamas set up so that a mouse hover will show embedded DDB data.

## CJKV-E Developments

The CJKV-E Dictionary has always had more competition as a Web resource, as Chinese ideographic dictionaries presently abound on the Internet. However, the CJKV-E is distinguished from the rest of these in its being the only online lexicon of its type that is (1) not merely a computerized aggregation, or a compilation by nonspecialists, and (2) not merely a reproduction of an older print dictionary. It is being actively developed in an ongoing manner by scholars in conjunction with the reading of classical texts. Besides its inherent digital advantages, the CJKV-E dictionary already surpasses many of its hard-copy counterpart dictionaries in a number of ways. The total number of entries in November 2016 was 52,000, with 12,250 of these being single-ideograph entries. As distinguished from the numerous computer-aggregated East Asian language dictionaries proliferating on the Web, each of the entries in this CJKV-E dictionary is human-edited, and usually contains far more detailed information than any other comparable Web lexicon, being developed while consulting a wide range of authoritative Chinese, Korean, and Japanese sources, and usually through the direct reading of primary classical texts. While a number of the Japanese-oriented modern *kanji* dictionaries that have appeared during recent decades have been of acceptable quality in terms of precision within their respective purviews, they are, from the perspective of the classical scholar, limited in their scope and orientation to modern vocabulary, and thus are not useful to those who are doing scholarly research/translation of pre-modern *han-wen* texts, who need to know all of the ancient semantic implementations and readings of a particular ideograph. During the past three years, the coverage of the CJKV-E has increased by more than 20,000 entries, based mainly on the work of an incredibly productive and reliable UTokyo PhD student named Yao Zhang.[35]

There is no limit to the intended future expansion in coverage of both works. Usage of the dictionaries and collaborative efforts along with contributions continue to grow. We are interested in developing and expanding these compilations in any direction where we can receive collaboration: from any linguistic/cultural region of Buddhist or East Asian studies where scholars would like to contribute

34 https://suttacentral.net.

35 https://u-tokyo.academia.edu/YaoZhang.

information. We have no limit on the length of articles, and we are happy to add images and any other sort of data that is appropriate. It is our hope, in terms of reflecting the history of the Buddhist and broader East Asian intellectual traditions, to provide as balanced and accurate an account as possible.

## References[36]

Hubbard, Jamie. 1995. "Upping the Ante: budstud@millenium.end.edu." *Journal of the International Association of Buddhist Studies* 18(2): 309–322.

Lancaster, Lewis R, and Sung-bae Park. 1979. *The Korean Buddhist Canon: A Descriptive Catalogue.* Berkeley: University of California Press.

Lanier, Jaron. 2010. *You Are Not a Gadget: A Manifesto.* New York: Alfred A. Knopf.

Lanier, Jaron. 2013. *Who Owns the Future?* New York: Simon and Schuster.

Lessig, Lawrence. 1999. *Code and Other Laws of Cyberspace.* New York: Basic Books.

Lessig, Lawrence. 2001. *The Future of Ideas: The Fate of the Commons in a Connected World.* New York: Random House.

Soothill, W.E, and L Hodous. 1997. *A Dictionary of Chinese Buddhist Terms: With Sanskrit and English equivalents and a Sanskrit-Pali Index.* Delhi: Motilal Banarsidass.

36 For more detailed background material on the history and development of the DDB and CJKV-E, we have published a few papers and have made a number of conference presentations on the topic over the years, which are available through my personal publications page at http://www.acmuller.net/research.html.

# Part Three: **Digital Analysis of Buddhist Documents**

Christopher Jensen

# Mapping Religious Practice in the *Eminent Monks:* Theoretical and Methodological Reflections

## Background

In the last thirty years, scholarship on Chinese religion (both Buddhist and otherwise) has moved away from the study of great men and great ideas, and toward a greater engagement with narrative, social history, and embodied practice, as well as the contingent and mutually constitutive nature of China's religious traditions: evolutionary developments that are perfectly preserved in the amber of McCrae, Teiser, and Verellen's (1995) "State of the Field" articles for the *Journal of Asian Studies.* Within contemporary scholarship on historical Chinese Buddhism, one of the most frequently-consulted sources employed by researchers delving into these topics has been the *Biographies of Eminent Monks*[1] corpus, as these texts provide a wealth of details on the particular circumstances of life for medieval Chinese Buddhist monks and lay devotees, whether one is interested in localized religious practice (Robson 2009), hagiographical ideals (Kieschnick 1997), Buddhist medicine (Salguero 2010) or even self-immolation (Benn 2007). In particular, given that a mere hundred and thirty years separates Huijiao's compilation of the first collection (*Gaoseng zhuan* [T. 2059]) in 519 CE and Daoxuan's compilation of the second (*Xu gaoseng zhuan* [T. 2060]) in 645 CE, these two texts in particular have proven themselves to be amenable to comparative analysis, as the accounts contained therein cover the period from the earliest introduction of Buddhism to China, through the chaos of the Northern / Southern dynasties, and into the reunification under the Sui and early Tang.

The attention lavished upon these collections by contemporary scholars parallels the esteem in which they were held in their original context(s) of compilation, as they were widely circulated, revered and attended to as models of exemplary conduct by both Buddhist monks and pious laypeople (Shinohara 1997; Kieschnick 1997). These two usage contexts differ substantially, however, in their respective positions on matters of historical accuracy. More specifically, medieval Chinese compilers and historiographers tended to approach their materi-

1 The three most influential, and frequently cited, of these texts are *Gaoseng zhuan* 高僧傳 (T. 2059), *Xu gaoseng zhuan* 續高僧傳 (T. 2060), and *Song gaoseng zhuan* 宋高僧傳 (T. 2061).

https://doi.org/10.1515/9783110519082-010

als as topoi, considering the ways that past episodes could illuminate current ideological concerns: an approach that Li (2000–2001) characterizes as the "moral-pragmatic" mode (185). In the context of the *Biographies*, Huijiao's rhetorical goal for compiling the collection (namely, proselytism) is laid bare in his introduction, where he avers: "For spreading the Way and explaining the Teaching, nothing surpasses eminent monks."[2] This focus on proselytism, which was also shared by Daoxuan, coloured their selection of biographical episodes, their organization, and the explicit logics outlined in the prose commentaries that close out each chapter. That said, and as noted by Kieschnick (1997), Daoxuan was also motivated to correct what he saw as a geographical bias in his predecessors' selection of sources (7): an issue that seems to be evidenced in the later collection as well (as will be discussed below).

In spite of these historiographical concerns, which partly inspired Kieschnick's decision to approach these materials thematically (*ibid.*, 1–4), the sheer volume of locational data present in the *Eminent Monks* corpus led me to wonder whether there might be a methodologically justifiable means of using these texts to map various aspects of medieval Chinese Buddhism, while simultaneously acknowledging the difficulties outlined above. In order to explore this issue, I turned to the voluminously-detailed, annotated versions of these texts prepared by Dharma Drum Buddhist College and made freely available online, within which each named individual and location is tagged with a unique ID, and all place names are linked with corresponding geolocation coordinates (Bingenheimer, *et al.* 2009). Considering this resource, I realized that the data contained therein would make it possible to map out every one of the 9,917 named locations in the corpus: a process that would yield a detailed map of these texts' geographical distributions and "centers of gravity." After deriving, plotting and analyzing this geographical distribution, it would – at least in theory – be possible to use these data as a baseline against which future studies could assess the distributions of pilgrimage routes, teaching centers, and other geographically-localized practices, in order to determine whether these distributions deviated meaningfully from that of the corpus as a whole.

As such, the present paper suggests a potential "middle way" between either assuming that the *Eminent Monks* texts, with the exception of their occasional tales of the miraculous, are essentially accurate historical documents (an outmoded style of scholarship effectively critiqued by Shinohara [1997]), and simply ignoring the wealth of geographical data they contain in order to focus on thematic issues. More specifically, while it is not possible to discern the extent to

2 T. 2059: 422c26 「而弘道釋教莫尚高僧.」 Translated by John Kieschnick 1997, 7.

which the events and locations mentioned in the *Gaoseng zhuan* and *Xu gaoseng zhuan* correspond to specific historical events, we do know that these popular texts were instrumental in creating and reinforcing the public perception of Buddhism in medieval China amongst their respective reading publics. As such, the present project endeavours to map the "imagined geographies" of these texts (to borrow a term from Edward Said) and, in so doing, explore the mental map(s) of Buddhist activity that these texts would have helped to inculcate amongst the medieval Chinese "discourse communities" that read, transcribed, and circulated them (Campany 2012).

To make this case, the present study is divided into five sections: first, a brief exploration of the constellation of theoretical issues surrounding the notion of "imagined geographies" and the process of mapping historical phenomena; second, a methodological overview of the techniques, tools and resources employed to assemble and analyze the geographical dataset; third, the analysis of "textual center(s) of gravity" of the *Gaoseng zhuan* and *Xu gaoseng zhuan*; fourth, a case study exploring the geographical distribution of a specific phenomenon (in this case, practices related to dreams) as a function of the overall geographical biases of the source texts; and, fifth, some brief conclusions. While this is very much a pilot project (both theoretically and methodologically), it is my hope that it will help to advance the disciplinary conversation related to geographical analyses of medieval Chinese Buddhism.

## Imagined Geographies, Mapping and the "Spatial Turn"

### *Theoretical background*

For the last several decades, anthropology and religious studies have begun to take cues from theoretical advances in cultural geography, increasingly attending to the distinction between geographical spaces and culturally-construed places (Gupta and Ferguson 1992; Matthews and Herbert 2004). This framework highlights the extent to which the most salient geographical units (from the smallest communities to the largest nations) exist primarily as imagined entities, whose ties to particular physical spaces are profoundly (and at times tendentiously) culturally situated.

One of the organizing metaphors of this shift, which owes its genesis to the incisive social and literary critic Edward Said, is the notion of "imagined geography" (as mentioned above): a term that he coined to describe the "poetics of space" whereby Westerners ascribe meaning and value to the physical spaces of "the Orient" (and their occupants) based on culturally-constructed discourses and modes of analysis (Said 1978). More specifically, Said argued that such systems exert a form of hegemonic control, whereby the systematizing intellectual products of Western scholars (e.g., translations, encyclopedias, scholarly articles) became the singular means through which Westerners accessed "the East." In this context, he argues that "truth, in short becomes a function of learned judgement, not of the material itself, which in time seems to owe even its existence to the Orientalist," but rather of these second- (or even third-) order representations of it (*ibid.*, 67). In this way, Said argued that the imaginative geographies of European academics came to play a constitutive role in centuries worth of artistic production, scholarly research agendas, and even colonial policy (Gregory 1995). In so doing, he provides a clear example of the ways that the construals of educated elites can, when broadly circulated and accepted, help to establish mental maps within their readerships that can, in turn, have significant socio-cultural effects.

In a similar fashion, Benedict Anderson suggests that notions of "imagined community" have undergirded the creation of modern nation states, wherein these unifying, identity-generative "communities" were the products of some combination of colonial experiences, shared linguistic heritage, and the retrospective creation of shared history (Anderson 1983). Anderson also argues for the centrality of knowledge production in the creation of these psycho-geographical places (to borrow a phrase from Derek Gregory [1995]), whereby such intellectual activities as performing censuses, making maps, and assembling / curating museum collections functioned to create "a totalizing classificatory grid, which could be applied with endless flexibility to anything under the state's real or contemplated control: peoples, regions, religions, languages, products, monuments, and so forth" (Anderson 1983, 184). Thus, Anderson's "imagined communities" and Said's "imagined geographies" seem to represent complementary faces of the same process, with Anderson focusing on the role of psycho-geographical imaginings within nations, and Said considering the effects of these processes when imposed upon the mental representations of geographical "others." Thus, both of these macro-level theorists can be seen commenting on the dynamic processes whereby mental models of spaces and places come to inform the social, political and intellectual activities of their inheritors.

Though the circumstances that inspired Said and Anderson to posit their related conceptions of imagined geographies / communities were profoundly situated in their respective, and predominantly modern, contexts of inquiry, an examination of the medieval Chinese context reveals some strikingly similar cultural processes. More specifically, I would argue that attending to this cultural process (i.e., scholarly knowledge production generating shared psycho-geographical places) is particularly apropos in medieval China, where the literary output of a class of educated elites served to at least partially define the ideological underpinnings of the era (Chan and Lo 2011). Though perhaps not generating the same sort of "totalizing discourse" as a colonial museum, these elites tended toward literary forms that purported to circumscribe and explicate the human world: namely, biographies, histories, encyclopedias, "strange tales," and various forms of collectanea. As Robert Campany argues in "Strange Writing," the compilation of such accounts always entailed a rhetorical and political negotiation between competing models of the Chinese state, highlighting shifting relationships between the country's cultural center(s) and its peripheral regions: Campany thereby dubs the process of editing and curating such narratives "cosmographic collecting," highlighting their role in charting out the worldviews of their readers (Campany 1996). He further subdivides these collections into two types: the *locative* (i.e., those written for the benefit of the rulers / elites of a centralized state and stressing the orderliness of a world subsumed under that state's authority) and the *anti-locative* (i.e., those that focus on the chaotic, liminal and/or peripheral, and thus offer an implicit critique of the purported religio-moral authority presumed by the ruler) (12–14). Though it would be possible to offer further evidence of relevant isomorphisms between the contexts about which Said, Anderson, and Campany were theorizing, I hope that the preceding brief discussion suffices to demonstrate the potential utility of employing the concept of "imagined geography" in the medieval Chinese context. Moreover, given that the *Eminent Monks* collections were self-consciously compiled as tools of monastic proselytism intended for literate elites, the foregoing discussion suggests that the episodes included in this corpus would predominantly be characterized in the locative mode, which in turn implies that these collections' imagined geographies would be centered upon the loci of secular power. I investigate this hypothesis below (in Section 3).

## Methodological background

Though many disciplines in the humanities and social sciences have been influenced by the recent "spatial turn," this theoretical shift has not always been accompanied by methodological innovation. In particular, GIS mapping technologies have been viewed with a measure of suspicion by traditionalist scholars, given the perceived epistemological and hermeneutical gulfs between the messy, fractious, incommensurable "data" of human lives and the seemingly unavoidable positivism implied by the granularity and precision of maps, coordinate systems, and other hallmarks of computer-assisted analysis (Knowles 2008; Bodenhamer 2010; Gregory and Geddes 2014). In spite of these concerns, however, interdisciplinary interest in the potential of these techniques and research orientations has grown exponentially over the last twenty years, spurred on by the raw potential of maps to elucidate spatial and temporal patterns that tabular or narrative data tend to obscure. Such advances have been accompanied by an ever-increasing methodological sophistication with regard to maintaining the traditional humanities focus on contingent complexity, while also consciously avoiding the "spurious level of precision" often implied by the assignation of GIS coordinates to geographical phenomena (Gregory and Geddes 2014, xiii). Though it is impossible in this limited space to summarize the broad and exciting range of theoretical and methodological advances produced within the burgeoning discipline of Historical GIS / Spatial Humanities,[3] I will instead conclude this section by considering the application of these technologies to imagined geographies, given the obvious methodological connection between such projects and the one I am proposing herein.

As suggested by Said, Anderson, and Campany, the line of demarcation between imagined geographies and their corresponding geographical spaces is often blurry at best, especially given the constitutive interplay between individuals' mental models and their social and political activities (Bodenhamer 2010). In spite of this, there have been a dearth of attempts to actually map out imagined geographies, no doubt due to the Gordian knot of challenges (pertaining to methods, sources, and theory) that accompany such a project. To date, the single most compelling example of such a project that I have encountered is Cameron Blevins' (2014b) "Space, Nation, and the Triumph of Region: A View of the World from Houston," which explicitly sets out to explore the imagined geographies of nineteenth-century Houstonians by text-mining almost a decade of local newspapers for references to named places and then analyzing the patterns in the resultant distribution. Though his primary analytical tool was simple frequency analysis (one of the methods that I also employ), he uses this technique to expertly explore emergent inter- and intra-regional linkages, drawing conclusions tied to politics, commercial shipping, and the effects of technology on American

3 For a helpful overview, see Ian N. Gregory's (2014) recent literature review "Further Reading: From Historical GIS to Spatial Humanities: An Evolving Literature" in *Toward Spatial Humanities: Historical GIS and Spatial History*, edited by Ian N. Gregory and Alistair Geddes, (Bloomington, IN: Indiana University Press), 186–202. The topic headings alone, which run the gamut from "Historical GIS" and "Time in GIS," to "Environmental and Agricultural History," "Demography," and "Transport and Mobility," highlight the breadth of topic areas and methodological orientations encompassed within this expansive interdisciplinary umbrella.

regionalism. Another commendable feature of his approach was the division of the project into two halves: one focused on practical, methodological issues (Blevins 2014a) and the other on the significance of these conclusions within his discipline (Blevins 2014b).[4] Emboldened by the success of Blevins' study, which provides a "proof of concept" for the sort of analysis that I propose in the present paper, we can now turn to the particular methods that I employ herein.

## Methodology

In addition to the theoretical considerations detailed above, the current project also depended upon successfully addressing a variety of technical challenges, including parsing the location data from Dharma Drum's TEI-tagged XML versions of the *Eminent Monks* texts, extracting the spatial coordinates of the named sites from Dharma Drum's *Buddhist Authority Database* (http://authority.dila.edu.tw/place/), plotting these coordinates to a map, and then evaluating the distribution of mapped locations: stages of analysis following Kemp's (2010) model of a typical GIS workflow. Given my hope that the conclusions of this study will be useful to other scholars of medieval China, I endeavoured to make this project as replicable as possible: for instance, this concern inspired me to rely entirely upon freely available, open-source software solutions and packages, as well as "bespoke code" (Hsu, 2014, ¶ 23) that I wrote explicitly for this project, which I have made available online via a publicly accessible GitHub repository: https://github.com/ChristopherJonJensen/GIS-GSZ.

First, in order to extract the 9917 references to named locations found in the *Eminent Monks* corpus and tagged by the Dharma Drum initiative, it was necessary to parse the XML versions of both the tagged biographies and the Dharma Drum Buddhist Authority Database, which I accomplished with the R scripts mentioned above. Then, in order to visualize and track patterns in the data, I employed R's *ggmap* package, designed by David Kahle and Hadley Wickham, which allows for the seamless integration of maps from various sources with the extremely versatile *ggplot2* system (Kahle and Wickham 2013). In particular, in order to identify clusters in the distribution of locations mentioned in the *GSZ* corpus, I made use of the same method that Wu, Tong and Ryavec (2013) have successfully employed to calculate regional patterns in Chinese monastery distri-

4 In the interests of brevity and in deference to potential readers who may have a general interest in this project but no coding background, I have followed Blevins in separating out the more technical material related to the project. For all R code and detailed instructions, please consult the associated github repository at: https://github.com/ChristopherJonJensen/GIS-GSZ.

bution based on gazetteer and archive data: kernel density estimation or KDE (183). This technique, which is used to calculate densities in statistical distributions as a form of 2D histogram, is built into the *ggmap* package via the *stat_density2d* and *geom_density2d* functions, which allowed me to perform the distribution analysis in the course of plotting the maps themselves.

## Results

Mapping all of the named locations in the *Gaoseng zhuan* and then performing a kernel density estimate yields the following result (Figure 1).[5] As can be seen, Daoxuan was absolutely correct to criticize Huijiao for selection bias in his compilation of the original *Eminent Monks* collection, given that the only cluster with any significant density, representing one-third of the approximately 3000 location references in the text, is found in a very small geographical area in and around Jiankang (i.e., the capital of the Liang dynasty, under whom it was compiled).[6] In Figure 2, in contrast, we can see that Daoxuan's purported attempt to rectify Huijiao's regional bias a century and a half later seems to have been only marginally more successful. In particular, and somewhat unsurprisingly, the "imaginary geography" of his collection also forms a single major cluster, albeit one centered around Chang'an: the Sui/Tang capital (modern day Xian, as seen in the contemporary maps below). That said, he did not wholly neglect the regions near Jiankang, as can be seen in the weaker (though still visible) secondary cluster centered there. This seems like an artifact of his text's compositional history, given that the reunification of China under the Sui, which established their capital Chang'an as that of the entire empire (589 CE) (Lewis 2009), occurred approximately halfway through the period covered by Daoxuan's collection (519 – 645 CE). That said, it may also attest to the continued activity of the disciples of the great monks described in the original *Gaoseng zhuan*, some of whom would likely have stayed on at their previous monastic residences in

5 It should be noted that the coverage areas of these two maps exclude approximately 10% of the locations mentioned in both texts, all of which are found in Central and South Asia. That said, given their relative scarcity and wide geographical dispersion, they do not represent any form of cluster whatsoever, which I believe is sufficient grounds to justify their exclusion.

6 This count was arrived at by the simple expedient of charting a map centered on the Jiankang region (lon: 118.778, lat: 32.0514) (http://authority.dila.edu.tw/place/?fromInner=PL000000008975) and those sites within 150 km of it, which excluded 2307 of 3130 locations. It would obviously be possible to perform these calculations in code, but for the present preliminary project, I considered this level of precision to be sufficient.

spite of the capital's shift away from them. Regardless, the relative weakness of the Jiankang cluster, which is very faint in spite of the comparably equal compositional periods before and after the movement of the capital, could be taken as evidence that Daoxuan either chose to concentrate on episodes in and around Chang'an, perhaps in deference to his target audience, or was responding to a massive geographical shift in the typical locations of imperial patronage activity. It should be noted that these options are not mutually exclusive.

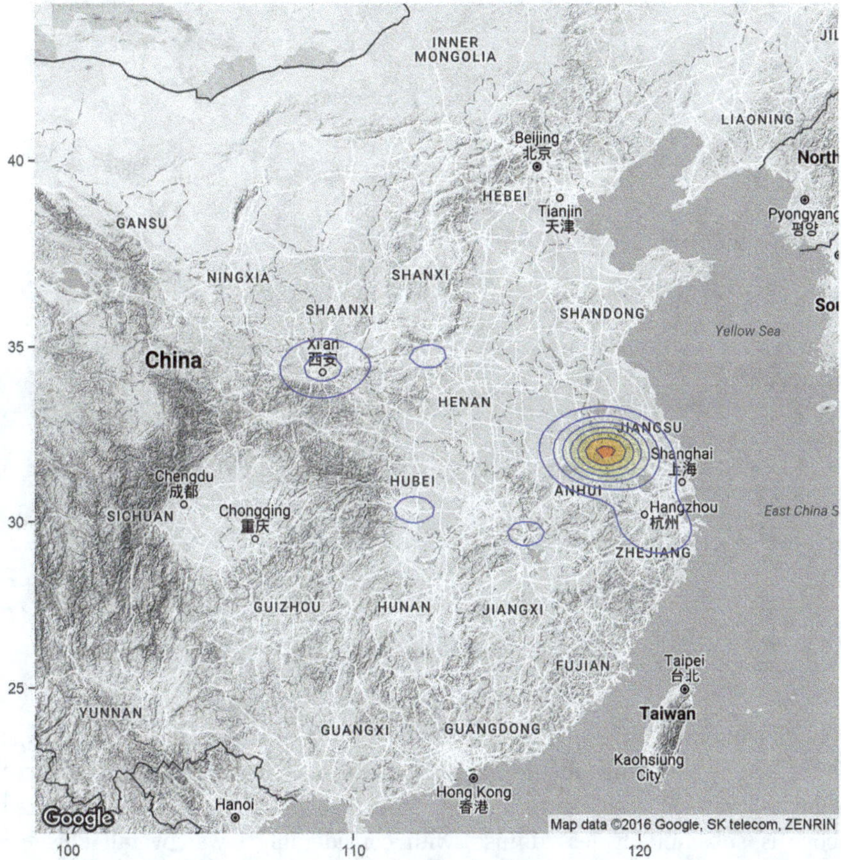


**Fig. 1:** Cluster Analysis of Locations Mentioned in *Gaoseng Zhuan*
(Plotted with Kahle and Wickham's *ggmap* [2013])

These two datasets, when considered in concert (i.e., with pronounced clusters at both Jiankang and Chang'an), bear a strong resemblance to the kernel density estimate map of Buddhist sites from the later Tang and Five Dynasties

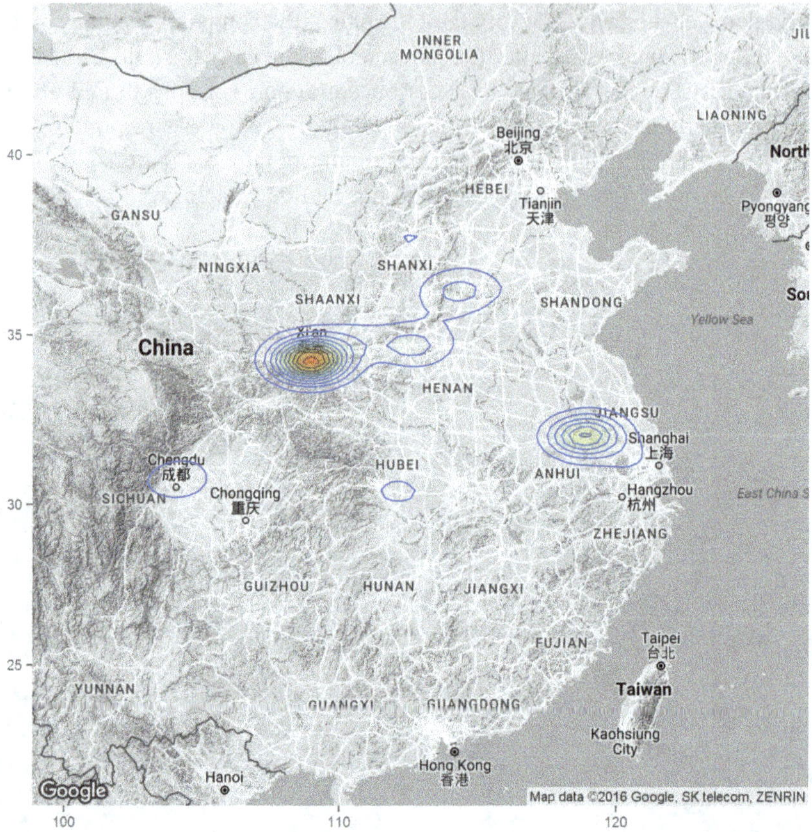


**Fig. 2:** Cluster Analysis of Locations Mentioned in *Xu gaoseng zhuan* (Plotted with Kahle and Wickham's *ggmap* [2013])

periods computed by Wu, Tong and Ryavec (2013), even though their map was derived via the far more labour intensive process of charting toponym references in local gazetteers (see Figure 3). That said, the *Eminent Monks* data pictured above is substantially less diffuse, with considerably fewer overall clusters. Just as a survey of contemporary American cinema would present an imaginary landscape in which New York and Los Angeles loom much larger than their actual demographics would warrant (given the concentration of writers and directors who dwell in both cities), the imagined geography of medieval Chinese Buddhism – at least as recorded in the *Biographies* corpus – seems substantially skewed toward the dwelling places of famous monks, many of whom dwelt in large monastic complexes supported by capital elites. Given the self-stroking cycle between tales of idealized monks and official patronage (Shinohara 1992; Shinohara 1997), it is perhaps unsurprising that these sites loomed large in the public imagination, distorting and simplifying the more nuanced perspective that Wu, *et al.* arrived at by considering the actual distribution of temples and monasteries during a slightly later period.

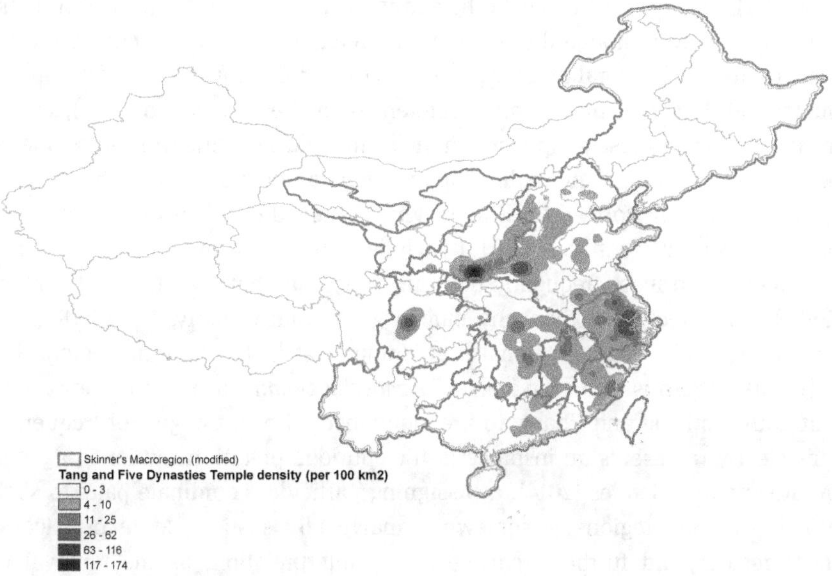


**Fig. 3:** Cluster Analysis of Temple Distributions in Tang / Five Dynasties (Wu, Tong and Ryavec [2013], p. 181, *reprinted with permission*)

The skewed geographical distribution of sites in the *Eminent Monks* corpus confirms the methodological intuition that inspired the present project: namely, that any attempt to discuss perceived patterns within these data without considering the geographical biases of the texts themselves is in danger of seriously overstating the significance of its findings. For a simplistic example, imagine a hypothetical study that excitedly notes that a large percentage of monks described in the "Exegetes" section of the *Gaoseng zhuan* are depicted as having practiced at monasteries in and around Jiankang. While this has the superficial semblance of being a meaningful finding, it is entirely possible that such a distribution would amount to nothing more than chance and selection bias, given the fact that around a third of *all* locations mentioned in the text fit this pattern.

Performing a simple frequency analysis of the data that produced the foregoing analysis (as per Blevins [2014a, 2014b]) provides additional insights, which will be explored individually for both of the source texts under consideration. For both ease of use and readability, I have chosen to concentrate specifically on those locations that were cited at least ten times in their respective texts. These results are presented Table 1, which lists the top ten locations (both general and religious) mentioned in each text. While the utility of attending to the top ten locations mentioned in such diverse texts seems meagre at best, it should be noted that both feature strikingly long-tailed distributions. For example, even though the *GSZ* includes reference to 869 discrete toponyms, the "top twenty" general and religious sites explored below account for approximately 30% of the total location references in the text (933 of 3133), which means that even these simple summaries can yield meaningful results. One of the first notable things about the "top ten" general locations is that the Dharma Drum team that performed the XML-tagging of named locations did not differentiate between different scales of toponym, which means that Jiankang was not only mentioned more frequently than any other city, but that it was also mentioned more frequently than any named geographical entity, from individual temples to entire macro-regions (e.g., India [印度], the Western Regions [西域]). This pattern is also seen in the *Xu gaoseng zhuan*, save that in the second text both Jiankang and Chang'an are mentioned with this degree of frequency. This clearly represents an instance of the spurious precision cautioned against by Gregory and Geddes (2014), as assigning particular coordinate pairs to such broadly defined regions is somewhat analytically suspect. More practically, these results lend further credence to my interpretation, as the removal of these spurious locations would only strengthen the clusters reported upon above, as very few of these spurious points are found within the existing mapped clusters.[7]

The coexistence of specific and general place names within the text (as mentioned above) is obviously explicable by their status as historical records, given that many of the monastic lives detailed therein describe individuals who were

7 Note: it would be possible, though methodologically problematic, to remove these specious identifiers. While virtually anyone would agree that assigning a single coordinate pair to the "Western Regions" is essentially meaningless, at what level of precision does this cease to be the case? Province? Commandery? Town? Even after making this (somewhat arbitrary) decision, attempting to parse out the locations thereby excluded would be a tremendous practical challenge, requiring a researcher to manually evaluate each of the 2605 unique named locations in the corpus. Given that the pattern described above is visible even in spite of these spurious points, I aver that – at least in the case of a pilot project like the present paper – the ease of replicability granted by employing the entire data-set is sufficient to offset the increased noise that it creates in the data.

born, studied in, or otherwise passed through India and the Western Regions, prior to arriving in China. That said, the juxtaposition of specificity in the Chinese case and extreme vagueness in the case of "foreign" regions, especially when the specific Chinese location mentioned is the capital, is precisely what one would expect of a cosmographic collection in the centripetally-directed, locative mode. Under such a system, narratives describing peripheral regions flowed into the imperial court, and were then collected and contextualized within the imperial context. As Campany (1996) notes, this editorial / curatorial mode is one in which "ultimate value is given to emplacing anomaly and domesticating the other, for these are the acts by which the cultural center is constructed" (14). While Campany's argument was made in the context of anomaly accounts *(zhiguai),* I would argue that the multifarious similarities in style, substance and authorial intent between *zhiguai* and Buddhist hagiographies justify this analogy. Regardless, none of this necessarily suggests any premeditation on the parts of Huijiao and Daoxuan; instead, I would argue that this pattern could have also emerged naturally from the selection of episodes that highlighted the relationship between these monks and their (potential) imperial patrons. That said, these collections attest, whether intentionally or otherwise, to the persistent reification of the bonds between individual monks and their imperial capitals through the imagined geographies that they helped to create and promulgate.

In addition, the simple rhetorical move of focusing on events that link the political center to the periphery is a good example of the process whereby prominent Buddhists, such as Huijiao and Daoxuan, attempted to place Buddhism into a dialectical relationship with the capital and its elite citizens (Kieschnick 1997, 7; Shinohara 1997). This process, whereby previously foreign models of sanctity came to be understood and propagated within the Chinese context (Keischnick 1997), is reflected in the gradual increase in the usage of specific, non-Chinese toponyms in the *Continued Biographies* as compared to its antecedent. For example, the river Ganges 恆河, Nalanda Monastery 那爛陀寺, and Oḍḍiyāna 烏仗那國 are all mentioned ten times in the *XGSZ*, compared to one, zero and two times (respectively) in *GSZ*. Conversely, the general toponym "Western Regions" (西域) is the fourth most common in *GSZ*, occurring sixty-one times, whereas it is only used twenty-four times in *XGSZ* (32nd most common); this is entirely consistent with the increasingly frequent use of specific "foreign" toponyms in the later text, which greatly decreased the utility of the general term. Both of these cases provide evidence of the process by which the imagined geography of medieval China expanded to encompass an increasingly detailed atlas of distant locales: locations that the vast majority of readers would only ever encounter textually and with which they were connected by shared Buddhist commitments.[8] This is in keeping with Daoxuan's aim, expressed both in *XGSZ* and in his other writings, of reconceptualizing China's place in the sacred geography of Buddhism, in order to transform it from a soteriologically peripheral realm, ever inferior to an idealized "India," to a site of new religious revelations, related (but not subordinate to) specific locations in South Asia (Nicol 2016; Young 2015).

A final intriguing observation can be made by examining the top ten religious sites named in each collection. With the exception of the Realm of Ultimate Bliss (極樂世界), which obviously has no corresponding geo-location, it is striking that there are no other commonalities between these lists of frequently cited locations. More broadly, and in keeping with the shifting religious geographies of medieval Chinese Buddhism, it is also notable that the *XGSZ* "top ten" list contains five entries utterly absent from the *GSZ*, whereas in the reverse situation, the *XGSZ* contains references to all but one of the most common religious locations from *GSZ*. The most likely explanation is that this represents an accurate picture of the vagaries of official patronage, through which new temples were built, and older temples renovated and renamed (Weinstein 1987), which implies that many of the sites present in *XGSZ* but absent from *GSZ* had not existed (at least under their later names) one hundred and fifty years earlier. That said, the persistence of many of these older sites within the later text suggests that Daoxuan, in compiling it, may have been caught between two editorial goals: reporting on the laudable activities of eminent monks from these older sites, and focusing on those temples and monasteries that were in close proximity to the new capital.

8 For a fascinating example of this process of (predominantly textual) negotiation, see Stuart Young (2015), *Conceiving the Indian Buddhist Patriarchs in China*, (Honolulu: University of Hawai'i Press).

**Tab. 1:** Location Frequencies by Text

| **General Toponyms in *Gaoseng zhuan* (T. 2059)** | | | |
|---|---|---|---|
| | Refs. | Name | Refs. in *XGSZ* |
| 1 | 188 | 建康 Jiankang | 171 |
| 2 | 82 | 關中 Guanzhong ("between the passes") | 67 |
| 3 | 70 | 長安 Chang'an | 181 |
| 4 | 61 | 西域 The Western Regions | 23 |
| 5 | 46 | 印度 Yindu (India) | 65 |
| 6 | 44 | 吳郡 Wu region | 29 |
| 7 | 40 | 洛陽 Luoyang | 73 |
| 8 | 39 | 中國 Zhongguo ("the Middle Kingdom") | 108 |
| 9 | 28 | 江南 Jiangnan | 62 |
| 10 | 26 | 龜茲 Qiuzi (Kucha) | 1 |

| **Religious Sites in *Gaoseng zhuan* (T. 2059)** | | | |
|---|---|---|---|
| | Refs. | Name | Refs. in *XGSZ* |
| 1 | 55 | 廬山 Lushan (Mt. Lu) | 27 |
| 2 | 33 | 瓦官寺 Waguansi | 12 |
| 3 | 32 | 中興寺 Zhongxingsi | 0 |
| 4 | 29 | 建初寺 Jianchusi | 30 |
| 5 | 28 | 上定林寺 Shang Dinglinsi | 8 |
| 6 | 24 | 祇洹寺 Qihuansi (Jetavana Temple) | 1 |
| 7 | 22 | 極樂世界 Jile shijie (Amitabha's Pure Land) | 39 |
| 8 | 21 | 天寧寺 Tianningsi | 3 |
| 9 | 17 | 長沙寺 Changshasi | 9 |
| 10a | 16 | 定林下寺 Dinglinxiasi | 9 |
| 10b | 16 | 東安寺 Dong'ansi | 7 |
| 10c | 16 | 草堂寺 Caotangsi | 4 |

**General Toponyms in *Xu gaoseng zhuan* (T. 2059)**

| | Refs. | Name | Refs. in *GSZ* |
|---|---|---|---|
| 1 | 181 | 長安 Chang'an | 70 |
| 2 | 171 | 建康 Jiankang | 188 |
| 3 | 144 | 大興 Daxing (Chang'an under the Sui Dynasty) | 0 |
| 4 | 103 | 中國 Zhongguo ("the Middle Kingdom") | 39 |
| 5 | 76 | 鄴縣 Ye district | 4 |
| 6 | 73 | 洛陽 Luoyang | 40 |
| 7 | 67 | 關中 Guanzhong ("between the passes") | 82 |
| 8 | 65 | 印度 Yindu (India) | 46 |
| 9 | 64 | 長安縣 Chang'an district | 0 |
| 10 | 62 | 江南 Jiangnan | 28 |

**Religious Sites in *Xu Gaoseng zhuan* (T. 2059)**

| | Refs. | Name | Refs. in *GSZ* |
|---|---|---|---|
| 1 | 95 | 大興善寺 Daxingshansi | 0 |
| 2 | 69 | 大莊嚴寺 Dazhuangyansi | 0 |
| 3 | 49 | 終南山 Zhongnanshan (Mt. Zhongnan) | 3 |
| 4 | 47 | 天臺山 Tiantaishan (Mt. Tiantai) | 2 |
| 5 | 39 | 極樂世界 Jile Shijie (Amitabha's Pure Land) | 22 |
| 6 | 38 | 莊嚴寺 Zhuangyansi | 9 |
| 7 | 36 | 總持寺 Zongchisi | 0 |
| 8 | 34 | 大開業寺 Dakaiyesi | 0 |
| 9 | 33 | 開善寺 Kaishansi | 6 |
| 10 | 33 | 慧日道場 Huiri daochang | 0 |

Note: This list was compiled by using the unique IDs assigned in the Dharma Drum / Academic Sinica datasets. The names listed here are those used as in the "primary name" field in their respective database entries.

## Case Study: Oneiric Practice

In order to test the methodological viability of attending to the skewed distribution of toponyms in the *Eminent Monks*, we now turn to my sample data set: accounts related to oneiric practice in both of the texts under consideration. In so doing, I return to the notion of "discourse communities" introduced above, which hypothesizes that different historical communities of Buddhists would have preserved and highlighted (or, contrastingly, minimized and elided) biographical materials based on the extent to which said narratives were compatible with their particular, localized ideologies and standards of practice (Campany 2012). As such, I was interested in approaching "oneiric practice" in this context, which I accomplished by seeking to explore the tendency of different communities of Buddhists to include stories about dreams (*meng* 夢) in their biographies. To this end, rather than focusing on what could be termed "first-order" oneiric practice, such as occurrences of specific types of dream incubation or monastic dream interpretation, I cast my net broadly, excluding only nominal uses (e.g., references to "Yunmeng marsh" [T. 2060: 561c6])[9] and usages within Huijiao and Daoxuan's explicitly commentarial materials, and thereby amassed a collection of all monastic biographies that mention dreams. I term this "second-order" oneiric practice: namely, the preservation and promulgation of biographical episodes related to dreams. As an aside, this approach had the added benefit of maximizing the sample size.

Given that Huijiao and Daoxuan made frequent use of monastic epitaphs in compiling these collections (Kieschnick 1997, 10–11), my admittedly coarse means of ascribing accounts to particular discourse communities (and thus to particular locations) was to specify the location of each monk by a single coordinate – namely, the site of their death.[10] Two advantages of this approach are, first, that it allowed for much greater precision than attempting to specify locations based solely on the narrative materials, given that the canonical biographies do not always proceed chronologically and that there is no guarantee that the monks' every relevant movement would have been recorded therein;

**9** To be clear, when Huijiao or Daoxuan make reference to this famous site, they are simply using its name (Yunmeng 雲夢), which happens to include the character *meng* ("dream").

**10** It should be noted that in a previous version of this paper, I employed a different mode of analysis, whereby I read through each account and attempted to determine where each described episode had taken place. Given the incompleteness and vagueness of many of these biographies, I noted at the time the provisional nature of any conclusions. I am grateful to Dr. Eric Greene for suggesting that focusing on sites of death would almost certainly provide more reliable results (personal communication).

and, second, these locations were extremely simple to track down, given that both Huijiao and Daoxuan's biographical collections include tables of contents wherein each monk is listed by era and place of death. The foregoing process resulted in 228 mappable data-points, 65 in *GSZ* and 163 in *XGSZ*, wherein each reference was tagged with the site of the monk's location of death. While this approach has its obvious drawbacks, in that it ignores any additional bias that would have been introduced during the compiling / editing process by Huijiao and Daoxuan, as well as overemphasizing the role of each monk's mortuary location in defining their subsequent biographies, I believe that it nonetheless represents the most reasonable method for generating a general picture of a medieval discourse community's hagiographical output, and, by proxy, of its "imagined geography."

When we compare Figure 4 with Figure 1 (i.e., the clusters of oneiric practice locations vs. all named locations in *GSZ*), we see a more-or-less identical distribution: a single, major cluster at Jiankang. Likewise, Figure 5 and Figure 2 (i.e., those pertaining to *XGSZ*) are similarly comparable, with visible clusters of approximately the same magnitude in both Jiankang *and* Chang'an. Though the outlines of the KDE clusters are slightly more capacious in both cases, this is simply an artifact of the process being run on substantially smaller samples. While it would be possible to define these relationships more formally,[11] in this case, it is visually apparent. As such, I would argue that, when it comes to second-order oneiric practice (as defined above), it would be methodologically irresponsible to use the *Eminent Monks* corpus as a means of arguing for any specific tradition of localized practice, even within the Jiankang and Chang'an clusters, given that it would be impossible to distinguish between that result and one emerging solely from underlying textual bias.

I must admit that I found this result somewhat surprising, given that I had believed I was detecting an emergent pattern when translating these materials, based on (for example) the sheer number of oneiric experiences reported in Zhiyi's biography. While the foregoing analysis obviously does not discount the fact that the discourse community surrounding Zhiyi considered visionary dreams to be meaningful events worthy of discussion and propagation, it does suggest that they were (seemingly) no more likely to discuss such experiences

---

**11** Though it was not necessary to do so for this preliminary exploration, I would propose that one could precisely calculate all locations at a given distance from any site by using the gdist() function in R's Imap package, which allows for the calculation of the geodesic distance between two sets of geolocation coordinates. I intend to formalize this process in future papers on this topic.

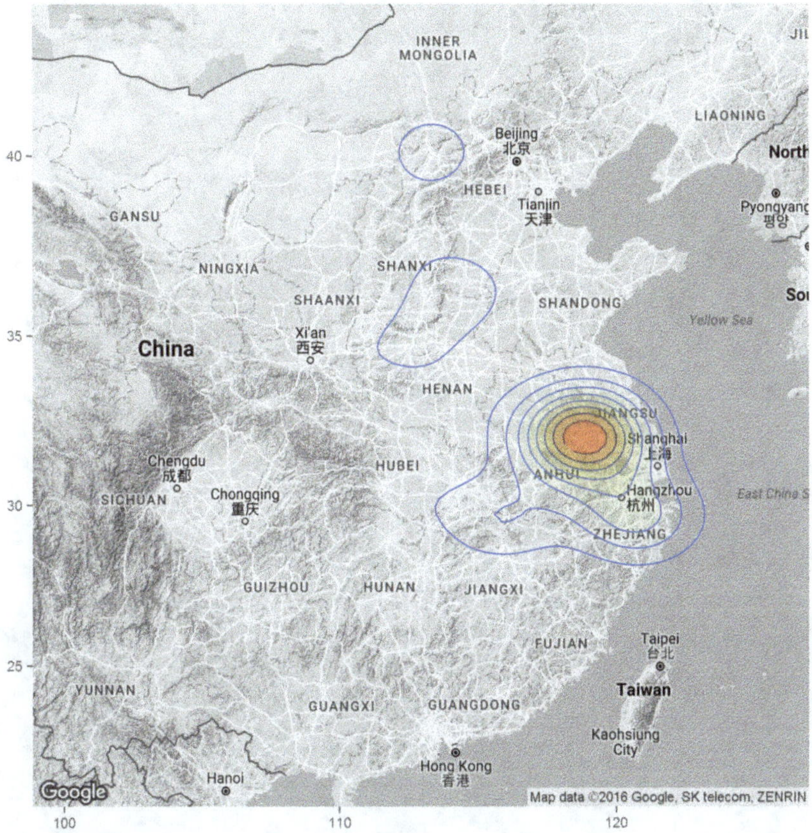


**Fig. 4:** Cluster Analysis of Second-Order Oneiric Practice in *Gaoseng zhuan* (Plotted with Kahle and Wickham's *ggmap* [2013])

than any other group of medieval Chinese monks:[12] an intriguing possibility in and of itself.

---

**12** It is notable that the results of my previously mentioned analysis, which employed the more methodologically problematic technique of attempting to discern the locations where each oneiric practice occurred based on the nearest relevant toponym included in the text of the biographies themselves, implied that certain locations in the Eastern cluster (i.e., the Jiankang area) seemed to be over-represented in the *XGSZ*'s coverage of these matters. When the two results are considered in tandem, one potential reading is that certain locations were sufficiently associated with first-order oneiric practice that they were equally likely to be described by monks from all discourse communities (second-order practice). This matter deserves further attention.

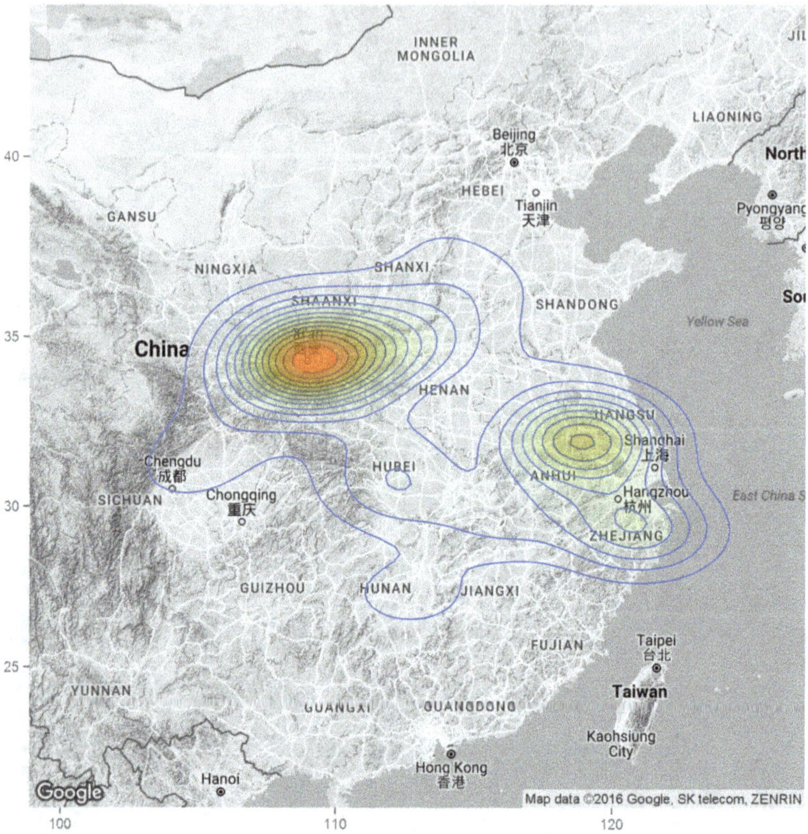


**Fig. 5:** Cluster Analysis of Second-Order Oneiric Practice in *Xu gaoseng zhuan* (Plotted with Kahle and Wickham's *ggmap* [2013])

## Conclusions

I believe that the present project highlights the sorts of compelling findings that can emerge at the intersection of traditional historical scholarship and data-driven digital analysis. More specifically, it demonstrates the applicability of the notion of "imagined geographies" to the medieval Chinese context and offers a preliminary attempt to graphically map out such geographies using data from the *Eminent Monks* corpus. Also, our test case, the type of "second-order" oneiric practice described above, serves as an important proof of concept, as it represents an instance where the distribution of a subset of the location data correlates closely with that of the entire dataset, implying that any perceived pattern might simply be an artifact of the editors' selection bias.

I look forward to future studies that employ the method proposed herein in order to investigate the geographical basis of any of the myriad textual and praxis traditions described in the *Eminent Monks*, and hope that the present paper has offered some useful insights into how this invaluable corpus can be used to draw more robust conclusions about spatial distributions in the medieval Chinese Buddhist context and the imaginative geographies that such distributions helped to inculcate and reify.

# References


高僧傳 *Gaoseng zhuan*. T. 2059.

續高僧傳 *Xu gaoseng zhuan*. T. 2060.

Anderson, Benedict. 2006. *Imagined Communities: Reflections on the Origin and Spread of Nationalism*. Revised Edition. London and New York: Verso.

Ayers, Edward L. 2010. "Turning Toward Space, Place, and Time." In *The Spatial Humanities: GIS and the Future of Humanities Scholarship*, edited by David J. Bodenhamer, John Corrigan, and Trevor M. Harris, 1–13. Bloomington, IN: Indiana University Press.

Benn, James A. 2007. *Burning for the Buddha: Self-Immolation in Chinese Buddhism*. Honolulu: University of Hawai'i Press.

Bingenheimer, Marcus, Hung Jen-Jou, and Simon Wiles. 2009. "Markup meets GIS – Visualizing the 'Biographies of Eminent Buddhist Monks.'" In *Proceedings of the International Conference on Information Visualization*. Accessed at: http://dh.obdurodon.org/GaosengZhuanGIS.pdf

Bodenhamer, David J. 2010. "The Potential of Spatial Humanities." In *The Spatial Humanities: GIS and the Future of Humanities Scholarship*, edited by David J. Bodenhamer, John Corrigan, and Trevor M. Harris, 14–30. Bloomington, IN: Indiana University Press.

Blevins, Cameron. 2014(a). "Mining and Mapping the Production of Space: A View of the World from Houston." *The Spatial History Project*. Accessed at: http://web.stanford.edu/group/spatialhistory/cgi-bin/site/pub.php?id=93

Blevins, Cameron. 2014(b). "Space, Nation, and the Triumph of Region: A View of the World from Houston." *Journal of American History*. Vol. 101(1): 122–147.

Campany, Robert Ford. 1996. *Strange Writing: Anomaly Accounts in Early Medieval China*. Albany, NY: State University of New York Press.

Campany, Robert Ford. 2012. *Signs from the Unseen Realm: Buddhist Miracle Tales from Early Medieval China*. Honolulu: University of Hawai'i Press.

Chan, Alan K. L. and Yuet-Keung Lo (eds.). 2011. *Interpretation and Literature in Early Medieval China*. Albany, NY: State University of New York Press.

Fields, Gary. 2011. "Enclosure Landscapes: Historical Reflections on Palestinian Geography." *Historical Geography* 39: 182–207.

Gregory, Derek. 1995. "Imaginative Geographies." *Progress in Human Geography*. 19(4): 447–485.

Gregory, Ian N. and Alistair Geddes. 2014. Introduction to *Toward Spatial Humanities: Historical GIS and Spatial History*, edited by Ian N. Gregory and Alistair Geddes, ix-xix. Bloomington, IN: Indiana University Press.

Gupta, Akhil and James Ferguson. 1992. "Beyond 'Culture': Space, Identity, and the Politics of Difference." *Cultural Anthropology* 7(1): 6–23.

Hsu, Wendy F. 2014. "Digital Ethnography Toward Augmented Empiricism: A New Methodological Framework." *Journal of Digital Humanities* 3(1). http://journalofdigitalhumanities.org/3–1/digital-ethnography-toward-augmented-empiricism-by-wendy-hsu/

Kahle, David and Hadley Wickham. 2013. "ggmap: Spatial Visualization with ggplot2." *The R Journal* 5 (1): 144–161.

Kemp, Karen K. 2010. "Geographic Information Science and Spatial Analysis for the Humanities," In *The Spatial Humanities: GIS and the Future of Humanities Scholarship*, edited by David J. Bodenhamer, John Corrigan, and Trevor M. Harris, 31–57. Bloomington, IN: Indiana University Press.

Kieschnick, John. 1997. *The Eminent Monk: Buddhist Ideals in Medieval Chinese Hagiography.* Honolulu: University of Hawai'i Press.

Knowles, Anne Kelly. 2008. Introduction to *Placing History: How Maps, Spatial Data, and GIS Are Changing Historical Scholarship*, edited by Anne Kelly Knowles, 1–26. Redlands, CA: ESRI Press.

Lewis, Mark Edward. 2009. *China Between Empires: The Northern and Southern Dynasties.* Cambridge, MA and London: The Belknap Press of Harvard University Press.

Li Youzheng. 2000–2001. "Modern Theory and Traditional Chinese Historiography." *NOAG* 167–70: 181–204.

Matthews, John A. and David D. Herbert. 2004. *Unifying Geography: Common Heritage, Shared Future.* London and New York: Routledge.

McRae, John. 1995. "Buddhism. (Chinese Religions: The State of the Field, Part II, Living Religious Traditions: Taoism, Confucianism, Buddhism, Islam and Popular Religion)." *Journal of Asian Studies* 54(2): 354–371.

Nicol, Janine. 2016. *Daoxuan (c. 596–667) and the Creation of a Buddhist Sacred Geography of China: An Examination of the* Shijia fangzhi 釋迦方志. PhD dissertation, SOAS.

Said, Edward. 1994. *Orientalism.* New York: Vintage Books.

Salguero, C. Pierce. 2010. *Buddhist Medicine in Medieval China: Disease, Healing and the Body in Crosscultural Translation (2nd to 8th Centuries CE).* Johns Hopkins University, Baltimore MD.

Shinohara Koichi. 1992. "Quanding's Biography of Zhiyi, the Fourth Patriarch of the Tiantai Tradition." In *Speaking of Monks: Religious Biography in India and* China, edited by Phyllis Granoff, 97–232. Oakville, ON: Mosaic Press.

Shinohara Koichi. 1997. "Biographies of Eminent Monks in a Comparative Perspective: The Function of the Holy in Medieval Chinese Buddhism." *Chung-Hwa Buddhist Journal* 7: 477–500.

Teiser, Stephen F. 1995. "Popular Religion. (Chinese Religions: The State of the Field, Part II, Living Religious Traditions: Taoism, Confucianism, Buddhism, Islam and Popular Religion)." *Journal of Asian Studies* 54(2): 378–395.

Verellen, Franciscus. 1995. "Taoism. (Chinese Religions: The State of the Field, Part II, Living Religious Traditions: Taoism, Confucianism, Buddhism, Islam and Popular Religion)." *Journal of Asian Studies* 54(2): 322–346.
Weinstein, Stanley. 1987. *Buddhism Under the T'ang*. Cambridge: Cambridge University Press.
Wu, Jiang, Daoqin Tong, and Karl Ryavec. 2013. "Spatial Analysis and GIS Modeling of Regional Religious Systems in China: Conceptualization and Initial Experiments." In *Chinese History in Geographical Perspective*, edited by Jeff Kyong-McClain and Yongtao Du, 179–196. Lanham, MD: Lexington Books.
Wu, Jiang. 2010. "Mapping Chinese Buddhist Monasteries: A Relational Database of Seventeenth-century Chinese Buddhism." Working Paper. Department of East Asian Studies, The University of Arizona. Accessed online at: https://arizona.academia.edu/JiangWu
Young, Stuart. 2015. *Conceiving the Indian Buddhist Patriarchs in China*. Honolulu: University of Hawai'i Press.

Christopher Handy

# A Context-Free Method for the Computational Analysis of Buddhist Texts

## Introduction to the Problem

This study demonstrates a practical method for extracting recurrent strings from digitized texts in cases where grammar, vocabulary and other information about the texts are partly or entirely unknown. My method involves building concordances of words and phrases from digitized input sets of texts, using a simple but effective pattern-recognition algorithm. The algorithm can be generalized to work with information in any language, but I restrict this study to just three major languages of the Buddhist tradition: classical Sanskrit, classical Tibetan and classical Chinese. I utilize free text files available in online databases so that my examples can be verified easily. I also provide C source code examples of the algorithm, available at a web link mentioned later in this paper.[1]

In modern English, and in many other modern languages, words in texts are separated by spaces, non-inflected, and essentially discrete particles that can be read as individual strings into a computer. A practical consequence of this linguistic feature is that computer spell-checkers, text search algorithms, and similar functions are computationally friendly (fast processing and small storage size for texts). Most computer programming languages in use today have string-analysis functions based on European languages using a standard roman character set. Unicode standards make it easier to input and output non-roman scripts, but the general string functions in C and Unix (and in later

Thanks to Lance Adams for providing use of his high-performance computing environment, a Linux cluster of 128 logical processors, which greatly reduced the processing time required for this project. While my computer program is able to run on an ordinary desktop computer (or notebook computer), having this extra power was of great benefit in testing the limits of the algorithm, allowing me to process entire corpora in a reasonable amount of time.

1 At the time this article was written, I was not aware of the very similar Tacl project by Michael Radich and Jamie Norrish, which is written in Python and specifically created to find patterns in Chinese Taishō texts from the CBETA project. As the documentation and interface for Tacl are more developed than those for my program, aks, scholars interested in trying these techniques for Chinese texts may find it easier to use that program instead. Full source code and documentation are available here: https://github.com/ajenhl/tacl and https://pythonhosted.org/tacl/

https://doi.org/10.1515/9783110519082-011

programming languages influenced by their shared paradigm) treat strings primarily as collections of individual roman characters.

Three languages of the Buddhist literary tradition – Sanskrit, Tibetan and Chinese – lack word boundary delimiters in their traditional manuscripts. A human being familiar with these languages can identify individual words in such manuscripts, but the texts have no spaces between words, such that we cannot locate words without prior knowledge of the language. As a result of this problem, digital concordances for Sanskrit, Tibetan and Chinese often require some amount of manual part-of-speech tagging before sending datasets to the computer. Numerous studies of Sanskrit, Tibetan and Chinese texts using such hybrid methods (e.g., Huet 2006, Hackett 2000, Zhan et al. 2006) have yielded useful information, but are unable to deal with unknown texts without some level of human intervention. Therefore, these tools are limited by the tagging efforts of human researchers. This limit is problematic in the large-scale analysis of Buddhist texts, in which we frequently find that we have only partial information about the contents of a set of texts. So, an ongoing issue even prior to automated semantic analysis or translation projects is the practical matter of how to find the boundaries of words. It is desirable to have a reliable parser that works on a variety of dynamic parsing rules, and which requires no user interaction.

Any language is necessarily composed of sets of repeating forms which in some way represent meaning. In natural languages, these sets of standard forms are always dynamic, mutating across time, region, and context. Dictionaries are therefore artificial constructs that act as maps to a language, but which do not restrict the actual expression of language in the world. If we accept that the very idea of a language presumes some level of relatively-fixed forms (i.e., the understanding that language patterns are maintained in a meaningful way over time, despite being dynamic overall), we can think of the vocabulary and speech patterns in a language as part of a concordance of frequently-appearing character strings within individual texts. This way of thinking about language is the key to my very simple method for processing texts.

## Sanskrit *akṣaras* and Strings

The basic unit of a written Sanskrit text is the *akṣara*, a consonant-vowel cluster represented in a single glyph. The Sanskrit syllabary contains 48 major consonant and vowel units that are combined to form these *akṣaras*. In general, an *akṣara* is a combination of between zero and five consonants and at least one vowel. While exceptions to these rules exist, we can use this basic definition to get a sense of how many possible *akṣaras* we might expect to find in Sanskrit texts. With 34 consonants (C) and 14 vowels (V), we can attempt a rough approximation of the total number of possible *akṣaras*:[2]

1 V: 14 *akṣaras*
1C + 1 V: 34 x 14 = 476 *akṣaras*
2C + 1 V: $34^2$ x 14 = 16,184 *akṣaras*
3C + 1 V: $34^3$ x 14 = 550,256 *akṣaras*
4C + 1 V: $34^4$ x 14 = 18,708,704 *akṣaras*
5C + 1 V: $34^5$ x 14 = 636,095,936 *akṣaras*
Total possible *akṣaras*: 655,371,570

There are not actually 655 million observed *akṣaras*. One reason is that certain sequences of consonants and vowels simply make no sense in Sanskrit. For example, the combination *ttttta* follows the rules proposed above, but does not ever seem to appear in Sanskrit texts. Likewise, we do not see the combinations *kcscbi*, *tjkmu*, *cmkmo*, or any of various other consonant-vowel clusters that do not agree with the rules of the language. The actual number of unique *akṣaras* appearing in these texts ranges from a few hundred to about three thousand, much smaller than the above calculations would suggest. However, it is impossible to construct a rule that accounts for every observed *akṣara* only, while leaving out "illegal" *akṣaras*, as the texts in question often do include *akṣaras* that are not technically permitted by the language. These appear due to scribal errors, regional differences of language, poetic license, or any number of other reasons. We cannot therefore rule out the possibility of finding *ttttta* or some other "illegal" *akṣara* construction in a text.

It is important to realize that the basic unit of the Sanskrit manuscript is this *akṣara* unit and not the roman characters that often make up a manuscript's digital counterpart. Most string-searching functions for digital computers treat individual roman characters as the smallest units within a string, and yet when dealing with Sanskrit strings, this notion can lead to erroneous conclusions. Consider the following two strings: *buddha* and *budda*. A typical string function created to analyze roman characters would take the first string to be composed of six characters, and the second to be composed of five characters: {*b*, *u*, *d*, *d*, *h*, *a*} and {*b*, *u*, *d*, *d*, *a*}. Breaking the strings into their constituent *akṣaras*, we see that they are composed of two *akṣaras* each: {*bu*, *ddha*} and {*bu*, *dda*}. This small difference is not negligible when it comes to doing text processing at large scales,

2 Special endings of characters were not taken into account here. The total number of consonants and vowels may be counted differently depending on specific purposes.

since statistics about the text will be skewed by the framework of roman-character analysis instead of *akṣara* analysis. We must therefore take the *akṣara* to be the basic atomic unit of the Sanskrit text if we are to analyze reliably the common words and phrases found in our sample corpora. For example, this selection from a digitized Mahāyāna Buddhist text, *Ārya Ṁaitreya-Vyākaraṇaṃ*, is easily read by humans but inappropriate for our purposes:

> śāriputro mahāprajñaḥ dharmasenāpatibibhuḥ|
> lokānāmanukampāya śāstāraṁ paryapṛcchata||1||
> sūtrāntare purā'khyātaṁ yaṁ lokanāyakasya ca|
> buddhasyānāgatasya hi maitreyanāma śāsanaṁ||2||
> vyākhyāhi tadvalaṁ cāpi ṛddhiṁ sarvārthavardhanaṁ|
> śrotumicchāma eva ca nāyakasya narottama||3||

whereas the following representation, easier for the computer to parse, is much better:

```
śā ri pu tro ma hā pra jñaḥ dha rma se nā pa ti bi bhuḥ
lo kā nā ma nu ka mpā ya śā stā raṁ pa rya pṛ ccha ta
sū trā nta re pu rā khyā taṁ yaṁ lo ka nā ya ka sya ca
bu ddha syā nā ga ta sya hi mai tre ya nā ma śā sa naṁ
vyā khyā hi ta dva laṁ cā pi ṛ ddhiṁ sa rvā rtha va rdha naṁ
śro tu mi cchā ma e va ca nā ya ka sya na ro tta ma
```

The first selection above is from the Digital Sanskrit Buddhist Canon version of the *Ārya Ṁaitreya-Vyākaraṇaṃ*, available at <http://www.dsbcproject.org/canon-text/content/26/261>. I obtained the second selection by creating a computer program in the language C to break *akṣara*s from the source text, in accordance with the rules I mentioned previously for *akṣara* formation. My algorithm reads characters from a text file until it encounters a vowel or other appropriate terminating character (e. g., *ḥ* or *ṁ*), and then stores the complete string of roman characters in a custom structure defined as "akshara" in the program. Spaces, periods, asterisks, and any other symbols that are not part of the Sanskrit syllabary are ignored. This method of processing only characters legally allowed in the language helps to filter out problems of line breaks, editors' notes, and other extraneous information.

After converting a text in this way, certain questions about the nature of the texts can be answered quite easily. While the rule for 5C+1 V *akṣara*s suggests over 655 million potential unique *akṣara* glyphs, my own observation after running my program is that only a few hundred to a few thousand unique *akṣara*s actually appear in any single text. We can utilize this fact – that the total unique *akṣara*s in a given text is so small – in at least two distinct ways, to create something like a "fingerprint" for a given text. First, since the number of unique *akṣaras* is finite and also relatively small, the observed set of *akṣaras* in a text can provide a quick basis for comparison between two texts. It may be true, for example, that Sanskrit Mahāyāna texts utilize certain *akṣaras* that never appear at all in the Sanskrit texts of mainstream Buddhism, due to specialized vocabulary or for some other reason. Or, we might find that the authors of our texts have significantly different writing styles that can be measured in this simple way. Second, we can search the texts based on these *akṣaras* in a way that is faster and more true to the original nature of the manuscripts themselves. We can then create sets of commonly-occurring *akṣara* sequences, and use these as a basis for extracting the vocabulary and common phrases found in the texts. Retrieving such information from the texts is a useful starting point in genre analysis and other applications.

## Strings of Connected *akṣaras*

My C program runs through every possible string of 'n' *akṣaras* in every text of the sample set, where 'n' is any number desired by the user. I refer to strings of connected *akṣaras* as n-grams, a term borrowed from computational linguistics. N-grams can be named by their specific 'n' size as 1-gram, 2-gram, 3-gram and so forth. My program counts each n-gram (sequence of *akṣaras*) in a given text, and then creates a concordance file for that text. These concordance files are then combined to form a concordance file for the entire corpus. For example, searching on 'n'=4 among a sample set of major Sanskrit Mahāyāna texts, I found the sequence *bo-dhi-sa-ttva* appearing frequently in many different texts. If this sequence appears more frequently in Mahāyāna texts than in mainstream texts, it could be used as an identifier for the Mahāyāna genre.

We do not really know which sequences will be the most useful, however, until we begin processing a corpus. That makes this concordance method somewhat different from a standard concordance, because we do not know the appropriate words of the genre in advance, and we are also not necessarily looking for words themselves as tokens. The n-grams are formed from sequences of 'n' *akṣaras*, and their boundaries determined by those *akṣaras*, so the n-grams themselves do not always constitute words. In the case of genre classification, it may be that partial words, or strings that fall between word boundaries, or strings that extend beyond word boundaries, work better as tokens. Or, it may be the case that exact words form more appropriate tokens. It is likely that some combination of the above will lead to the most suitable fingerprint for our text genre, so we must assume that any string of connected *akṣaras* is relevant. Therefore, we will record every single string of n-length *akṣaras*. This process is necessarily redundant, and requires later filtering of the data, but it ensures that nothing is overlooked.

Given the following *akṣara* sequence,

```
śā ri pu tro ma hā pra jñaḥ dha rma se nā pa ti bi bhuḥ
```

with an n-gram length of 4, my program outputs the following to its concordance file:

śāriputro
riputroma
putromahā
tromahāpra
mahāprajñaḥ
hāprajñaḥdha
prajñaḥdharma

and so forth to the end of the file. It does not matter if the above n-grams are complete words or not. The program is ignorant about the meaning of the text, simply recording everything it finds in the file. After the concordances are created, they are then sorted based on how many instances of each n-gram appear. In the source text used for the above selection, the 4-gram *śā-ri-pu-tro* appears only once in the entire text, and so that sequence does not appear to be very significant in terms of the content of the text. However, it may still be useful for establishing a genre theme (e. g., all stories about the monk Śāriputra).

The initial n-gram file created using this method will necessarily be larger than the original source file, by a factor of the 'n' value. For example, the complete text file for the *Ārya ṃaitreya-vyākaraṇaṃ* is only 14 kilobytes, but the 4-gram file is approximately 56 kilobytes. At small n-gram values this size increase does not pose much of a problem, but eventually becomes significant for very large values of 'n'. In my experience, the most common token words in Sanskrit are below 8 *akṣaras*, and so I have limited my exploration of these texts to n-grams from 1 to 8 in this sample demonstration. However, the size of the file is reduced dramatically after the initial indexing, and the algorithm used to process the n-grams takes approximately the same length of time to complete regardless of the 'n' value, so even very large n-grams can be processed using this method. Since the source files are stored as UTF-8 Unicode characters, they tend to be small, mostly under 1 MB each. Therefore, it is even possible to use values of 'n' up to 'n'=50 or greater without much concern about file size.

## Measuring *akṣara* Sequence Frequency

I applied my algorithm to two different sets of Sanskrit Buddhist texts available online: a set of 17 texts from the *Mūlasarvāstivāda Vinaya* (hereafter abbreviated MSV), and a set of 37 major Mahāyāna texts. The MSV texts are from GRETIL, the Göttingen Register of Electronic Texts in Indian Languages (http://gretil.sub.uni-goettingen.de), and the Mahāyāna texts are from the Digital Sanskrit Buddhist Canon (http://www.dsbcproject.org).

Below, I provide two tables listing sample data from the output of my *akṣara* concordance program. These tables show the most frequent 2-gram, 4-gram and 8-grams for each of the 37 texts in our sample Mahāyāna corpus with number of occurrences in parentheses, and the same information for each of the 17 texts in our MSV corpus. Since the program outputs the frequency of every single n-gram in the text, it generates much more data than what is listed below. This process leads to a great deal of extraneous data, but it is automatically sorted in such a way that such data are easy to disregard. By sorting on the frequency of occurrences, we can easily remove any *akṣara* sequences that occur only once, or below any threshold of our choice. From these tables, we can observe that some Mahāyāna texts share certain themes. For example, variations of the term *bodhisattva* occur frequently enough to be the top 4-gram or 8-gram in many of the Mahāyāna texts below. This fact should not be surprising to anyone familiar with Mahāyāna literature, but when we keep in mind that the computer has no idea what it is looking for, it is useful to know that such terms naturally bubble to the surface.

| **Mahāyāna text** | **2-gram** | **4-gram** | **8-gram** |
|---|---|---|---|
| *Ajītasenavyākaranaṃ Sūtra* | bhaga (91) | mahāśrāva (38) | nandimitramahāśrāva (16) |
| *Aparimitāyuḥ Sūtra* | pari (48) | parimitā (34) | mobhagavateetcaspa (28) |
| *Arthaviniścayasūtram* | prati (124) | hāpuruṣa (62) | yathābhūtaṁprajānāti (39) |
| *Ārya-maitreya-vyākaraṇaṁ* | ṣyati (52) | bhaviṣyati (21) | maitreyasyānuśāsane (4) |
| *Āryanityatā* | mara (26) | pitebhikṣa (9) | vasānaṁnāstijātasyā (7) |
| *Āryapratītyasamutpādo* | samu (7) | tītyasamu (6) | tītyasamutpādonāma (2) |
| *Āryarāṣṭrapālaparipṛcchā* | **bodhi** (103) | rāṣṭrapāla (55) | rāṣṭrapāla**bodhisattvā** (30) |
| *Āryasāgaranāgarājaparipṛcchā* | mahā (8) | ṣṭamakṣaya (4) | ṣṭamakṣayajñānaṁprava (4) |
| *Āryasaṁghāta* | bhaga (44) | bhaiṣajyase (150) | gavantametadavoca (49) |

*Continued*

| Mahāyāna text | 2-gram | 4-gram | 8-gram |
|---|---|---|---|
| *Āryatriratnānusmṛtisūtram* | prati (11) | triratnānu (3) | ryatriratnānusmṛtisū (3) |
| *Āryatriskandha* | namo (23) | śriyenamo (5) | ḍitābhijñāyatathāga (2) |
| *Āryavimalakīrtinirdeśo* | **bodhi** (335) | śāriputra (86) | licchavirvimalakīrti (44) |
| *Bhaiṣajyaguruvaidūrya.*[3] | tasya (81) | tathāgata (41) | ṣajyaguruvaidūryapra (32) |
| *Bhavasaṅakrāntisūtram* | mavi (15) | mahārāja (11) | yatravipākasyaprati (2) |
| *Catuṣpariṣat* | **bodhi** (24) | yāṁviharaṁ (11) | dhisattvobhagavānuru (10) |
| *Daśabhūmikasūtram* | dhisa (452) | **bodhisattva** (316) | yathābhūtaṁprajānāti (48) |
| *Daśabhūmikasūtre gāthāvibhāgaḥ* | sarva (158) | **bodhisattva** (90) | vataratiapramāṇaṁ (18) |
| *Gaṇḍavyūhasūtram* | sarva (4448) | **bodhisattva** (1619) | kṣetraparamāṇurajaḥ (201) |
| *Guṇakāraṇḍavyūhasūtram* | samā (723) | jagaddhite (103) | triratnabhajanaṁkṛtvā (34) |
| *Kāraṇḍavyūhaḥ* | nāma (339) | lokiteśva (176) | sarvanīvaraṇaviṣka (61) |
| *Karuṇāpuṇḍarīka-sūtram* | **bodhi** (797) | samyaksaṁbo (317) | nuttarāyāṁsamyaksaṁbo (195) |
| *Kāsyapaparivartasūtram* | kāśya (304) | damucyate (75) | dyathāpināmakāśyapa (47) |
| *Lalitavistaraḥ* | **bodhi** (1068) | **bodhisattva** (449) | tihibhikṣavobodhisa (33) |
| *Madhyamaka-śālistambasūtram* | vati (58) | bhavatia (29) | syāpinaivaṁbhavatia (11) |
| *Mahāmeghasūtram* | samu (143) | samudrame (121) | siṁhāsanasamudrame (20) |
| *Mahāparinirvāṇa* | bhaga (291) | mantrayate (43) | yuṣmānānandobhagava (34) |
| *Mahāvadānasūtram* | vāca (77) | tasminkāle (21) | ddhastadāgāthayovāca (7) |
| *Nairātmyaparipṛcchā* | prāhuḥ (13) | mahāyāni (8) | bodhicittasyalakṣaṇa (7) |
| *Saddharmalaṅkāvatārasūtram* | hāma (1103) | mahāmate (738) | naraparaṁmahāmate (66) |
| *Saddharmapuṇḍarīkasūtram* | bhaga (875) | śrāvakayā (14) | ṭīnayutaśatasaha (146) |

3 *Bhaiṣajyaguruvaidūryaprabharajasūtram*

*Continued*

| Mahāyāna text | 2-gram | 4-gram | 8-gram |
|---|---|---|---|
| *Śālistambasūtram* | tia (72) | bhavatia (36) | pinaivaṁbhavatiahaṁ (17) |
| *Samādhirājasūtram* | samā (586) | **bodhisattvo** (112) | māra**bodhisattvo**mahā (38) |
| *Sarvatathāgatādhiṣṭhānavyūham* | sarva (107) | tathāgata (44) | gavantametadavoca (12) |
| *Sukhāvatīvyūhaḥ(saṁkṣip-tamātṛkā)* | thāga (57) | śāriputra (41) | śāriputrabuddhakṣetra (6) |
| *Sukhāvatīvyūhaḥ[vistaramātṛkā]* | buddha (158) | samyaksaṁbo (69) | ttarāṁsamyaksaṁbodhima (55) |
| *Suvarṇaprabhāsasūtram* | pari (275) | varṇaprabhā (102) | suvarṇaprabhāsottama (53) |
| *Vinayaviniścaya Upāliparipṛcchā* | **bodhi** (48) | mahāyāna (26) | sthitānāṁ**bodhisattvā**nāṁ (9) |

The MSV corpus also exhibits certain patterns. While the term *bodhisattva* is entirely absent from the MSV table below, we do see that the term *kathayati* ("he tells") occurs frequently enough to be the top 2-gram in several MSV texts. When we compare the MSV texts with the Mahāyāna texts, we can see that there is also some overlap between terms. For example, the 2-gram *bhaga* (probably from *bhagavān*, "lord" and its variations) appears as a top 2-gram several times in both the Mahāyāna and MSV corpora.

| MSV text | 2-gram | 4-gram | 8-gram |
|---|---|---|---|
| *Pravrajyāvastu* | thaya (169) | **kathayati** (79) | tasyamamaitadabhava (22) |
| *Poṣadhavastu* | poṣa (164) | nimittaṃvā (88) | prātimokṣasūtroddeśa (30) |
| *Pravāraṇāvastu* | vāra (307) | pravāraṇā (123) | yāpravāraṇayāpravā (30) |
| *Varṣāvastu* | raṇī (85) | sminnāvāse (50) | nāpattirvarṣācchedea (28) |
| *Carmavastu* | **yati** (120) | **kathayati** (69) | ṇaṃbhikṣavobhagavata (15) |
| *Bhaiṣajyavastu* | bhaga (840) | tahastama (13) | nabhagavāṃstenopasaṃ (41) |
| *Cīvaravastu* | **yati** (348) | **kathayati** (217) | gavantamidamavoca (26) |
| *Kaṭhinavastu* | cīva (203) | cīvaraṃka (52) | stīrṇakaṭhinādāvāsā (43) |
| *Kośāmbakavastu* | tkṣipta (52) | kānuvarta (38) | tpannaḥkalahobhaṇḍanaṃ (18) |
| *Karmavastu* | karma (154) | dharmakarma (70) | kurvantiadharmakarma (18) |

*Continued*

| MSV text | 2-gram | 4-gram | 8-gram |
|---|---|---|---|
| *Pāṇḍulohitakavastu* | prati (491) | praticchannā (189) | ttipratirūpāyāḥprati (116) |
| *Pudgalavastu* | māpa (236) | pattimāpa (104) | vaśeṣāmāpattimāpa (102) |
| *Pārivāsikavastu* | rivā (83) | pārivāsi (36) | śukravisṛṣṭisamutthi (11) |
| *Poṣadhasthāpanavastu* | poṣa (109) | ṣadhasthāpa (67) | rmikaṃpoṣadhasthāpana (42) |
| *Śayanāsanavastu* | bhaga (216) | nāthapiṇḍa (96) | nāthapiṇḍadogṛhapa (47) |
| *Adhikaraṇavastu* | kara (323) | dhikaraṇa (141) | tadadhikaraṇaṃvyupa (28) |
| *Saṃghabhedavastu* | bhaga (1422) | **kathayati** (623) | lenatenasamayena (99) |

# Shared and Unique Sequences within Corpora

We can combine lists of the frequently-recurring sequences from each text into a master list of sequences for each corpus, producing a list of all recurring *akṣara* sequences in the Mahāyāna corpus along with their frequency, and the same for the MSV corpus. Below are the most common 4-grams and 8-grams in the Mahāyāna and MSV corpora:

| Mahāyāna 4-gram | Mahāyāna 8-gram | MSV 4-gram | MSV 8-gram |
|---|---|---|---|
| bodhisattva (3343) | nuttarāyāṁsamyaksaṁbo (451) | kathayati (1367) | bhagavataārocaya (166) |
| tathāgata (2096) | ttarāyāṁsamyaksaṁbodhau (436) | bhagavanā (550) | vaśeṣāmāpattimāpa (166) |
| kulaputra (1346) | nuttarāṁsamyaksaṁbodhi (320) | gavānāha (520) | ghāvaśeṣāmāpattimā (166) |
| śatasaha (1298) | samyaksaṁbodhimabhisaṁ (303) | sakathaya (499) | gavataārocayanti (166) |
| bodhisattvā (1289) | ttarāṁsamyaksaṁbodhima (302) | samayena (458) | nakālenatenasama (164) |
| samyaksaṁbo (901) | rāṁsamyaksaṁbodhimabhi (297) | kathayanti (405) | kālenatenasamaye (164) |
| bodhisattvo (874) | thāgatorhansamyaksaṁbu (266) | saṃlakṣaya (372) | lenatenasamayena (163) |

*Continued*

| Mahāyāna 4-gram | Mahāyāna 8-gram | MSV 4-gram | MSV 8-gram |
|---|---|---|---|
| athakhalu (860) | kṣetraparamāṇurajaḥ (262) | damavoca (372) | vobhagavataāroca (159) |
| lokadhātu (812) | ddhakṣetraparamāṇura (260) | lakṣayati (356) | kṣavobhagavataāro (159) |
| sahasrāṇi (746) | traparamāṇurajaḥsa (259) | bhagavatā (346) | tatprakaraṇaṃbhikṣavo (153) |
| mahāmate (740) | buddhakṣetraparamāṇu (250) | midamavo (332) | tprakaraṇaṃbhikṣavobha (152) |
| buddhakṣetra (647) | gavantametadavoca (241) | ghāvaśeṣā (311) | raṇaṃbhikṣavobhagava (152) |
| tasahasrā (637) | bhagavantametadavo (236) | gṛhapati (303) | karaṇaṃbhikṣavobhaga (152) |
| dhisattvasya (616) | ṭīnayutaśatasaha (224) | praticchannā (298) | bhikṣavobhagavataā (152) |
| tadavoca (610) | koṭīnayutaśatasa (224) | tisakatha (292) | ṇaṃbhikṣavobhagavata (151) |
| sarvasattva (599) | paramāṇurajaḥsamā (205) | tadabhava (288) | gavantamidamavoca (150) |
| sattvomahā (578) | myaksaṁbodhimabhisaṁbu (205) | rvavadyāva (280) | ārocayantibhagavā (135) |
| tathāgatā (571) | ṭīniyutaśatasaha (196) | saṃghāvaśe (278)* | tenakālenatenasa (135) |

After generating these lists, I used some standard Unix commands (sort, join, uniq and comm) to sort and join the lists together to form three more specialized lists of n-grams: 1) A list of all n-grams that occur in *both* corpora, 2) A list of all n-grams that occur *only* in the Mahāyāna corpus, and 3) A list of all n-grams that occur *only* in the MSV corpus. All three of these lists tell us different things in our search for common features of the Mahāyāna genre. List 2 is perhaps the most useful here, as it gives us sequences that absolutely are not found in the MSV corpus. A selection of the most-frequent n-grams in the Mahāyāna-only list is given here:

| | | |
|---|---|---|
| mahāyāna | Mahāsāha | bodhicaryā |
| bodhimaṇḍa | Yānasūtra | sugatāna |
| jinaputra | lokamukhaṃ | gatadharma |

| | | |
|---|---|---|
| gatadharma | Daśabuddha | ekaikasmā |
| vyāhāreṇa | sattvacaryāṃ | gandharvaka |
| pariśuddhi | gaṅgānadī | kulaputro |
| bodhisattvai | Vakapratye | sattvakoṭī |

Many of the sequences above are things we might expect to see when looking at Mahāyāna text. Certainly it is no surprise to find the word *mahāyāna* among the Mahāyāna-unique sequences in the list. However, its presence does not tell us very much about what Mahāyāna texts are as a genre. Unfortunately, the vast majority of n-grams that my program reports as unique to the Mahāyāna corpus occur less than fifty times in the entire set, some only appearing once. These items, which are frequently just fragments of overlapping rare words, do not tell us much of anything about the Mahāyāna in its origins or otherwise. It would seem that creating absolute lists of words that are either entirely members of a set or excluded from that set is not an ideal way to approach the problem of genre identification, although this method does appear to be a viable way of creating a list of vocabulary terms in a more general way.

## Applications in Tibetan Language

We can apply the same method to Tibetan texts, with some slight modification to the syllable-parsing portion of the algorithm. Tibetan, like Sanskrit, is composed of sequences of consonant-vowel syllables. Individual syllables are written as discrete glyphs, with space between each glyph, but no additional spaces or other consistent markings to indicate word boundaries. As with Sanskrit, we are faced with the difficult problem of determining where words actually begin and end. However, unlike Sanskrit, it is customary when preparing digital versions of Tibetan texts to retain these distinct syllables as they appear in the original manuscripts, and not edit the file to produce words.

For the purposes of this experiment, I am using the digital editions of the *Degé Kangyur* from the Asian Classics Input Project (http://asianclassics.org). My primary reason for choosing this specific collection is very simple – it is available to the public for free. In addition, ACIP provides its texts in roman transliteration and also in Tibetan Uchen script using Unicode characters. As my initial program was created for processing roman characters, I began my analysis using the ACIP roman transliteration. For the sake of completeness, I also modified the program slightly to allow it to process the Tibetan character version as well. I present these two sets of data below. As we shall see, there is some discrepancy between the two collections. I have not yet determined if this is due to a parsing problem in the program or inconsistencies between the two text collections. In any case, the results are consistent enough to demonstrate the basic ideas of this context-free method for text analysis. Other collections of texts may prove to yield better results at a later time, but as the current research is a proof of concept, I did not consider it necessary to spend time investigating that matter. In the following sections, I apply my algorithm to two sets of texts from these roman and Tibetan script versions of the *Degé Kangyur* – one is a set of *'dul ba* (=Sanskrit *vinaya)* texts, and the other is a set of *mdo mang* (=Sanskrit *sūtra)* texts. These text collections were chosen as being roughly parallel to my earlier experiment on Sanskrit *vinaya* and Mahāyāna texts.

# Tibetan Syllables as Atomics

Classical Tibetan comprises 30 consonants and 4 vowels. The minimum syllable length represented as a unique glyph is one consonant or vowel. A syllable in Tibetan is much the same as an *akṣara* in Sanskrit, being the absolute description of a unique glyph. However, the rules for opening and ending Tibetan syllables necessitate different rules in the computer for determining syllable boundaries. Fortunately, it is common practice to preserve the individuality of Tibetan syllables within digitized roman-character texts by means of whitespace, or in Tibetan script by means of the *tsheg* symbol, a small dot (་). It is still necessary to tell our program to extract only this syllable information and not any extra notations or other markings provided by the texts' editors.

As a brief example, here is a selection from one of the *'dul ba* texts named kl00001e1.txt:

```
@1 A *, ,'DUL BA KA PA BZHUGS SO, ,
@1B *, ,'DUL 'DZIN CHEN PO GNAS BRTAN NYE BAR 'KHOR, ,
#, ;@1B [DD] #, ,RGYA GAR SKAD DU [DD] BI NA YA BASTU, BOD [DD]
SKAD DU, 'DUL BA GZHI, BAM PO DANG PO, DKON
MCHOG GSUM LA PHYAG 'TSAL LO, ,GANG GIS
'CHING RNAMS YANG DAG RAB BCAD CING, ,MU
@2 A [DD] #, ,STEGS TSOGS RNAMS THAMS CAD RAB BCOM STE, ,SDE DANG
BCAS PA'I
BDUD RNAMS NGES BCOM NAS, ,BYANG CHUB 'DI BRNYES DE LA PHYAG
'TSAL LO, ,KHYIM
```

From the above selection it is clear that the ACIP edition of the *Degé Kangyur* uses capitalized roman characters A–Z to represent unique Tibetan glyphs, as well as the apostrophe character as a representation of the *'a-chung* (འ). My algorithm treats connected sets of these characters, separated on each end by whitespace, as individual syllables. Any other characters are stripped out. Below is a syllable-corrected version of the same text:

A 'DUL BA KA PA BZHUGS SO
B 'DUL 'DZIN CHEN PO GNAS BRTAN NYE BAR 'KHOR
B DD RGYA GAR SKAD DU DD BI NA YA BASTU BOD DD
SKAD DU 'DUL BA GZHI BAM PO DANG PO DKON
MCHOG GSUM LA PHYAG 'TSAL LO GANG GIS

We can see that there are certain problematic characters, in this case A, B, and DD, that are not always representative of syllables from the original manuscript but nevertheless included in the program's list of syllables. It is possible to strip these out using more complex processing rules (for example, the unwelcome 'A' and 'B' above are preceded by the '@' symbol, and so we could check for the code '@' + numeral + roman character and filter these out), but I have found that generally these additions to the text are statistically insignificant and naturally removed during the frequency-measuring portion of the algorithm. So, while the above selection is not a perfect representation of the original manuscript, it is for all practical purposes close enough that such extraneous characters do not significantly alter the output.

## Strings of Connected Tibetan Syllables

As with our Sanskrit example, we can create n-grams of any length from these Tibetan syllables. Once again, we have no idea prior to performing the frequency analysis which n-grams will be representative of Tibetan words and phrases. However, since the nature of language in general is based on the simple idea of repeating patterns, we can be confident that patterns occurring frequently in the collection of texts will be representative of meaning. So, just as with Sanskrit, we will parse each text redundantly in terms of all of its possible n-grams, from size 1 to 8 (an underscore has been added by the program to make the syllables easier for humans to read):

| 1-gram | 2-gram | 3-gram | 4-gram |
|---|---|---|---|
| A | A_'DUL | A_'DUL_BA | A_'DUL_BA_KA |

*Continued*

| 1-gram | 2-gram | 3-gram | 4-gram |
|---|---|---|---|
| 'DUL | 'DUL_BA | 'DUL_BA_KA | 'DUL_BA_KA_PA |
| BA | BA_KA | BA_KA_PA | BA_KA_PA_BZHUGS |
| KA | KA_PA | KA_PA_BZHUGS | KA_PA_BZHUGS_SO |
| PA | PA_BZHUGS | PA_BZHUGS_SO | PA_BZHUGS_SO_B |

| 5-gram | 6-gram |
|---|---|
| A_'DUL_BA_KA_PA | A_'DUL_BA_KA_PA_BZHUGS |
| 'DUL_BA_KA_PA_BZHUGS | 'DUL_BA_KA_PA_BZHUGS_SO |
| BA_KA_PA_BZHUGS_SO | BA_KA_PA_BZHUGS_SO_B |
| KA_PA_BZHUGS_SO_B | KA_PA_BZHUGS_SO_B_'DUL |
| PA_BZHUGS_SO_B_'DUL | PA_BZHUGS_SO_B_'DUL_'DZIN |

| 7-gram | 8-gram |
|---|---|
| A_'DUL_BA_KA_PA_BZHUGS_SO | A_'DUL_BA_KA_PA_BZHUGS_SO_B |
| 'DUL_BA_KA_PA_BZHUGS_SO_B | 'DUL_BA_KA_PA_BZHUGS_SO_B_'DUL |
| BA_KA_PA_BZHUGS_SO_B_'DUL | BA_KA_PA_BZHUGS_SO_B_'DUL_'DZIN |
| KA_PA_BZHUGS_SO_B_'DUL_'DZIN | KA_PA_BZHUGS_SO_B_'DUL_'DZIN_CHEN |
| PA_BZHUGS_SO_B_'DUL_'DZIN_CHEN | PA_BZHUGS_SO_B_'DUL_'DZIN_CHEN_PO |

Again, as with our Sanskrit texts, we can count the frequency of each n-gram's appearance within a text and sort these lists of n-grams to find those that are most significant. The table below shows the most frequent 2-grams and 4-grams from a selection of these *'dul ba* texts:

| ***'dul ba*** **text** | 2-gram | 4-gram |
|---|---|---|
| kl00001e1.txt | DGE_SLONG (2671) | SO_SOR_THAR_PA'I (672) |
| kl00001e2.txt | PA_DANG (1827) | BCOM_LDAN_'DAS_KYIS (578) |
| kl0001e3inc.txt | DGE_SLONG (2031) | BCOM_LDAN_'DAS_KYIS (523) |
| kl0001e4inc.txt | PA_DANG (1713) | BCOM_LDAN_'DAS_KYIS (407) |

*Continued*

| *'dul ba* text | 2-gram | 4-gram |
|---|---|---|
| kl00002e1.txt | DGE_SLONG (346) | TSE_DANG_LDAN_PA (101) |
| kl00003e1.txt | DGE_SLONG (2089) | TSE_DANG_LDAN_PA (647) |
| kl00003e2inc.txt | DGE_SLONG (2636) | TSE_DANG_LDAN_PA (749) |
| kl00003e3.txt | DGE_SLONG (2550) | BCOM_LDAN_'DAS_KYIS (879) |
| kl00003e4.txt | PA_DANG (1679) | BCOM_LDAN_'DAS_KYIS (591) |
| kl00004e.txt | DGE_SLONG (465) | DGE_SLONG_MA_GANG (211) |

For the sake of comparison, we can also examine the same output from the ACIP Tibetan script version of these texts. There are unfortunately a number of discrepancies between the most-frequent strings for the roman character and Tibetan character versions of the texts. I am not yet sure of the reason for these discrepancies.

| *'dul ba* text | 2-gram | 4-gram |
|---|---|---|
| KL00001-001(eTB).txt | དགེ་སློང་ (2622) | སོ་སོར་ཐར་པའི་ (667) |
| KL00001-002(eTB).txt | པ་དང་ (1796) | བཅོམ་ལྡན་འདས་ཀྱིས་ (560) |
| KL00001-003(eTB).txt | དགེ་སློང་ (1993) | བཅོམ་ལྡན་འདས་ཀྱིས་ (515) |
| KL00001-004(eTB).txt | པ་དང་ (1686) | བཅོམ་ལྡན་འདས་ཀྱིས་ (404) |
| KL00002-001(eTB).txt | དགེ་སློང་ (342) | ཚེ་དང་ལྡན་པ་ (100) |
| KL00003-001(eTB).txt | དགེ་སློང་ (2042) | ཚེ་དང་ལྡན་པ་ (622) |
| KL00003-002(eTB).txt | དགེ་སློང་ (2595) | ཚེ་དང་ལྡན་པ་ (733) |
| KL00003-003(eTB).txt | དགེ་སློང་ (2500) | བཅོམ་ལྡན་འདས་ཀྱིས་ (858) |
| KL00003-004(eTB).txt | པ་དང་ (1656) | བཅོམ་ལྡན་འདས་ཀྱིས་ (581) |
| KL00004(eTB).txt | དགེ་སློང་ (457) | དགེ་སློང་མ་གང་ (211) |

From the above data we can see that the strings "DGE_SLONG" (from *dge slong*, "monk"), "PA_DANG" (*pa dang*, a connecting clause) "BCOM_LDAN_'DAS_KYIS" (*bcom ldan 'das kyis*, third case form of "Buddha") and TSE_DANG_LDAN_PA (*tse dang ldan pa*, "venerable") are significant words in *'dul ba* texts. This observation is not particularly surprising, but it does help us to create maps of frequently-occurring words that can be applied toward automated genre analysis utilities. For the sake of comparison, we can look for the frequently-occurring n-grams within *mdo mang* (*sūtra*) texts, where we find that the term *byang chub sems dpa'* (= *bodhisattva*) tends to bubble to the top (though not always the very top):

| ***mdo mang* text** | **4-gram** | **8-gram** |
|---|---|---|
| kl00094e.txt | **BYANG_CHUB_SEMS_DPA'** (111) | **BYANG_CHUB_SEMS_DPA'**_MCHOG_TU_DGA'_BA'I (25) |
| kl00095e.txt | **BYANG_CHUB_SEMS_DPA'** (608) | SLONG_DAG_DE_LTAR_**BYANG_CHUB_SEMS_DPA'** (36) |
| kl00096e.txt | **BYANG_CHUB_SEMS_DPA'** (55) | **BYANG_CHUB_SEMS_DPA'I**_RAB_TU_'BYUNG_BA (25) |
| kl00097e.txt | **BYANG_CHUB_SEMS_DPA'** (63) | PA_JI_LTAR_NA_**BYANG_CHUB_SEMS_DPA'** (30) |
| kl00098e.txt | **BYANG_CHUB_SEMS_DPA'** (29) | **BYANG_CHUB_SEMS_DPA'**_SEMS_DPA'_CHEN_PO (11) |
| kl00108e.txt | **BYANG_CHUB_SEMS_DPA'** (187) | **BYANG_CHUB_SEMS_DPA'**_SEMS_DPA'_CHEN_PO (88) |
| kl00353.txt | **BYANG_CHUB_SEMS_DPA'** (353) | **BYANG_CHUB_SEMS_DPA'**_SEMS_DPA'_CHEN_PO (22) |
| kl00357.txt | **BYANG_CHUB_SEMS_DPA'** (27) | **BYANG_CHUB_SEMS_DPA'**_SEMS_DPA'_CHEN_PO (8) |

In the Tibetan script version of these texts, we see a similar pattern. Again, there are some discrepancies between the roman character and Tibetan script output from my program. The first text in particular does not seem to have a suitable parallel for its roman character companion:

| *mdo mang* text | 4-gram | 8-gram |
|---|---|---|
| KL00094(eTB).txt | བྱང་ཆུབ་ཏུ་ནི་ (977)* | བྱང་ཆུབ་ཏུ་ནི་སེམས་བསྐྱེད་དོ་བདེ་ (679)* |
| KL00095(eTB).txt | བྱང་ཆུབ་སེམས་དཔའ་ (591) | སློང་དག་དེ་ལྟར་བྱང་ཆུབ་སེམས་དཔའ་ (36) |
| KL00096(eTB).txt | བྱང་ཆུབ་སེམས་དཔའ་ (55) | བྱང་ཆུབ་སེམས་དཔའི་རབ་ཏུ་འབྱུང་བ་ (24) |
| KL00097(eTB).txt | བྱང་ཆུབ་སེམས་དཔའ་ (60) | པ་ཇི་ལྟར་ན་བྱང་ཆུབ་སེམས་དཔའ་ (29) |
| KL00098(eTB).txt | བྱང་ཆུབ་སེམས་དཔའ་ (29) | བྱང་ཆུབ་སེམས་དཔའ་སེམས་དཔའ་ཆེན་པོ་ (11) |
| KL00108(eTB).txt | བྱང་ཆུབ་སེམས་དཔའ་ (108) | བྱང་ཆུབ་སེམས་དཔའ་སེམས་དཔའ་ཆེན་པོ་ (87) |
| KL00353(eTB).txt | བྱང་ཆུབ་སེམས་དཔའ་ (232) | བྱང་ཆུབ་ཏུ་སེམས་བསྐྱེད་པར་གྱུར་ཏོ་ (9)* |
| KL00357(eTB).txt | བྱང་ཆུབ་སེམས་དཔའ་ (26) | བྱང་ཆུབ་སེམས་དཔའ་སེམས་དཔའ་ཆེན་པོ་ (8) |

## Interpretation of Data and Potential Applications

The nature of the Tibetan language to split individual words along these syllable boundaries makes this n-gram method particularly useful for creating word tables directly from the n-grams. While not all n-grams will result in words (some will necessarily be too short and represent only partial words, while others will extend beyond the boundaries of individual words), those n-grams are statistically likely to drop to the bottom of the list, as they will tend to be less represented than actual words. Further processing of these data can allow us to develop more complex combinations of different sized n-grams to create genre codes in order to categorize unknown input texts. As this article is intended only to illustrate the basic concept of n-gram extraction, I have not illustrated these further possible projects here.

In the tables above, I have indicated some very basic ways that these n-gram data can be used as a window into the patterns of a particular genre. The numbers and strings above are taken directly from my program output. However, I should point out that the *mdo mang* (*sūtra*) data in the above tables have been selected by hand in order to illustrate frequent appearance of the term *byang chub sems dpa'* (བྱང་ཆུབ་སེམས་དཔའ་ ), and do not reflect the absolute most frequent terms.

## Special Problems in Chinese

The situation with Chinese texts should in some ways be much more simple than building up syllables in Sanskrit and Tibetan, but possibly more time-consuming in certain respects due to an increased need to read from memory. Chinese glyphs are best represented in the computer not by romanized text, but by individual Unicode characters in Chinese script. There are several reasons that this is the case, but mainly what it comes down to is the fact that romanized Chinese words do not preserve all necessary information about their originating characters, even when tone markers are included. For example, the modern Chinese word 八 ("eight") is represented as the roman character string *bā* (*ba* + first tone marker). The characters 粑 ("cake"), 疤 ("scar") and 笆 ("basketry") are also represented in pinyin transliteration by exactly the same string, *bā*, since they all have exactly the same pronunciation in spoken Chinese. In the context of speech, such homophones are rarely a problem, and in written Chinese the distinct characters eliminate any ambiguity. However, their roman representation is what we can call "data lossy" – having only the romanized form does not always allow us to reconstruct the correct Chinese character. The above examples are also not outliers, and in fact most Chinese phonemes can be mapped onto more than one character, each with a unique meaning.

The complete set of Chinese glyphs numbers over 80,000, but the character diversity in any given text is much lower, and general literacy for a human being learning Chinese today is closer to 3,000 characters. The computer should be prepared for the possibility of encountering any Chinese character in a text, and so the Unicode standard for Chinese characters is the most suitable way to interact with such texts. The individual units of speech in Chinese are individual characters, which function not unlike the *akṣara*s as in Sanskrit or syllables in Tibetan, and so the program must parse texts at the level of single characters.

Chinese characters are not only the atomics for words, but often represent words themselves. While some Sanskrit and Tibetan words are also a single *akṣara* or syllable in length, there are far more instances in which a Chinese word is represented by a single character. Keeping this fact in mind, the n-gram method used for Sanskrit and Tibetan is potentially less useful, since many of the words we encounter in Chinese will be 1-grams. However, we can still expect to find words larger than one character, as well as common phrases of varying lengths. In order to test the limits of what my program can do, I applied the same algorithm to sample sets of Chinese text, albeit with some differences in the parsing rules. I explain these differences below.

## Some Experiments with the Taishō Canon

The largest digitized collection of Buddhist texts available in Chinese is the Taishō canon, which is available online at the CBETA Project (http://www.cbeta.org/). I downloaded this entire collection and converted it to UTF-8 format, the same format I used for my Sanskrit and Tibetan datasets. In the interest of keeping some level of consistency, I chose as my sample set the T24 section of the CBETA collection, which includes 59 texts from T. 1448 through T. 1504. These texts are compiled from the *vinaya* sections of several Buddhist lineages.

As with all digitized manuscripts, the Taishō canon available at CBETA includes its own special editorial features in addition to the actual manuscript characters. These other characters include text and line numbers, end of phrase indicators, and other extraneous data that would be unwelcome in our text processing application. The following selection from the beginning of the file for T. 1448 shows the basic structure consistent throughout the collection:

```
T24n1448_p0001a01(00)║
T24n1448_p0001a02(00)║    No. 1448
T24n1448_p0001a03(00)║
T24n1448_p0001a04(12)║根本說一切有部毘奈耶藥事卷第一
T24n1448_p0001a05(00)║
T24n1448_p0001a06(00)║        大唐三藏義淨奉　制譯
T24n1448_p0001a07(00)║初攝頌曰。
T24n1448_p0001a08(00)║  開許用諸藥　　膏油治疥病
T24n1448_p0001a09(00)║  眼藥及風痼　　畢隣婆蹉等
T24n1448_p0001a10(00)║爾時薄伽梵。在室羅伐城。逝多林。給孤獨園。
```

As we would like to have only the Chinese characters themselves without any extra data, my algorithm is instructed to ignore any roman characters, arabic numerals, underscores, and other unwanted characters. The parsed output then appears as follows:

根本說一切有部毘奈耶藥事卷第一大唐三藏義淨奉制譯初攝頌曰開許用諸藥膏油治疥病
眼藥及風痼畢隣婆蹉等爾時薄伽梵在室羅伐城逝多林給孤獨園

As with our Sanskrit and Tibetan texts, we can then read these files from beginning to end, storing 1-grams, 2-grams, 3-grams, up to whatever limit we like. To maintain consistency with the previous experiments, I instructed my program to produce n-grams from size 1 to 8, like so:

1-grams: 根 本 說 一 切 有 部 毘 奈 耶 藥 事
2-grams: 根本 本 說 說一 一切 切有 有部
3-grams: 根本說 本說一 說一切 一切有 切有部 有部毘
4-grams: 根本說一 本說一切 說一切有 一切有部 切有部毘 有部毘奈
5-grams: 根本 說一切 本 說一切有 說一切有部 一切有部毘
6-grams: 根本說一切有 本說一切有部 說一切有部毘 一切有部毘奈
7-grams: 根本說一切有部 本說一切有部毘 說一切有部毘奈 一切有部毘奈耶
8-grams: 根本說一切有部毘 本說一切有部毘奈 說一切有部毘奈耶

After generating all possible n-grams from all of the input texts, we can search for common strings as before. However, due to the aforementioned idiosyncrasies of written Chinese, the repetition of character strings above 1 or 2 characters is much less common. The chart below illustrates some common strings found in select texts from the input sample of T. 1448 – 1504. These texts are the five largest from the input dataset:

| Text | 1-gram | 2-gram | 3-gram | 4-gram | 5-gram |
|---|---|---|---|---|---|
| T. 1448 | 大 (1066) | 婆羅 (291) | 婆羅門 (275) | 一婆羅門 (19) | 世尊及苾芻 (19) |
| T. 1450 | 時 (2291) | 汝等 (215) | 婆羅門 (107) | 爾時世尊 (172) | 佛告諸苾芻 (112) |
| T. 1451 | 不 (3859) | 如是 (1046) | 作是念 (294) | 得越法罪 (194) | 芻以緣白佛 (112) |
| T. 1452 | 佛 (1026) | 諸苾 (358) | 時諸苾 (197) | 時諸苾芻 (197) | 以緣白佛佛 (178) |
| T. 1453 | 苾 (1203) | 苾芻 (1203) | 苾芻尼 (280) | 大德僧伽 (164) | 鄔陀夷苾芻 (97) |

Even from this small selection, we can see a few recurring themes. The 3-gram 婆羅門 (*pó luó mén*, "*brāhmaṇa*") in texts T. 1448 and T. 1450 gives some indication about the subject matter here, and as before could be useful in determining genre. We can see other repeating terms that may be less useful in this regard, such as 如是 (*rú shì*, "thus"), but which could still help to create a linguistic fingerprint of a set of texts as distinct from another set. In many cases the repeating strings are common phrases that occur only in a Buddhist context, and which could help in the automated cataloguing of large sets of unknown texts. In Chinese this capability would be especially useful, as the variety of Chinese texts available digitally is far more varied in content than texts in Sanskrit and Tibetan.

We can take this idea further by again comparing n-gram frequency across multiple subsets. By combining the n-gram frequency data from all texts within a section of the CBETA collection, we can form master frequency lists for each section. Since the sections are roughly divided according to literary genre, this method may give us a better idea of major differences across different genres within the Taishō canon. Below, I provide the four most common 1-grams, 2-

grams, 4-grams and 8-grams for a select set of collections within the Taishō canon:

| Collection | 1-gram | 2-gram | 4-gram | 8-gram |
|---|---|---|---|---|
| T01 | 不 (21400) | 比丘 (7863) | 所以者何 (879) | 如來無所著等正覺 (246) |
| | 有 (21078) | 如是 (7848) | 沙門瞿曇 (799) | 聞佛所說歡喜奉行 (242) |
| | 是 (20109) | 世尊 (4876) | 尊者阿難 (557) | 我聞如是一時佛遊 (216) |
| | 者 (16553) | 沙門 (3014) | 爾時世尊 (544) | 誦我聞如是一時佛 (199) |
| T02 | 是 (21383) | 比丘 (11395) | 爾時世尊 (2592) | 衛國祇樹給孤獨園 (1505) |
| | 不 (18528) | 如是 (7862) | 所說歡喜 (1803) | 舍衛國祇樹給孤獨 (1505) |
| | 時 (16702) | 世尊 (7260) | 聞佛所說 (1756) | 聞佛所說歡喜奉行 (1380) |
| | 如 (16470) | 爾時 (6083) | 佛所說歡 (1699) | 如是我聞一時佛住 (1275) |
| T03 | 是 (16212) | 菩薩 (5812) | 藐三菩提 (1094) | 阿耨多羅三藐三菩 (1092) |
| | 如 (15204) | 如是 (5750) | 三藐三菩 (1094) | 耨多羅三藐三菩提 (1092) |
| | 不 (14458) | 爾時 (4446) | 阿耨多羅 (1093) | 成阿耨多羅三藐三 (349) |
| | 無 (14028) | 一切 (3834) | 耨多羅三 (1093) | 多羅三藐三菩提心 (241) |
| T04 | 不 (16280) | 比丘 (3117) | 是故說曰 (1052) | 舍衛國祇樹給孤獨 (138) |
| | 是 (11786) | 是故 (2268) | 爾時世尊 (520) | 衛國祇樹給孤獨園 (137) |
| | 者 (11086) | 世尊 (2248) | 即說偈言 (347) | 在舍衛國祇樹給孤 (137) |
| | 人 (10931) | 爾時 (2141) | 亦復如是 (300) | 佛在舍衛國祇樹給 (134) |
| T05 | 無 (62288) | 菩薩 (16385) | 波羅蜜多 (15657) | 增語是菩薩摩訶薩 (3781) |
| | 不 (45758) | 蜜多 (15657) | 薩摩訶薩 (15368) | 薩摩訶薩不不也世 (2952) |
| | 若 (42183) | 羅蜜 (15657) | 菩薩摩訶 (15368) | 菩薩摩訶薩不不也 (2952) |
| | 薩 (31835) | 波羅 (15657) | 若波羅蜜 (10007) | 摩訶薩不不也世尊 (2952) |
| T08 | 不 (30632) | 波羅 (16532) | 般若波羅 (11852) | 阿耨多羅三藐三菩 (2176) |
| | 菩 (29114) | 羅蜜 (16492) | 若波羅蜜 (11851) | 耨多羅三藐三菩提 (2170) |
| | 是 (28812) | 菩薩 (16387) | 菩薩摩訶 (6444) | 須菩提菩薩摩訶薩 (878) |
| | 無 (27650) | 般若 (12207) | 薩摩訶薩 (6439) | 阿耨多羅三耶三菩 (878) |
| T09 | 一 (19709) | 一切 (14366) | 一切眾生 (2769) | 阿耨多羅三藐三菩 (544) |
| | 無 (18855) | 菩薩 (9990) | 菩薩摩訶 (2089) | 耨多羅三藐三菩提 (544) |
| | 佛 (16633) | 眾生 (8800) | 薩摩訶薩 (2088) | 子是為菩薩摩訶薩 (267) |
| | 法 (15684) | 如來 (4534) | 令一切眾 (1187) | 佛子是為菩薩摩訶 (267) |
| T10 | 一 (30535) | 一切 (21590) | 一切眾生 (3496) | 阿耨多羅三藐三菩 (495) |
| | 無 (29172) | 菩薩 (17716) | 菩薩摩訶 (2369) | 耨多羅三藐三菩提 (495) |
| | 切 (21625) | 眾生 (11979) | 薩摩訶薩 (2368) | 謂菩薩生如是心我 (316) |
| | 諸 (20996) | 如是 (6543) | 一切諸佛 (1211) | 薩生如是心我已得 (316) |
| T11 | 無 (25990) | 菩薩 (10722) | 薩摩訶薩 (2303) | 阿耨多羅三藐三菩 (770) |
| | 如 (21719) | 如是 (7850) | 菩薩摩訶 (2303) | 耨多羅三藐三菩提 (770) |
| | 是 (21493) | 一切 (7281) | 文殊師利 (1033) | 舍利子菩薩摩訶薩 (331) |
| | 不 (19870) | 如來 (6397) | 一切眾生 (802) | 得阿耨多羅三藐三 (154) |
| T12 | 是 (31334) | 菩薩 (10028) | 菩薩摩訶 (1900) | 阿耨多羅三藐三菩 (1052) |

*Continued*

| Collection | 1-gram | 2-gram | 4-gram | 8-gram |
|---|---|---|---|---|
| | 不 (28306) | 如是 (9206) | 薩摩訶薩 (1896) | 耨多羅三藐三菩提 (1050) |
| | 如 (27667) | 如來 (7684) | 亦復如是 (1640) | 得阿耨多羅三藐三 (369) |
| | 無 (27300) | 眾生 (7624) | 一切眾生 (1385) | 善男子菩薩摩訶薩 (334) |
| T13 | 無 (23427) | 菩薩 (9957) | 菩薩摩訶 (1686) | 阿耨多羅三藐三菩 (898) |
| | 是 (22261) | 一切 (9957) | 薩摩訶薩 (1680) | 耨多羅三藐三菩提 (898) |
| | 不 (21834) | 眾生 (7919) | 一切眾生 (1109) | 多羅三藐三菩提心 (263) |
| | 如 (19803) | 如是 (7743) | 阿耨多羅 (905) | 發阿耨多羅三藐三 (248) |
| T14 | 無 (58875) | 南無 (36603) | 如來南無 (4964) | 阿耨多羅三藐三菩 (607) |
| | 佛 (44990) | 佛南 (28455) | 王佛南無 (2403) | 耨多羅三藐三菩提 (607) |
| | 南 (37115) | 如來 (9873) | 佛南無無 (2148) | 中華電子佛典協會 (332) |
| | 如 (19559) | 菩薩 (7861) | 菩薩南無 (1460) | 曰智慧是為六何謂 (242) |
| T15 | 不 (21311) | 菩薩 (7368) | 文殊師利 (1282) | 阿耨多羅三藐三菩 (359) |
| | 無 (21014) | 一切 (5846) | 不可思議 (1125) | 耨多羅三藐三菩提 (359) |
| | 是 (19035) | 如是 (4631) | 菩薩摩訶 (645) | 童子菩薩摩訶薩復 (171) |
| | 如 (15385) | 眾生 (3574) | 薩摩訶薩 (644) | 子菩薩摩訶薩復有 (171) |
| T20 | 二 (21775) | 二合 (13659) | 薩摩訶薩 (1271) | 中華電子佛典協會 (368) |
| | 一 (19536) | 一切 (8879) | 菩薩摩訶 (1271) | 觀世音菩薩摩訶薩 (277) |
| | 合 (15837) | 菩薩 (7256) | 真言曰唵 (1048) | 項本資料庫可自由 (184) |
| | 三 (12616) | 真言 (6195) | 娑嚩二合 (987) | 電子佛典普及版完 (184) |
| T21 | 一 (15785) | 二合 (7689) | 娑嚩二合 (1151) | 中華電子佛典協會 (456) |
| | 二 (15538) | 一切 (5164) | 此陀羅尼 (784) | 項本資料庫可自由 (228) |
| | 如 (11616) | 如是 (4365) | 嚩二合引 (767) | 電子佛典普及版完 (228) |
| | 不 (11430) | 菩薩 (3513) | 電子佛典 (684) | 電子佛典協會版權 (228) |
| T22 | 比 (38638) | 比丘 (37618) | 若比丘尼 (1663) | 默然故是事如是持 (509) |
| | 丘 (37624) | 諸比 (9580) | 六群比丘 (1570) | 從今是戒應如是說 (482) |
| | 不 (33402) | 丘尼 (8891) | 白佛佛言 (1517) | 今是戒應如是說若 (449) |
| | 是 (25496) | 如是 (8760) | 告諸比丘 (1456) | 是戒應如是說若比 (442) |
| T23 | 不 (30543) | 比丘 (22825) | 種種因緣 (1156) | 應如是說若復苾芻 (409) |
| | 是 (28299) | 苾芻 (8356) | 僧伽婆尸 (1054) | 學處應如是說若復 (372) |
| | 比 (23647) | 如是 (6004) | 伽婆尸沙 (1054) | 處應如是說若復苾 (368) |
| | 丘 (22827) | 丘尼 (4509) | 白佛佛言 (1011) | 制其學處應如是說 (363) |
| T24 | 不 (27289) | 苾芻 (8486) | 爾時世尊 (695) | 波逸底迦若復苾芻 (279) |
| | 者 (23089) | 比丘 (6489) | 白佛佛言 (611) | 苾芻以緣白佛佛言 (206) |
| | 是 (18720) | 世尊 (5131) | 時諸苾芻 (601) | 者波逸底迦若復苾 (191) |
| | 有 (16271) | 如是 (4908) | 波逸底迦 (551) | 逸底迦若復苾芻尼 (182) |

It is not immediately clear what, if anything, we can deduce from the above data, yet we can be certain that patterns exist among the different sizes of n-grams.

The string "阿耨多羅三藐三菩" appears as the most frequent 8-gram in T08, T10, T11, T12, T13 and T14, for example, while the string "中華電子佛典協會" appears as the most frequent 8-gram in T20 and T21. This string is also the third most frequent in T14. We can also see patterns within the top n-grams of a given set, as in T03, where "阿耨多羅三藐三菩" and "耨多羅三藐三菩提" appear exactly the same number of times. This type of result is an indication that we should look at higher values of n in order to capture the complete phrase. We can also look back at the original texts in each collection to determine the full phrase that led to the creation of these particular n-grams.

In fact, "中華電子佛典協會" is part of the phrase "中華電子佛典協會版權宣告" that occurs in the header information for each file in the CBETA collection, and is not actually part of the original texts. If I had wanted to, I could have stripped these headers from the input files by using a separate script, but there are other ways to eliminate these kinds of false positives without requiring files to be specially prepared. Just as we can have a minimum threshold for n-gram frequencies to reduce "garbage" strings that occur only once within a text, we can also have a maximum frequency or key frequencies (e.g., frequency exactly matches number of files in set) that indicates potentially misleading data.

In the case of "阿耨多羅三藐三菩" and "耨多羅三藐三菩提" we can easily see that the complete string captured partly by each of these should be a 9-gram, "阿耨多羅三藐三菩提" – the meaning is equivalent to the term *anuttara-samyak-sambodhi* in Sanskrit, often translated into English as "supreme correct enlightenment." This phrase is a common feature of Mahāyāna texts, and could be used along with other strings to build up a genre fingerprint for singling out Mahāyāna texts. In order for these results to be useful in advancing some argument about the text, however, it is necessary to perform a deeper analysis. Unfortunately, such an analysis is beyond the scope of the present paper, which is meant only to illustrate the basic function of the algorithm.

## Conclusions

Recent advances in computing have enabled researchers to digitize large amounts of Buddhist texts in various languages. Analysis of these texts is, however, still mainly limited to traditional methods that do not take advantage of the unique capabilities of the computer. A major problem with closing this gap involves the automation of word boundary selection for the purpose of constructing text concordances. I have presented here a novel method for constructing such concordances without requiring user input, by searching for repeating character strings. This brute-force technique is suitable for analyzing very large corpora, as it is relatively fast, context-independent, and generates datasets that can be read by humans or fed back into the computer for further analysis. While my technique is not limited to Buddhist materials, the Buddhist texts available to us in Sanskrit, Tibetan and Chinese present excellent test cases for this concept. I have demonstrated some ways that this technique can be applied to a few publicly-available text collections as a proof of concept. The specific data in this paper are not themselves especially revealing of anything new in terms of the content of their texts, but merely illustrate how an automated process can be used to extract meaningful information in cases where the content of texts is partially unknown, or where it would be inconvenient for a human being to search through large corpora.

My method is not intended to replace the many other excellent text analysis projects that rely on manual tagging of words, and it has certain limits to its application. The simple algorithm I have written is not a text translation engine, and has no idea about the meaning of the texts it parses. This lack of capability is in some ways a positive feature, however, because the program is not biased in any way about the nature of the data it finds. It is a pattern-recognition machine of the simplest kind, and can be applied to texts in any language.

One of my main goals in creating the program discussed in this paper was to share with other scholars of Buddhism a general tool that could be used by anyone for a wide variety of purposes. I am hopeful that someone will utilize the technique described here to discover something more interesting in Buddhist texts than the above examples have done. To that end, I have made my program available online, together with its source code, so that it can be used without restriction by anyone who is interested. The URL is <https://github.com/handyc/aks>. While the program in its current form is very simple, I plan to continue developing it by adding features such as Levenshtein distance measurement and other text-comparison techniques.

## References

Hackett, Paul. 2000. "Automatic Segmentation and Part-Of-Speech Tagging For Tibetan: A First Step Towards Machine Translation." Columbia University Academic Commons, http://hdl.handle.net/10022/AC:P:10471.

Huet, Gérard. 2006. "Lexicon-directed Segmentation and Tagging of Sanskrit" In *Themes and Tasks in Old and Middle Indo-Aryan Linguistics*, edited by Bertil Tikkanen and Heinrich Hettrich, 307–325. Delhi: Motilal Banarsidass.

Zhan, Weidong, Chang Baobao, Duan Huiming and Zhang Huarui. 2006. “Recent Developments in Chinese Corpus Research” In *Language Corpora: Their Compilation and Application (Proceedings of the 13th NIJL International Symposium)*, 19–30. Tokyo

James B. Apple

# Digital Filiation Studies: Phylogenetic Analysis in the Study of Tibetan Buddhist Canonical Texts

## Introduction

In this chapter I briefly explain the critical editing and restitution of Tibetan Buddhist canonical texts through the text critical analysis of manuscripts supported with computer technology. The chapter succinctly outlines the principles and methodology involved in applying phylogenetics to investigating the genealogy of texts found in Tibetan Kanjurs. In the following sections I discuss the current known history of Tibetan Kanjurs to account for the textual witnesses under philological consideration, outline the principles of text criticism for editing Tibetan versions of Buddhist canonical texts, and explain the method of applying phylogenetic analysis to critical editions of Tibetan texts. The chapter concludes with a brief example that illustrates the techniques involved in utilizing phylogenetic analysis in text criticism.[1]

## Tibetan Kanjurs

The primary textual sources for critical editions of Tibetan Buddhist texts are preserved in Tibetan Kanjurs. A Kanjur (Tibetan *bka' 'gyur*)[2] is an authorative collection of the Tibetan translations of the "Word of the Buddha." There is not a single authorized Kanjur as no two are exactly alike, but rather multiple Kanjurs which carry a great amount of resemblance. Kanjurs[3] consist of massive compendiums of Tibetan *sūtra* and *tantra* translations that were gathered together after a

1 Restored new editions have completely revolutionized scholarly understanding of Buddhist history and practices (Cantwell and Mayer 2007, Silk 1994, Harrison 1992a). In the case of Mahāyāna sūtras, although they have greatly contributed to Buddhist culture and Asian civilization, less than five percent of this literature has been systematically studied or translated into a modern European language (Haberman and Nattier 1996, Nattier 1997, Raman 1998).

2 The Tibetan term kangyur (Tib. *bka' 'gyur*) is commonly known under its Mongol pronunciation "kanjur." On the general characteristics of Kanjurs see Apple 2016.

3 On the necessity of employing the plural "Kanjurs" as opposed to "the Kanjur," see the work of Peter Skilling 1997, 2009, 2013.

https://doi.org/10.1515/9783110519082-012

number of centuries (Skilling 1997) and cataloged by Tibetan scholar-librarians beginning in the late 13th century (Schaeffer and van der Kuijp 2009). At the beginning of the 14th century, a collection of various copies of all the Tibetan translations of Indian *sūtras* (*mdo*) and *śāstras* (*bstan bcos*) was made at the Kadampa (*bka' gdams pa*) monastery of Narthang (*snar thang*), the so-called the old Narthang edition of the Kanjur. According to Tibetan tradition, the "Old Narthang" Kanjur was disseminated in manuscript copies, of which two main groups or recensions can be discerned.[4]

The first branch is the so-called Tshal pa Kanjur edition that was named after Tshal Gung-thang monastery in Central Tibet (*dbus*) and was published between 1347–1351. The Tshal-pa edition serves as a basis for the block prints of the Yongle (**Y**, 1410 c.e.), Kangxi Taiwan (**K2**, 1669), 'Jang sa tham/Lithang (**J**, 1608–21), Peking (**Q**, 1717–20), and Cone (**C**, 1721–31) among extant Kanjurs in this lineage of affliation.[5]

---

4 We can infer from historical anecdotes that in the 18th century, based on Kaḥ thog si tu's pilgrimage guide to Tibet, there were at least 185 sets of Kanjur in the provinces of U-Tsang and Khams, and that 23 sets of Tibetan Kanjurs and Tanjurs were examined at Wu-t'ai-shan in 1940. Modern scholarship on the study of Tibetan Buddhist canonical literature is currently aware of over twenty different Kanjurs (Tauscher and Lainé 2008). At the present time there are at least eight xylographic editions (Cone (1721–31), Derge (1733), Lithang (1614–21), Lhasa (1934), Narthang (1730–32), Peking (1717–20), Urga (1908–10), and Yongle (1410) (Harrison 1992 and Eimer 1992) of the Kanjur, another seven manuscript editions; Berlin (1680), London Shel-dkar, Newark Batang (15th/16th century), Ulan Bator (1671), Phug brag, Stog Palace (18th century), Tokyo Manuscript (1858–1878). as well as numerous local manuscript Kanjurs (e.g. Gondhla, Hemis, Tholing, Mustang) that are increasing in number due to the efforts of the University of Vienna's Resources for Kanjur Studies Tibetan Manuscripts Project. The pioneering efforts of Helmut Eimer and Paul Harrison, followed up by the recent work of Silk (1994), Skilling (1997), and Zimmermann (2002), have advanced scholarly understanding of the relationships between this massive amount of extant textual material and have provided the groundwork for the ongoing scholarly effort to delineate a historical genealogy for texts preserved in Tibetan Kanjurs and Tanjurs.

5 Note that the recently published *bKa' 'gyur dpe bsdur ma*, "Comparative Edition of the Kangyur" (*krung go'i bod rig pa zhib 'jug ste gnas kyi bka' bstan dpe sdur khang* ['The Tibetan Tripitaka Collation Bureau of the China Tibetology Research Center'], 2006–2009), a publication involving immense scholarly effort and preparation, twenty years in the making, provides access to the Yongle Kanjur (printed in 1410) among the eight editions that comprise its philological pedigree (See *Bka' 'gyur dpe bsdur ma'i gsal bshad mun sel sgron me*, pp. 2–16). However, all eight editions utilized for this work are genealogically stemming from the Tshal pa line and this critical edition completely leaves out readings from other important, and perhaps more ancient, textual lines of recension that would provide evidence for earlier Tibetan archetypes. The *bKa' 'gyur dpe bsdur ma* is also a product of Chinese Communist sponsored research that, subconsciously or not, pays homage to Tibetan literary productions that are culturally and histor-

The second branch is derived from the Them spangs ma manuscript. According to Tibetan tradition, the Them-spangs-ma Kanjur was copied in 1431 from a manuscript in Narthang and brought to dPal-'khor-chos at Gyantse (*rgyal rtse*) (Zimmermann 2002, 186). Manuscript Kanjurs in this group include the London Manuscript copy of Shel-dkar rdzong (**L**), the Stog Palace Manuscript (**S**), the Kawaguchi or Tokyo Manuscript (**T**) Kanjur, and the recently available Ulan Bator Manuscript Kanjur (**U**). In addition to these Tshal pa and Thems spangs ma branches, there are a number of independent branches, such as the Phug brag,[6] Newark Batang, and Tabo manuscripts, that are not related to the old Narthang. This includes newly discovered Kanjurs and proto-Kanjurs from Western Tibet such as the Basgo Kanjur (**Ba**), Hemis I Kanjur (**He**), Hemis II Kanjur (**Hi**), and Gondlha proto-Kanjur (**Go**).

Subsequent block print editions, such as those from Derge, Cone, Narthang, and Lhasa, have proven to be contaminated editions that have been edited from earlier witnesses within the Tshal pa and Thems spangs ma branches. Such editions might read well, but they are historical products of traditional Tibetan editorial practices and one would be naïve to utilize these late editions uncritically for text critical analysis. [7]

ically linked to perceived Chinese cultural sovereignty over Tibetan culture. Every one of its exemplars are from blockprint editions, none are based on hand-copied manuscripts preserved in the Thems spangs ma and other branches from Western Tibet. Besides the fact that hand-copied manuscripts of Kanjurs were more valued in traditional Tibetan culture (Eimer 2007), they also provide variant readings that often correlate with readings found among the Tibetan Dunhuang fragments.

**6** The Phug-brag (F) Kanjur was copied at Phug-brag monastery in Western Tibet between 1696 and 1706. Previous studies (Harrison 1992, Silk 1994, Schoening 1995) have determined that the Phug-brag is an independent tradition in that it shares readings with both the Tshal-pa lineage and Them-spangs-ma but seems to be based on editions distinct from these two main groups.

**7** Andrew Skilton (2000:21) notes that scholars should not make the mistaken assumption that editions of Tibetan Kanjurs are free from contamination or other textual problems merely because they are readily available or easy to read in terms of orthography and grammar. One only has to view a pristine copy of the Derge xylograph Kanjur digitally available from the Tibetan Buddhist Resource Center to think that one has a satisfactory or adequate text. The potential low expectation of the educated public who can read Tibetan might assume that "what is already there, on the page, the *lectio recepta* [or *textus receptus*], commands automatic respect" (Kenney 1974:23–25), particularly when an edition such as the one from Derge is highly esteemed by the Tibetan tradition and serves as the base for a highly expensive and labor intensive recently published "critical edition" Kanjur. But later blockprint editions such as the Derge have been shown to be contaminated and conflated, and even though they may read well, they do not have much use for text critical purposes.

## The Critical Editing of Mahāyāna sūtras found in Tibetan canonical collections (Tib. bka'-'gyur)

Critical editions of Tibetan Buddhist canonical works are usually established through stemmatic textual criticism utilizing the processes of recension (*recensio*) and emendation (*emendatio*) based upon a collation of non-derivative extant Tibetan exemplars of manuscripts.[8] Stemmatic textual criticism seeks to detect the transmission history of a given text from variants transmitted in different versions. All variants are recorded in an apparatus, providing a detailed record of all readings in extant manuscripts and fragments. The recorded variants in the apparatus document all alternative readings, such that a reader may choose a reading that is different from the one established by the editor in the main body of the critical edition. The variants may be recensional or transmissional. Recensional variants reveal extensive and deliberate editorial changes to a text and may involve extensive alterations to the wording of a text or the use of different terminology. Transmissional variants are errors resulting from scribal lapses or attempts to improve or update a text, and may consist of single readings (*lectiones singulares*) attested in only one witness (Harrison 1992a). The history of the variants or indicative errors is represented graphically in a pedigree of witnesses known as a *stemma codicum*. Stemmatic textual criticism is concerned with the reconstruction of historical facts from variant readings which are introduced into a text during its history of transmission.

## Phylogenetic Analysis

The formulation of a stemmatical hypothesis based on textual criticism may be supplemented with cladistic computer assisted methods to investigate the genealogy of textual witnesses. Cladistic analysis enables an editor to infer a refined estimation of the genealogical relations among extant textual witnesses not initially discernable through text critical techniques. Cladistic analysis, also known as phylogenetic analysis, has been successful in analyzing textual traditions in English, Sanskrit, and Tibetan literature (Apple 2014b) as well as

8 Classical stemmatic textual criticism, developed by Maas (1958) and West (1973) and actively practiced in a variety of literary fields in Europe (Trovato 2014), has previously been successfully employed for the philological and historical analysis of Tibetan Buddhist Canonical editions of Indian Mahāyāna sūtras (Harrison 1992a, Braarvig 1993, Silk 1994, Zimmermann 2002, Habata 2013, Apple 2014b, Kritzer 2014).

in other areas of human culture such as textiles and art objects (Marwick 2012).[9] Cladistic software is currently used in the field of evolutionary biology called "phylogenetic systematics."

Phylogenetic systematics aims at a classification of the species of living beings according to their evolutionary history. Phylogenetic systematics tries to reconstruct this process. Cladistics is a method applied by systematic biologists to create evolutionary trees of species. Through the long course of reproduction and divergence in the evolutionary past, the multitude of species has come into existence by means of "descent with modification" (Darwin 1872). Evolutionary biology and textual criticism have in common the principle that species or texts share derived characters in their evolutionary history that indicate relationships between ancestors and descendants (Maas 2008b, Macé et al 2012). The aim of the cladistic method is to reconstruct this process, which is only inferable but not observable. Cladistics start with the determination of differences between species (so-called characters), which allows classification into two or more groups and inference of the evolutional process. Phylogenetic techniques utilize all genealogical informative variants in textual witnesses and apply algorithms that carry out thousands of combinations to discern probable relations between witnesses. These probable relations are represented in a bifurcated genealogical tree that depict a hypothetical model of a text's development. Along these lines, supplementary algorithmic procedures such as the "consistency index" (Maas 2008b, 2009, 2014) and "bootstrapping" (Felsensteing 1985; Hillis and Bull 1992; Apple 2014b) provide verifiable means to assess confidence in analysis derived from phyologenetic techniques. In brief, computer based algorithmic procedures enable an editor to discern the genealogical relations of textual witnesses at an exponential level of calculation that supersedes linear human cognition. Just as one can effect the present and predict the future through algorithmic data processing at exponential levels, an editor can discern the past genealogical relations between textual witnesses through phylogenetic analysis. The technology complements traditional text historical analysis with a highly accurate and alternative mode of accounting for genealogical development and transmission of texts (Roos and Heikkilä 2009).

9 The phylogenic analysis of texts has successfully been applied to the analysis of *The Canterbuy Tales* (Barbrook et al 1998), the Middle Dutch drama, *Lanseloet van Denemerken* (Salemans 2000), the transmisison of *Little Red Ridinghood*, and the *Carakasaṃhitā*, a 2nd century Indian Sanskrit medical text (Maas 2009).

## Case Study: The Tibetan version of the *Āryāvalokiteśvaraparipṛcchā-saptadharmaka*

I have so far critically edited Tibetan versions of the *Jayamatisūtra* (Apple 2015), *Mañjuśrīvihāra* (Apple 2014c), *Vīradattaparipṛcchā*, *Avaivartikacakrasūtra* (2014a), and *Avalokiteśvaraparipṛcchā-sapta-dharmaka* (Apple 2014b) utilizing stemmatic text criticism supplemented with phylogenetic analysis.

As a case study for illustrating phylogenetic analysis applied to critical editions of Tibetan Mahāyāna sūtras I have selected the *Avalokiteśvaraparipṛcchā-sapta-dharmaka*, or in English, *The Inquiry of Avalokiteśvara on the Seven Qualities.*[10] *The Inquiry of Avalokiteśvara on the Seven Qualities* (hereafter, APSD) was initially translated from an Indian language, most likely Sanskrit, into Tibetan by Atiśa and the Tibetan monk dGe-ba'i blo-gros. The translation took place in all probability at the monastery of Tho-ling in West Tibet, where the rulers of mNga'-ris first officially welcomed Atiśa and where dGe-ba'i blo-gros was active (Apple 2014c; Chattopadhyaya 1967, 325). As the following analysis indicates, the earliest preserved copies of this *sūtra* in Tibetan are found in Western Tibet.

The twelve available witnesses of the Tibetan text were collated and analyzed in order to establish the critical edition of the Tibetan translation. The variant readings were noted in a positive apparatus.[11] As the APSD is a short text all variants except single readings were recorded in the apparatus. Single readings, i. e., variants attested by only one witness (*lectiones singulares*), were relegated to end notes. The twelve available witnesses of the APSD were collated and found to have 144 variant readings. Among the 144 variant readings, 84 were single or unique readings that were due to spelling and punctuation. The edition therefore consisted of 60 variant readings that were genealogically informative. These variant readings clearly indicated group relations between the Tshal pa based witnesses (**CDJNQY**) and the Them spang ma based witnesses (**LSZ**). The relations of **F, Go**, and **He** were initially determined to be independent of these two groups. Further analysis on philological grounds indicated that Go and He were related and preserved quite ancient readings.

Along these lines, phylogenetic analysis works best when examining genealogically informative variants that are shared between textual witnesses that

10 As the Indian version is no longer extant the title is a reconstruction based on the title given in Tibetan manuscripts. An annotated English translation of this scripture is in Apple 2014c.
11 In general, a positive apparatus is one in which the instances of both accepted and rejected readings are recorded.

have not been subject to textual hybridization.[12] A criticism against classical stemmatics, as well as phylogenetic analysis, is that these methods cannot account for textual hybridization, or so-called "contamination," a process where two (or more) text versions are blended into one when a copyist changes from one exemplar to another. However, this critique is not valid, for just as biology has successfully developed techniques to account for horizontal gene transfer, phylogenetic based textual studies have developed methods to identify, and account for, horizontal textual recombination (Howe et al 2012). These methods include the application of the *law of parsimony* (see below) and Chi-Squared Method Analysis (Windram et al 2005; Philipps-Rodriguez et al 2009; Howe et al 2012), a statistical measure developed by Maynard Smith (1992) for detecting recombination in DNA sequences, and successively applied to Dante's *Monarchia* (Windram et al 2008).

The genealogically informative variants of eight textual Kanjur witnesses (F, Go, He, J, L, Q, S, Z) were exported from the word processing program *Classical Text Editor* (Hagel 1997–2013) in the form of a data matrix and were analysed by the software program *Phylogenetic Analysis Using Parsimony (*and Other Methods)*, or PAUP* (Swofford 2003).

In its application in textual criticism, PAUP* (Swofford 2003) is applied to a collation of manuscripts. The exact text of all the different manuscripts indicated above is entered into a computer and PAUB* records all the differences among them. The cladistic analysis of variant readings quickly provides an estimation of the genealogical relation of all witnesses (Maas 2008; Macé and Baret 2006) and the manuscripts are then grouped according to their shared characteristics. PAUP* projects encoded variant readings into genealogical trees that graphically represent a hypothesized development of a text through time (Barbrook et al 1998, Maas 2008, Apple 2014b). A phylogenetic analysis of a matrix of textual witnesses may produce millions of different genealogical trees. In order to determine which trees represent the most probable of genealogical rela-

12 Textual hybridization, also referred to as "textual contamination" by twentieth century classical scholars, is the process by which a copyist utilizes "two (or more) text versions combined into one" (Maas 2010:67). Textual hybridization is well known in the history of Tibetan Kanjurs, as Tibetan scholars and editors often favored "harmonized" (Harrison 1992:xxix) textual readings that would account for variants in different manuscript traditions to achieve a "complete" text (Mass 2008:234). However, in aiming to reconstruct the oldest inferable ancestor known hybridized textual traditions need to be removed from the analysis. In this instance, the Kanjurs of Cone (**C**, 1721–31), Derge (**D**, 1733), and Narthang (*snar thang*, **N**, 1730–32) were removed from consideration for phylogenetic analysis as they are known to be textual hybrids based on previous studies. The readings of the Yongle Kanjur (**Y**, 1410 CE) were also removed as I did not directly view the manuscript but only noted the readings found in the *dpe bsdur ma* edition.

tions, phylogenetics relies upon the law of parsimony, also known as Occam's razor (Maas 2008b, 230), which states that the simplest explanation that can explain data is the best. In the cladistic analysis of texts, the most parsimonious account of a text's development is that variants shared between two or more textual witnesses are introduced only once in the transmission of a text and then subsequently copied, rather than occurring several times in the history of the text's transmission (Maas 2008b, 230; Maas 2010, 70). The applied analysis from PAUP* generated an unrooted genealogical tree that is depicted in the phylogram illustrating the hypothetical relations among the eight witnesses of APSD (Figure 1). A phylogram is a tree-like branching diagram in which ancestors are depicted as junctures where lines meet, and where lines of descent are represented as branches. The phylograms in Figures 1 and 2 are unrooted. That is, as no assumptions about the oldest inferable ancestor have yet been made, the tree-like diagram is not yet depicted with a root, or genealogical basis for determining descent. Along these lines, the phylograms depicted in Figures 1 and 2 differ based on the algorithm utilized for their generation.

The method of maximal parsimony is not the only algorithm to discern relations in the data. As outlined by Phillips-Rodriguez *et al* (2010, 33–34), the Neighbour-joining (NJ) algorithm "proceeds by estimating the mean number of differences in specimens that have descended from a common ancestor, and then assigns a numeric value to the distance between each pair of them to make a pairwise distance matrix." Along these lines, "boostrap analysis" (Felsenstein 1985) is a common procedure of assessing confidence in analysis derived from phyologenetic techniques. Bootstrapping is a procedure that randomly resamples the original data set together with alternative replicates of the data matrix to test the viability of a tree against computer generated alternative virtual data sets. In this instance data was resampled 500 times, with each resampling being subject to parsimony analysis. The computer program then generated a single majority-rule consensus tree with bootstrap proportions being depicted between clades, or groups that share a common ancestor. In genealogical analysis, it has been claimed that "bootstrap proportions of ≥ 70 % usually correspond to a probability of ≥95 %" in group relations (Hillis and Bull 1993). Figure 2 illustrates an unrooted distance matrix diagram with the application of Neighbor-Joining and Bootstrap algorithms.

Figures 1 and 2 depict unrooted trees that indicate group relations but do not provide a hypothesis for the development of the text over time. In order to root a genealogical tree one must identify a point on the tree which is thought to serve as the base point (or apex position depending on the orientation of the tree) from which all witnesses are inferred to derive their ancestry. This point is called the archetype in textual criticism, the point of the oldest inferable ancestor of the

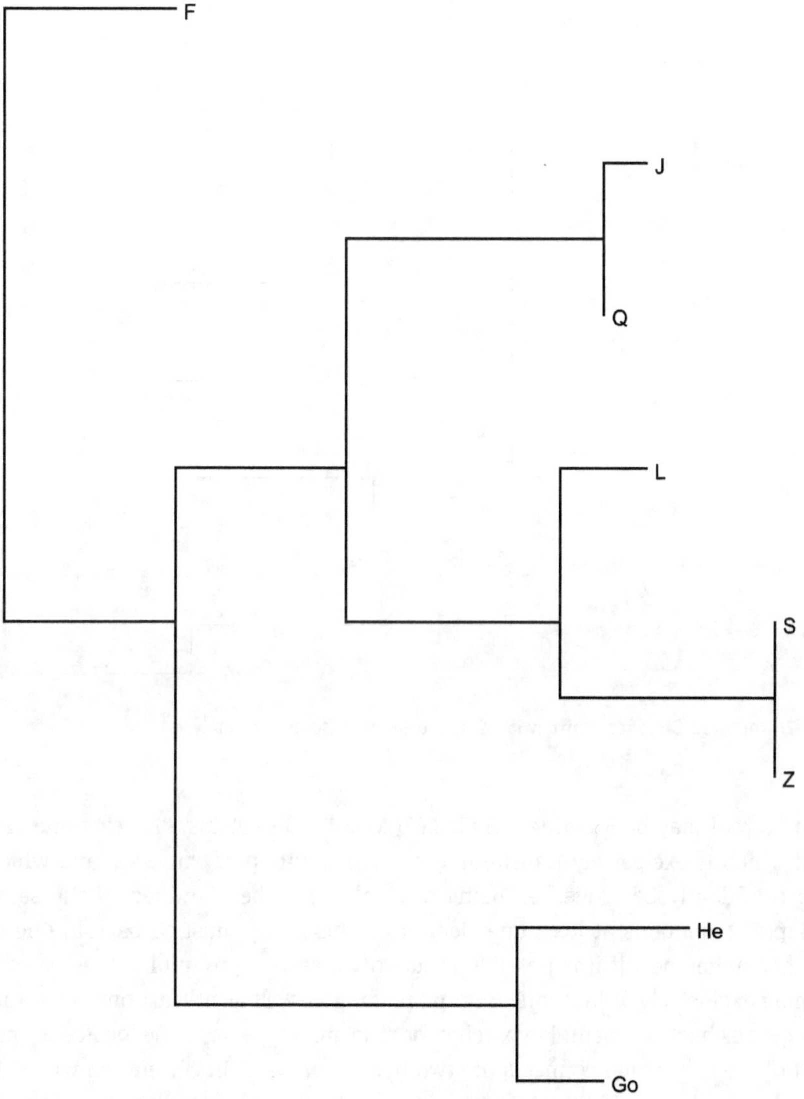


**Fig. 1:** Unrooted Phylogram of *Āryāvalokiteśvaraparipṛcchā-saptadharmaka* (APSD) Tibetan Version witnesses

text. Rooting a tree does not affect the structure of the tree as the connections between all nodes and branches are maintained. However, as noted by Maas (2008, 232), there is no exclusively numeric calculation to discern at which

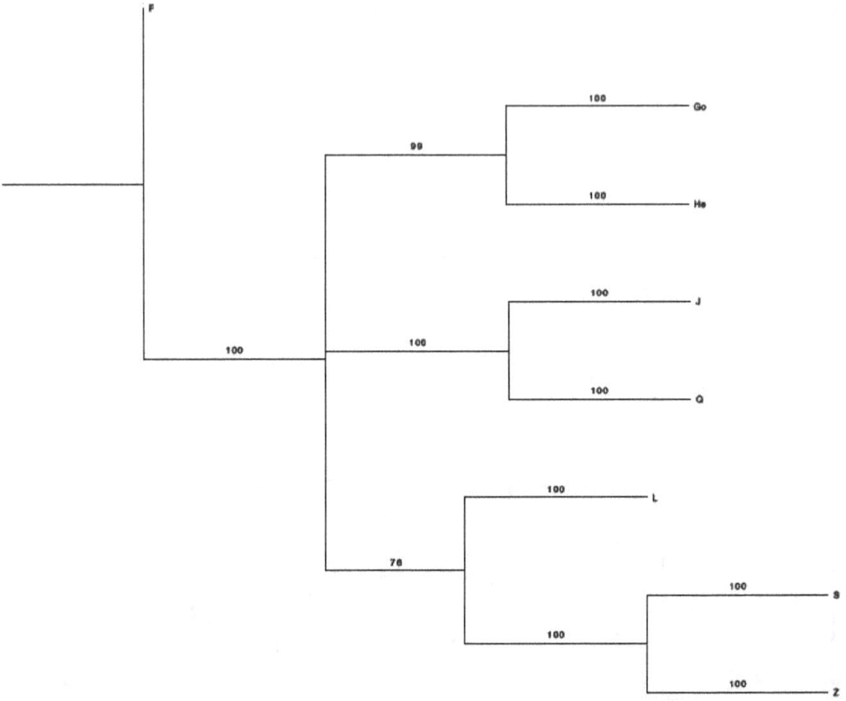


**Fig. 2:** Unrooted Distance Matrix with Neighbor-Joining Bootstrap Analysis

point a root may be identified. As Maas (2008, 232) explains, "At least one variant which is exclusively transmitted by a single group of witnesses and which can confidently be judged as being original has to be identified. If the same group also contains at least one clear error, this group must go back to one of the hyparchetypes. If it is possible to identify a second group of witnesses containing exclusively at least one original reading as well as at least one error, this group goes back to a seond hyparchetype. The archetype has to be located at that part of the tree which connects the two hyparchetypes." In correlation with this type of philological judgement, one may construct a rooted split network utilizing the software program SplitsTree (Huson and Bryant 2006) by employing an equal angle algorithm (Gambette and Huson 2008) that roots a phylogenetic tree based on a given outgroup. Based on the maximum parsimony analysis depicted in Figure 1, the outgroup selected for rooting the hypothetical tree was textual witness F (Phu brag). The rooted equal angle tree is presented in Figure 3.

A stemma may now be drawn to represent the transmission history of the APSD. A stemma graphically represents from top to bottom the archetype, the

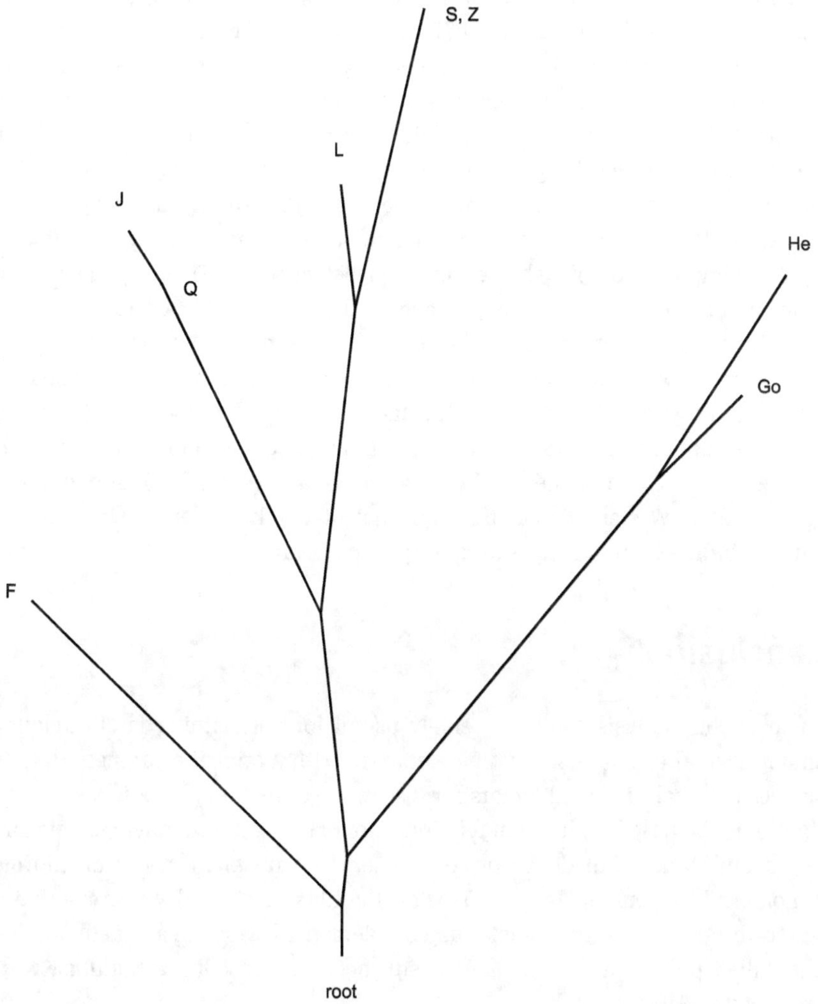


**Fig. 3:** Equal Angle Rooted Tree based on Maximum Parsimony

oldest inferable ancestor, with the available witnesses connected through intermediate textual witnesses based on the data resulting from the philological and phylogenetic analysis of variant readings. The stemma is a hypothetical construct that provides an estimate of the development of a text based on available data. The proposed stemma for APSD is provided in Figure 4.[13]

The stemma depicts the archetype having its beginning in the Western Tibetan monastery of Tho-ling. Copies and unknown intermediate witnesses were transmitted resulting in an initial split between the hyparchetype α ("alpha") and copies of the Phu brag witness. Further copies and unknown intermediate witnesses resulted in a split of hyparchetype α into the hyparchetype μ comprised of the readings shared between Go and He and the hyparchetype ψ ("psi") comprised of the shared readings between the Them spang ma and Tshal pa based Kanjurs. The hyparchetype μ ("mu") could possibly be a copy from Tabo or another Western Tibet monastic institution. The hyparchetype ψ would represent the so-called Old Narthang Kanjur, or the copies of texts that were held at Narthang monastery. In this case study, the phylogenetic analysis of APSD supplements the discerned relations based on philological analysis among known textual witnesses. The provisional analysis of APSD supports a hypothesis for a Western Kanjur tradition that may only be verified by more text critical studies of individual *sūtras* found in Tibetan Kanjurs.

## Conclusion

Phylogenetic analysis, while extremely useful for determining family relations among textual exemplars, must be employed with a critical awareness that recognizes external historical factors for discerning a text's genealogy. A genealogy should not be based on internal relations alone. In this sense, phylogenetic analysis complements, but does not supercede, the painstaking work of informed philological judgement. In sum, Tibetan Buddhist canonical works may be restored through text critical methods complemented with phylogenetic analysis but skilled philological judgement is still necessary in editing Buddhist works preserved in Tibetan.

---

**13** A stemma connects from top to bottom the oldest reconstructable ancestor, the archetype, with all available witnesses through intermediate witnesses, the variant readings of which have to be inferred from variants that are characteristic for a particular line of transmission. A stemmatical hypothesis is indispensable for the reconstruction of an archetypal text version. The stemmatic hypothesis is then compared against the known external evidence or historical record for the development of the text through time to gain knowledge of the text's transmission and historical composition. The constructed stemma is then compared against the current provisional historical record of Tibetan Kanjur transmission established in the studies of Eimer (1983), Harrison (1992b), and Apple (2014b).

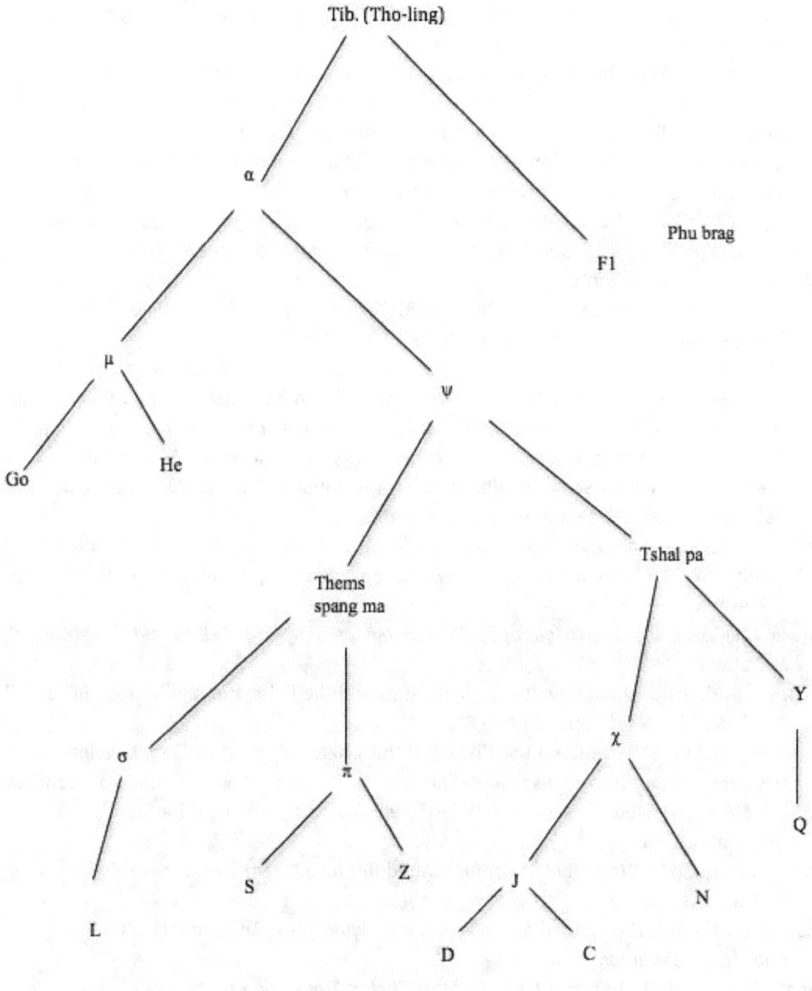


**Fig. 4:** Proposed Stemma of APSD

# References


Apple, James B. 2014a "Fragments and Phylogenetics of the Old Tibetan Version of the Avaivartikacakrasūtra from Dunhuang." Paper presented at *Canadian Society for the Study of Religion*, Brock University.

Apple, James B. 2014b. "Fragments and Phylogeny of the Tibetan Version of the *Mañjuśrīvihārasūtra:* A Case Study in the Genealogy of Tibetan Kanjurs." *Annual Report of The International Research Institute for Advanced Buddhology at Soka University for the Academic Year 2013*, 293–336. Tokyo: The International Research Institute for Advanced Buddhology, Soka University.

Apple, James B. 2014c. *The Sūtra of the Inquiry of Avalokiteśvara on the Seven Dharmas* [*Avalokiteśvaraparipṛcchāsaptadharmaka-nāma-mahāyānasūtra*], 84000:Translating the Words of the Buddha, Khyentse Foundation, http://84000.co/).

Apple, James B. 2015. "Redaction and Rhetoric in Mahāyāna Sūtras The Case of the *Jayamatiparipṛcchāsūtra*." *Indo-Iranian Journal* 58: 1–25.

Apple, James B. 2016. "Caractéristiques des Kanjurs tibétains." In *Sūtras bouddhiques: un heritage spiritual universal. Manuscrits et iconographie du Sūtra du Lotus*, 88–91. Paris: Les Indes savantes.

Barbrook, Adrian, Christopher Howe, Norman Blake and Peter Robinson. 1998. "The Phylogeny of the Canterbury Tales." *Nature* 394: 839.

Braarvig, Jens. 1993. *Akṣayamatinirdeśasūtra*. Volume I: Edition of Extant Manuscripts with an Index. Volume II: The Tradition of Imperishability in Buddhist Thought. Oslo: Solum.

Cantwell, Cathy, and Robert Mayer. 2007. *The Kīlaya Nirvāna Tantra and the Vajra Wrath Tantra. Two Texts from the Ancient Tantra collection*. Denkschriften-Österreichische Akademie Der Wissenschaften. Philosophisch-Historische Klasse. Wien: Verlag der Österreichischen Akademie der Wissenschaften.

Chattopadhyaya, Alaka. 1967. *Atīśa and Tibet; life and works of Dīpaṃkara Śrījñāna in relation to the history and religion of Tibet*. [Calcutta]: distributors: Indian Studies: Past & Present.

Darwin, Charles. 1872. *The Origin of Species by Means of Natural Selection*. Chicago: Rand, McNally.

d'Avray, David. 2012. "Contamination, Stemmatics and the Editing of Medieval Latin Texts." *Ars Endendi Lecture Series* 2: 63–82.

Eimer, Helmut. 1992. "A Note on the History of the Tibetan Kanjur." In *Ein Jahrzehnt Studien zur Überlieferung des tibetischen Kanjur*, 175–183. Wien Arbeitskreis für Tibetische und Buddhistische Studien. Arbeitskreis für Tibetische und Buddhistische Studien, Universität Wien.

Eimer, Helmut. 2007. "The Tibetan Kanjur Printed in China." *Zentralasiatische Studien* 36: 35–60.

Felsenstein. Joseph. 1985. "Confidence Limits on Phylogenies: An Approach using the Bootstrap." *Evolution* 39(4): 783–91.

Habata, Hiromi. 2013. *A Critical Edition of the Tibetan Translation of the Mahāparinirvāṇa-mahāsūtra*. Wiesbaden : Dr. Ludwig Reichert Verlag.

Haberman, David L. and Jan Nattier. 1996. "Whatever Became of Translation?" *Religious Studies News* 11(4): 13.

Hagel, Stefan. 1997–2013. *Classical Text Editor*. http://cte.oeaw.ac.at//

Harrison, Paul M. 1992a. *Druma-kinnara-rāja-paripṛcchā-sūtra: A Critical Edition of the Tibetan text (recension A) based on Eight Editions of the Kanjur and the Dunhuang Manuscript Fragment*. Tokyo: The International Institute for Buddhist Studies.

Harrison, Paul M. 1992b. "Meritorious Activity or Waste of Time? Some Remarks on the Editing of Texts in the Tibetan Kanjur", *Tibetan Studies: Proceedings of the 5th Seminar of the International Association for Tibetan Studies 1989*, 77–94. Narita.

Harrison, Paul M. 1996."A Brief History of the Tibetan Kanjur." In *Tibetan Literature. Studies in Genre*, edited by José Ignacio Cabezón and Roger R. Jackson, 70–94. Ithaca, New York: Snow Lion.

Hillis, David M. and Bull, James J. 1993. "An Empirical Test of Bootstrapping as a Method for Assessing Confidence in Phylogenetic Analysis." *Systematic Biology* 42(2): 182–192.

Howe, Christopher J., Ruth Connolly, and Heather F. Windram. 2012. "Responding to Criticisms of Phylogenetic Methods in Stemmatology." *Studies in English Literature 1500–1900* 52(1): 51–67.

Huson, Daniel H., and David Bryant. 2006. "Application of Phylogenetic Networks in Evolutionary Studies." *Molecular Biology and Evolution* 23 (2): 254–267. doi:10.1093/molbev/msj030.

Huson, Daniel. H. and Philippe Gambette. 2008. "Improved Layout of Phylogenetic Networks." *IEEE/ACM Transactions of Computational Biology and Bioinformatics* 5(2): 1–8.

Kenney, Edward. J. 1974. *The Classical Text: Aspects of Editing in the Age of the Printed Book.* Berkeley: University of California Press.

Kritzer, Robert. 2014. *Garbhāvakrāntisūtra: The Sūtra on Entry into the Womb.* Tokyo: International Institute for Buddhist Studies of the International College for Postgraduate Buddhist Studies.

Maas, Paul. 1958. *Textual Criticism.* Oxford: Clarendon Press.

Maas, Philipp A. 2008a. "Descent with Modification": The Opening of the *Pātañjalayogaśāstra.*" In *Śāstrārambha: Inquiries into the Preamble in Sanskrit,* edited by Walter Slaje, 97–119. Wiesbaden: Harrassowitz Verlag.

Maas, Philipp A. 2008b. "A Phylogenetic Approach to the Transmission of the Tibetan Kanjur-the *Akṣayamatinirdeśa* Revisited." In *Bauddhasāhityastabakāvalī: Essays and Studies on Buddhist Sanskrit Literature: Dedicated to Claus Vogel by Colleagues, Students, and Friends*, edited by Dimitrov, Dragomir, Michael Hahn, and Roland Steiner, 229–243. Marburg: Indica et Tibetica Verlag.

Maas, Philipp A. 2009. "Computer Aided Stemmatics—The Case of Fifty-Two Text Versions of *Carakasaṃhitā Vimānastāna* 8.67–157." In *Text Genealogy, Textual Criticism and Editorial Technique*, edited by Jürgen Hanneder and Philipp A. Maas, 63–119. Wiener Zeitschrift für die Kunde Südasiens 52.

Maas, Philipp A. 2014. "Sanskrit Textual Criticism—Aims, Methods, and Problems." Lecture held at Institute des Langues et Civilisations slaves et de l'Asie du Sud, University of Lausanne, Switzerland.

Macé, Caroline and Philippe V. Baret. 2006. "Why Phylogenetic Methods Work: The Theory of Evolution and Textual Criticism." In *The Evolution of Texts*, edited by Caroline Macé, 89–108. Pisa: Istituti editoriali e poligrafici internazionali.

Macé, Caroline, Ilse De Vos and Koen Geuten. 2012. "Comparing Stemmatoligical and Phylogenetic Methods to Understand the Transmisison History of the *Florilegium Coislinianum.*" *Ars Endendi Lecture Series* 2:107–129.

Marwick, Ben. 2012. "A Cladistic Evaluation of Ancient Thai Bronze Buddha Images: Six Tests for a Phylogenetic Signal in the Griswold Collection." In *Connecting Empires,* edited by Dominik Bonatz, Andreas Reinecke and Mai Lin Tjoa-Bonatz, 159–176. Singapore: National University of Singapore Press.

Nattier, Jan. 1997. "Buddhist Studies in the Post-Colonial Age." *Journal of the American Academy of Religion* 65(2): 469–485.
Phillips-Rodriguez, Wendy J., Christopher J. Howe and Heather F. Windram. 2009. "Chi-Squares and the Phenomenon of 'Change of Exemplar' in the *Dyūtaparvan*." In *Sanskrit Computational Linguistics, Lecture Notes in Computer Science 5402*, edited by Gérard Huet, Amba Kulkarni and Peter Scharf, 380–390. Berlin: Springer.
Raman, N. S. S. 1998. *Methodological Studies in the History of Religions: with Special Reference to Hinduism and Buddhism.* Shimla: Indian Institute of Advanced Study.
Roos, Teemu and Tuomas Heikkilä. 2009. "Evaluating Methods for Computer-Assisted Stemmatology using Artificial Benchmark Data Sets." *Literary and Linguistic Computing* 24(4): 417–433.
Salemans, Benedictus J.P. 2000. *Building Stemmas with the Computer in a Cladistic, Neo-Lachmannian Way. The Case of Fourteen Text Versions of Lanseloet van Denemerken.* Nijmegen: Nijmegen University Press.
Schaeffer, Kurtis R., and Leonard W. J. van der Kuijp. 2009. *An Early Tibetan Survey of Buddhist Literature: The Bstan pa rgyas pa rgyan gyi nyi 'od of Bcom ldan ral gri.* Cambridge, Mass: Dept. of Sanskrit and Indian Studies, Harvard University.
Schoening, Jeffrey D. 1995. *The Śālistamba Sūtra and Its Indian Commentaries.* Wien: Arbeitskreis für Tibetische und Buddhistische Studien Universität Wien.
Silk, Jonathan A. 1994. *The Heart Sūtra in Tibetan: A Critical Edition of the Two Recensions contained in the Kanjur.* Wien: Arbeitskreis für Tibetische und Buddhistische Studien, Universität Wien.
Simonsson, Nils. 1953. "Zur indo-tibetischen Textkritik." *Orientalia Suecana* 2: 129–152.
Simonsson, Nils. 1957. *Indo-Tibetische Studien: die Methoden der Tibetischen Übersetzer, untersucht im Hinblick auf die Bedeutung ihrer Übersetzungen für die Sanskritphilologie, 1.* Uppsala: Almqvist & Wiksells.
Skilling, Peter. 1997. "From bKa' bstan bcos to bKa' 'gyur and bsTan 'gyur." In *Tibetan Studies: Proceedings of the 7th Seminar of the International Association for Tibetan Studies, Graz 1995*, edited by Ernst Steinkellner, 87–111. Vienna: Verlag der Österreichischen Akademie der Wissenschaften.
Skilling, Peter. 2001. "The Batang Manuscript Kanjur in the Newark Museum: A Preliminary Report." *Annual Report of The International Research Institute for Advanced Buddhology University at Soka University* 4: 71–92.
Skilling, Peter. 2009. "Translating the Buddha's Words: Some Notes on the Kanjur Translation Project." Talk at Nonthaburi, March 11, 2009.
Skilling Peter, and Saerji. 2013. "The Circulation of the Buddhāvataṃsaka in India." *Annual Report of The International Research Institute for Advanced Buddhology at Soka University for the Academic Year 2012* 16: 193–216.
Skilton, Andrew. 2000. "The Letter of the Law and the Lore of Letters: The Role of Textual Criticism in the Transmission of Buddhist Scripture."*Contemporary Buddhism* 1(1): 9–34.
Smith, Maynard J. 1992. "Analysing the Mosaic Structure of Genes." *Journal of Molecular Evolution* 34: 126–29.
Swofford, David. L. 2003. *PAUP**. Phylogenetic Analysis Using Parsimony (*and Other Methods). Version 4. Sunderland, Massachusetts.

Tauscher, Helmut, and Bruno Lainé. 2008. "Western Tibetan Kanjur Tradition." In *The Cultural History of Western Tibet*, edited by Deborah Klimburg-Salter and Liang Junyan, 339–362. Wien: Arbeitskreis für Tibetische und Buddhistische Studien.

Timpanaro, Sebastiano, and Glenn W. Most. 2005. *The Genesis of Lachmann's Method.* Chicago: University of Chicago Press.

Trovato, Paolo. 2014. *Everything You Always Wanted to Know About Lachmann's Method: A Non-Standard Handbook of Genealogical Textual Criticism in the Age of Post-Structuralism, Cladistics, and Copy-Text.* Padova: Libreriauniversitaria.it.

West, Martin L. 1973. *Textual Criticism and Editorial Technique: Applicable to Greek and Latin Texts.* Teubner Studienbücher. Stuttgart: Teubner.

Windram, Heather F., Christopher J. Howe, and Matthew Spencer. 2005. "The Identification of Exemplar Change in the *Wife of Bath's Prologue* Using the Maximum Chi-Squared Method." *Literary and Linguistic Computing* 20(2): 189–204.

Windram, Heather F., Prue Shaw, Peter Robinzon, and Christopher J. Howe. 2008. "Dante's *Monarchia* as a Test Case for the use of Phylogenetic Methods in Stemmatic Analysis." *Literary and Linguistic Computing* 23(4): 443–463.

Zimmermann, Michael. 2002. *A Buddha Within: The Tathāgatagarbhasūtra: The Earliest Exposition of the Buddha-Nature Teaching in India.* Tokyo: The International Research Institute for Advanced Buddhology, Soka University.

# Appendix: Selected Digital Humanities Resources

## General Tools

| URL | Description |
|---|---|
| http://lexos.wheatoncollege.edu | Integrated text processing workflow |
| http://mallet.cs.umass.edu/index.php | Java-based package for statistical natural language processing, document classification, clustering, topic modeling, information extraction, and other machine learning applications to text. |
| https://www.r-project.org/ | The R Project for Statistical Computing |
| http://www.online-utility.org/text/analyzer.jsp | Online Word Frequency Counter |
| https://www.tensorflow.org/tutorials/word2vec/ | Word Vector Mapping Software |
| http://programminghistorian.org/lessons/corpus-analysis-with-antconc | Distant Reading and Corpus Analysis Tutorial |
| http://dh101.humanities.ucla.edu/wp-content/uploads/2014/09/IntroductionToDigitalHumanities_Textbook.pdf | Introduction to Digital Humanities Course |
| https://github.com/ajenhl/tacl/ | Search for matching text strings |
| https://github.com/BuddhistDigitalResourceCenter | General repository for Buddhological resources and code |
| http://www.tei-c.org/release/doc/tei-p5-doc/en/html/MS.html | Text Encoding Initiative Manuscript Description Module |
| https://www.rdocumentation.org/packages/stylo/versions/0.6.7 | R package for stylometric analysis, authorship attribution and other computational linguistics approaches |
| http://voyant-tools.org/ | Easy-to-use suite of tools for text analysis including word frequency, keyword in context, correlation scores, collocation analysis, lexical density, and various visual displays |
| http://tapor.ca/home | Text Analysis Portal for Research: Gateway for a variety of tools that can be used in sophisticated text analysis and retrieval |

https://doi.org/10.1515/9783110519082-013

*Continued*

| URL | Description |
|---|---|
| http://ecai.org/ | Electronic Cultural Atlas Initiative |

# Buddhological: General

| | |
|---|---|
| http://mbingenheimer.net/tools/indexTools.html | List of digital tools for Buddhist Studies |
| http://buddhanet.net | Hub for Buddhist texts, teachings, lectures, videos, education |
| http://religion.oxfordre.com/browse?t0=ORE_REL:REFREL005 | Oxford Research Encyclopedia of Religion: Buddhism |
| https://web.sas.upenn.edu/tlc/internet-resources/ | List of Resources for Thai, Lao and Cambodian Studies |
| http://www.ciolek.com/WWWVL-Buddhism.html#TOC | Buddhist Studies Virtual Library |

# Buddhological: Text Databases

| | |
|---|---|
| http://www.tipitaka.org | Pali Canon and Commentaries |
| http://www.cbeta.org | Chinese Canon |
| http://www.sutra.re.kr | Korean Canon |
| http://21dzk.l.u-tokyo.ac.jp/SAT | Chinese and Japanese Canon |
| http://www.dsbcproject.org | Sanskrit Canon |
| https://www2.hf.uio.no/polyglotta | Thesaurus Literaturae Buddhicae |
| http://databases.aibs.columbia.edu | Tibetan Canon |
| https://www.tbrc.org | Buddhist Digital Resource Center |
| http://gretil.sub.uni-goettingen.de/ | GRETIL – Göttingen Register of Electronic Texts in Indian Languages and Related Indological Materials from Central and Southeast Asia |
| http://www.asianclassics.org/ | Asian Classics Input Project (ACIP) |
| http://tibetan.works | Tibetan Canon (ACIP Mirror) |

| | |
|---|---|
| http://Hathitrust.org | Large Database of Digitized Books on many topics |
| http://www.sacred-texts.org | Older Translations of Public Domain Religious Texts in English |
| http://www.accesstoinsight.org | English Translations of Pali Texts |
| http://www.tibetan-knowledge.org | Tibetan Cultural and Textual Resource |
| http://sanskritweb.net | Sanskrit Texts and Transliteration Tools |
| https://gandhari.org | Gandhari Texts, Inscriptions, Dictionaries |
| http://uma-tibet.org | Translations of Tibetan Texts |
| http://laomanuscripts.net | Database of Manuscripts from Laos |
| http://lannamanuscripts.net | Database of Manuscripts from Lanna (Northern Thailand) |
| http://idp.bl.uk | International Dunhuang Project: Digital repository of manuscripts, paintings, textiles and artefacts from the Silk Road |
| https://dazangthings.nz/cbc | Chinese Buddhism Canonical Attributions Database |
| https://www.istb.univie.ac.at/kanjur/rktsneu/sub/index.php | Resources for Kanjur and Tanjur Studies |
| http://kanji.zinbun.kyoto-u.ac.jp/~wittern/can/can2/ind/canwww.htm | Database of Chinese Buddhist Texts |
| https://suttacentral.net/ | Early Buddhist Texts, Translations and Parallels |

# Buddhological: Lexical Resources

| | |
|---|---|
| http://www.buddhism-dict.net/ddb/ | Digital Dictionary of Buddhism |
| http://dsal.uchicago.edu/dictionaries/ | Digital Dictionaries of South Asia |
| http://authority.dila.edu.tw/ | Onomasticon of person, place names and Tripitaka catalogues from Buddhist sources; geospatial referencing of names and dates |
| http://www.sanskrit-lexicon.uni-koeln.de/ | Online Sanskrit Dictionaries |
| http://www.thlib.org/reference/dictionaries/tibetan-dictionary/translate.php | Online Tibetan to English Translation Tool |

| | |
|---|---|
| http://www.pktc.org/pktc/index.htm | Padma Karpo Translation Committee online resources for Tibetan Digital Libraries |
| http://www.itlr.net/testb.php?md=view | Indo-Tibetan Lexical Resource |
| http://www.buddha-vacana.org/toolbox.html | Pali Toolbox with dictionary, sample declensions and conjugations |

## Buddhological: MultiMedia Resources

| | |
|---|---|
| http://www.thlib.org/places/monasteries/sera/ | Virtual Sera Tibetan Monastery |
| http://digitalhimalaya.com | Multimedia Information from the Himalaya Region |
| http://www.dalailama.org | Multimedia Resource including videos of talks by Dalai Lama |
| http://tdm.sas.upenn.edu/ | Thai Digital Monastery |
| http://sydney.edu.au/arts/research/read/ | Research Environment for Ancient Documents |
| http://frogbear.org/ | From the Ground Up: Buddhism and East Asian Religions. Repository of texts, images, artifacts and practices |

## Bibliographies

| | |
|---|---|
| https://www.zotero.org/groups/h-buddhism_bibliography_project/items | H-Buddhism Zotero Bibliography |
| http://www.inbuds.net | INBUDS Article Database |
| http://databases.aibs.columbia.edu | Tibetan Canon Bibliography |
| https://east.library.utoronto.ca/internet-resources-guide/93 | List of East Asian Digital Resources |
| http://www.oxfordbibliographies.com/browse?module_0=obo-9780195393521 | Oxford Bibliographies: Buddhism. Comprehensive annotated bibliography for Buddhist studies |
| http://mbingenheimer.net/tools/bibls/transbibl.html | Bibliography of Translations from the Chinese Buddhist Canon into Western Languages |
| http://www.acmuller.net/descriptive_catalogue/ | The Korean Buddhist Canon: A Descriptive Catalogue |

# Index

agile 37, 40
algorithm 5, 15, 20, 25, 39 f., 43, 45–47, 57, 103, 149, 183, 186, 188 f., 194–196, 201 f., 206 f., 213, 216, 218
anthropology 28, 161
application programming interface 38 f.
archives 1, 3, 20 f., 77 f., 81, 88, 97–99, 106 f., 112, 115 f., 132, 141
Asian Classics Input Project 11, 34, 96–100, 102, 107, 146, 194, 196, 198, 228
avatar 20, 59–66, 68–70

Bartle, Richard 64
BibTEX 79
Biographies of Eminent Monks 15, 22, 159, 167, 171–173, 176 f.
Bodhisattva 8
Boellstorff, Tom 62 f., 65
Bu-ston 92 f.
Burrows, John 43 f.

Cabezon, Jose 28
canon 4, 7, 9–16, 20–23, 25, 30 f., 33 f., 48, 52, 54, 78 f., 81–83, 91, 99, 106 f., 111 f., 114, 117 f., 124, 129, 134, 136, 145 f., 150, 154, 175, 202–204, 209 f., 212, 220, 228–230
catalog 4, 14, 33, 78 f., 81, 98, 131, 137, 203
Chaṭṭha Saṅgāyana Tipiṭaka 25, 30 f.
Chang'an 166, 167, 170, 173, 174, 176
Chiang Mai 21, 127, 129, 131–133, 138–141
China 9, 12, 95, 97, 102–104, 112, 116 f., 131, 145, 159, 161, 163, 165 f., 171 f., 210
Chinese Buddhist Electronic Text Association 12, 14, 25, 32, 35, 77–79, 82 f., 99, 123, 146, 153, 183, 202 f., 206
Chinese font 95
CJKV-E 22, 145–150, 152–156
cladistic 22, 212 f., 215 f.
classification 39, 44, 51, 79, 103, 105, 119, 121, 187, 213, 227
clustering 165–170, 176–178, 183–185, 227
collaboration 3, 12, 17, 22, 31, 40, 100 f., 107, 113, 123, 127, 138, 143 f., 146, 150–152, 155
collocation 20, 44, 51–53, 227
commentaries 9, 17, 26, 34, 50, 52, 54, 81, 91–93, 104 f., 107, 119, 129, 160, 175, 228
computational linguistics 20, 31, 43, 78, 103, 187, 227
computing 2 f., 14, 20, 22, 26 f., 31, 33, 37, 43 f., 51, 57, 66, 93 f., 102, 107, 143, 183, 206, 227
concordance 3, 22, 150, 183 f., 187–189, 206
corpora 4–6, 14 f., 25–27, 29, 32–34, 39, 43–45, 47 f., 52, 54, 57, 91, 97, 102 f., 107, 124 f., 140, 159 f., 163, 165, 168–170, 176, 178 f., 183, 186 f., 189, 191–194, 207, 227
creative commons 127, 153 f.
cross-language 20, 78 f., 81, 103
crowd sourcing 32, 34, 39 f., 143
cyberspace 59

Daoxuan 159 f., 166 f., 171 f., 175 f.
databases 1, 10, 16, 20, 25 f., 28–30, 32–35, 37, 48, 52, 77–79, 98 f., 107, 136, 147, 152, 154, 165, 174, 183, 228–230
Devanagari 112, 121 f.
dharma 10, 16, 45, 53, 68, 82, 101, 118, 129, 188
Dharma Drum Buddhist College 150, 160, 165, 170, 174
dictionary 10 f., 13 f., 21, 30 f., 81, 95, 100–104, 143–145, 147–150, 152–155, 184, 229 f.
Digital Dictionary of Buddhism 13, 21, 33, 143, 145–150, 152–156, 229
Digital Sanskrit Buddhist Canon 12, 21, 111–117, 119, 121, 123–125, 186, 189
digitization 4, 9–13, 15, 21 f., 25, 32–34, 46, 93 f., 96, 98, 111–113, 115, 121, 123–

125, 131, 133–135, 137–140, 142, 145 f., 150, 153, 183, 186, 195, 202, 206, 229
Duff, Tony 11, 13, 94 f., 107
Dunhuang 98, 125, 211

e-text 25, 29–31, 33–35, 93 f., 96–99, 102, 106 f., 112, 115
encoding 15, 17, 37 f., 83, 91, 94 f., 97, 100, 121, 148 f.
Ethnography 59
extensible markup language 9, 17, 32, 37, 146–149, 154, 165, 170

fonts 11 f., 21, 94 f., 101, 121
funding 22, 25–27, 31 f., 35–37, 95, 100, 103, 130, 142, 150

Gāndhārī 13, 31, 114, 229
genealogy 23, 70, 209 f., 212 f., 215 f., 220
geographic information system 22, 99, 163–165, 195 f.
geomapping 165–168, 177 f.
glyphs 95, 186, 194, 196, 201
google books 6

H-Buddhism 146, 230
hathitrust 6
Hoben Mountain Zen Retreat 59, 68
Hundius, Harald 21, 127, 131 f., 135, 138, 142
hyparchetype 218, 220
hypertext markup language 100, 144, 147, 149, 153

India 10 f., 15, 26, 31, 56, 66, 91, 96 f., 105, 112, 114–117, 121, 124 f., 129, 145, 147, 170–174, 189, 210, 212–214, 228
interface 13, 30, 32 f., 66, 94, 98, 103, 105, 136, 138, 183
International Dunhuang Project 13, 25, 31, 98, 146, 229
International Image Interoperability Framework 38
Internet 4, 10, 12 f., 34, 38 f., 43, 59, 63, 99, 123 f., 129, 134, 141, 144, 155

Jiankang 166 f., 169 f., 173 f., 176 f.
Jockers, Matthew 4, 6

Kanjur 33, 99, 107, 118, 194–196, 209–211, 215, 220, 229
keyword in context 227
knowledge path 81, 83, 87 f.

Lancaster, Lewis 9, 12, 111, 146
Laos 10, 21, 31, 127–138, 140–142, 228 f.
lexicon 13, 20, 78 f., 81, 148, 150, 155
Lhasa 116, 125, 210 f.
Lifecycle 35
Linden Lab 59
lineages 91, 104–106, 202

machine learning 20, 25, 27, 30, 34, 40, 44, 47, 227
Mahāyāna 7–9, 12, 22 f., 86, 112–114, 117–119, 186 f., 189–195, 206, 209, 212, 214
manuscripts 8, 10, 12–14, 19, 21, 25, 27, 29–33, 37, 39, 98, 112–117, 123, 127–134, 137–142, 147, 184, 187, 194, 202, 209–212, 214 f., 229
mapping 20, 27, 29, 45, 54, 100, 159, 161, 163, 166, 227
markup 11, 15, 17, 144, 146–148
matrices 16
matricies 78, 91, 93–95, 215 f., 218
McDaniel, Justin 28, 142
Mechanical Turk 39
meditation 5, 8, 48–50, 66–69
metadata 4, 14, 17, 38, 78, 98, 123, 147
methodology 1, 20, 22, 63, 69, 159, 161, 163–165, 169, 175, 209
microfilm 21, 98, 115, 128, 131–135, 137 f., 141
monastic 10–12, 28, 34, 38, 59, 92, 97, 105 f., 112 f., 116, 119, 127 f., 130 f., 133 f., 140 f., 163, 165 f., 168–172, 175, 210 f., 214, 220, 230
monks 15, 68, 97, 105, 129 f., 140, 159 f., 163, 165 f., 168 f., 171 f., 175–179
mormonism 51
multi-user dungeons 62

multimedia 21, 28, 105, 230
Myanmar 10, 129, 131

n-grams 14, 46, 187–194, 196–200, 202–206
Narthang 210 f., 215, 220
Nepal 11, 21, 98, 105, 111–115, 117–119, 121, 124
Newar 114, 118 f.

Oneiric Practice 175, 177 f.
ontology 20, 38, 77–79, 81, 83, 85, 88
Optical Character Recognition 32, 34, 102

Pali 4, 7, 9 f., 12 f., 16, 22, 25 f., 30 f., 33–35, 46–48, 50, 52, 79, 81, 118, 127–129, 132, 134, 136, 228–230
parsing 20 f., 50, 103, 154, 165, 184, 194 f., 201
part-of-speech 103, 184
patterns 6, 15, 20, 22, 39, 43 f., 57, 83, 164 f., 169, 183 f., 191, 196, 200, 205 f.
Perfection of Wisdom 91, 107
philology 14, 22 f., 100, 209 f., 212, 214, 218–220
phylogenetics 22 f., 209, 212–216, 218–220
PNTMP 127 f., 132, 137 f., 142
preservation 2, 7, 9, 11, 19–21, 26, 31, 34–37, 91, 94, 98, 106, 111–116, 119, 124 f., 127–130, 132–134, 136 f., 140–142, 159, 175, 209–211, 214, 220
publication 7, 11, 34, 36, 68, 144, 156, 210
punctuation 45, 93 f., 97, 214

Radich, Michael 14, 26, 152, 183
retrieval 3, 9 f., 27, 29, 31, 79, 83, 85, 141, 227
romanization 33, 94, 96 f., 100, 136 f., 147

Sanskrit 7, 9, 12–15, 20–22, 26, 31, 35, 79, 81, 92, 94–96, 98, 100, 111–121, 123–125, 183–189, 194–197, 201–203, 206 f., 212–214, 228 f.
Śāstravid 26, 35
SAT Database 12, 25, 33, 99, 146, 154
scripts 10, 30, 101, 114, 129, 140 f., 165, 183
second life 20, 59–70
segmentation 79, 83, 103
semantics 13, 20 f., 26, 34 f., 44 f., 54 f., 66, 77 f., 83, 103, 106, 155, 184
Shakya, Min Bahadur 12, 111, 118, 121
sources 14, 21 f., 26, 32 f., 46, 91, 105, 112, 121, 127, 130 f., 134, 136, 140 f., 144 f., 150 f., 155, 159 f., 164 f., 209, 229
statistical 6, 15, 20, 22, 25, 29 f., 34, 39 f., 43 f., 47, 51, 55, 102, 166, 215, 227
stemma 212, 218–221
survey 19, 21, 26, 30, 59, 61, 63–65, 69, 127, 129–133, 135, 137 f., 168
sustainability 26, 35–37
sutra 7, 10, 43, 47–50, 78, 81–86, 107, 114, 117–119, 154, 189 f., 195, 199 f., 209 f., 212, 214, 220
syllable 101 f., 184–189, 192, 194–196, 200 f.

tagging 14, 17 f., 20, 39, 103, 106 f., 148, 170, 184, 207
Taisho 12, 25
Tensor Flow 40
term frequency – inverse document frequency 20, 44 f., 47 f., 52
text encoding initiative 14, 17, 37, 147, 227
text encoding intiative 9, 14 f., 37, 147–149, 165
textual criticism 23, 212 f., 215 f.
Thailand 9 f., 20 f., 28, 31, 127–129, 131–134, 137 f., 140–142, 228–230
thailand 131, 229
Theravada 70, 129, 134
Tibet 28, 91 f., 99 f., 104 f., 112, 116, 210 f., 214, 220
tibet 9, 11–13, 20–23, 25 f., 28, 33–35, 38, 70, 79, 81, 91–107, 111 f., 117 f., 125, 183 f., 194–196, 198–203, 207, 209–212, 214 f., 217, 220, 228–230
Tibetan and Himalayan Library 25, 33
Tibetan Buddhist Resource Center 25, 33 f., 38, 98 f., 102, 107, 211
Tibetan font 95, 100 f.
toponyms 170 f., 173–175
transcription 10, 14, 17, 34, 94–96, 106, 128

translation 9–12, 14 f., 21, 26, 46 f., 50, 69, 78, 82, 91, 93, 103–105, 111, 118, 125, 129, 134, 150, 155, 162, 184, 207, 209 f., 214, 229 f.
transliteration 11, 13, 100, 121, 194, 201, 229
Tripitaka 12, 32, 78 f., 81, 111, 117–120, 123–125, 146, 150, 210, 229

unicode 96 f., 100 f., 112, 121, 146, 183, 188, 194, 201
unix 94, 183, 193

vector space 20, 44 f., 54 f.
Vientiane 130 f., 137
Vinaya 128, 189
Vipassana Research Institute 25, 30
Virtual 20, 61 f., 64, 68, 228, 230

Wittern, Christian 12, 144, 146
Wordnet 79
Wylie Transcription 96
Wylie transcription 93–96, 100

Zen 11, 59–61, 65–70, 144

www.ingramcontent.com/pod-product-compliance
Lightning Source LLC
Chambersburg PA
CBHW051611230426
43668CB00013B/2063